3/13/12
$24.95

HOW TO
Design and Build a
Green Office Building

A Complete Guide
to Making Your New
or Existing Building
Environmentally Healthy

Author: **Jackie Bondanza**

Editor: **Martha Maeda**

How to Design and Build a Green Office Building: A Complete Guide to Making Your New or Existing Building Environmentally Healthy

Copyright © 2011 by Atlantic Publishing Group, Inc.
1405 SW 6th Ave. • Ocala, Florida 34471 • 800-814-1132 • 352-622-1875–Fax
Website: www.atlantic-pub.com • E-mail: sales@atlantic-pub.com
SAN Number: 268-1250

Bondanza, Jackie, 1980-
How to design and build a green office building : a complete guide to making your new or existing building environmentally healthy / by Jackie Bondanza.
   p. cm.
Includes bibliographical references and index.
ISBN-13: 978-1-60138-241-2 (alk. paper)
ISBN-10: 1-60138-241-3 (alk. paper)
1. Office buildings--Design and construction. 2. Sustainable buildings--Design and construction. 3. Buildings--Repair and reconstruction. 4. Green technology. I. Title. II. Title: Complete guide to making your new or existing building environmentally healthy.

TH4311.B66 2010
690'.523047--dc22

2010045679

PROJECT MANAGER: Shannon McCarthy
BOOK PRODUCTION DESIGN: T.L. Price • design@tlpricefreelance.com
PROOFREADER: C&P Marse • bluemoon6749@bellsouth.net
FRONT COVER DESIGN: Meg Buchner • megadesn@mchsi.com
BACK COVER DESIGN: Jackie Miller • millerjackiej@gmail.com

Printed in the United States

We recently lost our beloved pet "Bear," who was not only our best and dearest friend but also the "Vice President of Sunshine" here at Atlantic Publishing. He did not receive a salary but worked tirelessly 24 hours a day to please his parents. Bear was a rescue dog that turned around and showered myself, my wife, Sherri, his grandparents Jean, Bob, and Nancy, and every person and animal he met (maybe not rabbits) with friendship and love. He made a lot of people smile every day.

We wanted you to know that a portion of the profits of this book will be donated to The Humane Society of the United States. *–Douglas & Sherri Brown*

The human-animal bond is as old as human history. We cherish our animal companions for their unconditional affection and acceptance. We feel a thrill when we glimpse wild creatures in their natural habitat or in our own backyard.

Unfortunately, the human-animal bond has at times been weakened. Humans have exploited some animal species to the point of extinction.

The Humane Society of the United States makes a difference in the lives of animals here at home and worldwide. The HSUS is dedicated to creating a world where our relationship with animals is guided by compassion. We seek a truly humane society in which animals are respected for their intrinsic value, and where the human-animal bond is strong.

Want to help animals? We have plenty of suggestions. Adopt a pet from a local shelter, join The Humane Society and be a part of our work to help companion animals and wildlife. You will be funding our educational, legislative, investigative and outreach projects in the U.S. and across the globe.

Or perhaps you'd like to make a memorial donation in honor of a pet, friend or relative? You can through our Kindred Spirits program. And if you'd like to contribute in a more structured way, our Planned Giving Office has suggestions about estate planning, annuities, and even gifts of stock that avoid capital gains taxes.

Maybe you have land that you would like to preserve as a lasting habitat for wildlife. Our Wildlife Land Trust can help you. Perhaps the land you want to share is a backyard—that's enough. Our Urban Wildlife Sanctuary Program will show you how to create a habitat for your wild neighbors.

So you see, it's easy to help animals. And The HSUS is here to help.

2100 L Street NW • Washington, DC 20037 • 202-452-1100
www.hsus.org

Table of Contents

Table of Contents

Chapter 3: Planning and Designing Your Green Building Project........ 93

Chapter 4: Building Site and Orientation.................................129

Chapter 5: Energy Efficiency 149

Chapter 6: Water 169

Chapter 7: Green Interiors and Exteriors 183

Chapter 10: Financing Your Green Project............. 267

Chapter 11: Making Your Green Building Work 279

Introduction

Green building, though a relatively new industry, is rapidly expanding into every sector of the economy. Concepts like "energy efficiency," "sustainability," "zero landfill," "life cycle assessment," "low emitting," "xeriscaping," and "VOCs" that were rarely discussed two decades ago are now embodied in the mission statements of many corporations and private companies. Legislation now mandates that federal and state construction projects incorporate certain green building practices. Businesses and their clients recognize that steps must be taken immediately to counteract a global environmental and energy crisis. Individuals want to feel that they are living responsibly and minimizing their impact on the natural environment. At the same time, an increasing awareness of the harmful effects of poor working conditions and exposure to toxins on employees' health and long-term well-being has created a demand for office buildings that provide clean, wholesome environments for their occupants.

This book is an introduction to the principles, concepts, and important considerations of green office building and renovation. Some aspects of green building differ significantly from traditional building practices. If you are about to embark on a green office building or renovation project, this book will provide you with a clear understanding of the industry before you enter into negotiations with designers, architects, contractors, or builders. Regardless of your occupation or business, you will find information on how to integrate green building practices into your new or existing office building. Learn how building green can help you save money, improve employee productivity, conserve energy, use resources more efficiently, reduce your impact on the environment, and win the loyalty and enthusiastic support of your customers and investors.

The term "green building" encompasses several major objectives: energy and water conservation, sustainability, preservation of the environment, improvement of the surrounding community, cost savings, and the creation of an optimal working environment for employees. These objectives are accomplished, on a small or large scale, through a variety of design and building practices, selection of building materials and equipment, and implementation of green policies and procedures. Your goal might be to pursue just one of these objectives, or it might be a totally green project that fulfills all of them to the maximum extent possible. The scope of your project will be defined by the available financial and physical resources and your priorities. If you are not planning a new building or a major renovation, you can make your office greener by implementing a recycling program, changing to energy-efficient light bulbs, or giving incentives to encourage your employees to carpool.

Learn about planning and designing a green project; site selection; landscaping; recycling building materials and equipment; energy-efficient cooling and heating systems; natural lighting and low-energy lighting; water conservation and stormwater management; alternative energy sources; green interior design and interior air quality; and environmentally friendly policies in the workplace. Many innovative technologies are used in green building, and new products are constantly appearing on the market. To design and complete a successful green project, you will need to consult experienced professionals familiar with the philosophy and the techniques of green building. Depending on the size of your project, you might require specialists, such as solar contractors and lighting engineers.

Most people are aware that carbon dioxide emissions from automobiles, airplanes, and trains have a serious negative effect on our environment, but few realize the extent of the environmental damage caused by buildings. In 2007, buildings were responsible for 38.9 percent of total carbon dioxide emissions in the United States. Commercial buildings contributed 18 percent, and residences contributed 20.8 percent. Commercial buildings used almost ⅓ of the electricity consumed in the United States in 2006, and accounted for about 18 percent of all energy consumed by the United States in 2005. The U.N. Environment Programme (UNEP) recognizes that reducing carbon emissions and energy use in commercial buildings is the fastest and cheapest way to cut back global greenhouse gas emissions. National governments are anxious to promote energy efficiency and the use of renewable energy sources in commercial buildings to reduce dependency on imported fossil fuels and because rapidly developing urban centers face a looming energy crisis. Federal and local governments in many countries offer tax incentives, grants, and low-interest loans to encourage green building. The time is quickly coming when green building will be the global standard for construction.

Some aspects of green construction, such as collaboration among project team members from start to finish, pre-design brainstorming sessions, and the use of a third-party agency to commission a finished building have already influenced conventional building practices. Manufacturers of building materials are responding to the demand for environmentally responsible products, bringing down their cost. Buyers and tenants are willing to pay more for green real estate because they know their operating and maintenance costs will be much lower than for a conventional building.

Green building is a complex science, and a book like this cannot cover every topic in detail. Throughout the book and in the Appendices you will be directed to resources where you can find additional information. Once you have identified your goals and objectives, you will be able to consult green building professionals who can help you with the details of your green project.

Whether or not you choose to go ahead with a green building project, the information in this book will permanently alter your ideas about the way you consume natural resources. Once you have understood the philosophy and the principles behind green building, you will become conscious of the impact of your own activities on the environment. You will begin to participate in the growing awareness that human beings cannot continue their current lifestyles and that the earth is a finite resource that must be carefully managed.

CHAPTER 1:
What is Green Building?

The basic theory of green building is very simple: Any building construction should be done in such a way that life's essentials — air, water, and food — remain clean, and the natural cycle of life and its systems is maintained. Green building uses processes, designs, and products that do not deplete resources, disturb ecosystems, or disrupt natural life rhythms. Though it is almost impossible for human beings to live and work without having some negative effects on the environment, green building strives to minimize that impact as much as possible. Some green building practices seek to have a positive impact by using products that contribute to regenerating resources.

Conventional building design typically considers only the environmental impact of the finished structure. Green building takes a much wider view, calculating the environmental effect of every activity associated with a building, from inception until demolition. Green building considers the impact of new land development on the community, the energy and resources used to manufacture and transport the building materials to the site, the energy and water used to operate the building, the waste products produced during operation, how the building materials can be salvaged and waste disposed of when a building is demolished (green building prefers the term "deconstructed"), what will be done with the site afterward, and even the pollution generated by employees driving to work in the building.

Green building also considers the health and well-being of the building occupants. It is now documented that employees are more productive when their work environment is comfortable, well lighted, and provides access to daylight and outdoor views. Employees in such an environment suffer less from stress-related illness and take fewer sick days. Over time, exposure to even tiny amounts of toxic chemicals emitted by office furnishings and cleaning products can cause disease. Pollutants in the interior air of a building can cause respiratory distress, asthma, and allergic reactions. Some green projects, such as the construction of green areas in hotels, schools, and hospitals, are designed to create a toxin and allergen-free environment for building occupants.

This chapter introduces concepts that will help you to evaluate your green building project and make important choices during the design and building process.

Sustainability

A primary goal of green building is sustainability — making use of available resources in a way that does not deplete them for future generations and allows their use to continue indefinitely. Green building uses processes, designs, and products that do not deplete natural resources, and in some cases actively contributes to regenerating resources. A sustainable building minimizes its use of water and energy, improves the quality of life for its occupants and the community, cuts down on waste, and does not contribute significantly to the depletion of natural resources throughout the entire life of the building from planning until demolition.

Forests: sustainable natural ecosystems

A forest is prime example of a sustainable ecosystem. For hundreds of thousands of years, trees have sprouted, lived, and died. Living trees propagate themselves by spreading seeds or through underground root systems. Dead trees decompose into the soil and provide nutrients for new trees, which then participate  in the natural cycle of distributing oxygen and other gases into the air, absorbing sunlight, and retaining moisture. Natural events such as floods, droughts, and wildfires help to maintain the balance among different types of trees in the forest. The process is cyclical and sustainable because it continues, or sustains itself, on its own.

The terms "sustainable building" and "green building" are often used interchangeably. Sometimes "green building" is used to refer to buildings constructed for environmental reasons, and "sustainable building" to refer to those that are constructed to conserve costs and energy.

Renewable resources

A renewable resource can be replenished naturally at a rate that is greater than the rate at which it is consumed. Wind and solar power are considered renewable sources of energy because wind and sunshine are abundant and natural, and energy from these sources is easily accessible and has the potential to be replenished at a faster rate than it is consumed. Bamboo is considered a renewable building material because it grows rapidly, reaching a mature height of 75 feet in two months, and its cultivation does not require the use of pesticides.

Carrying capacity

Carrying capacity refers to the number of individuals who can be supported in a given area within natural resource limits, and without degrading the natural social, cultural, and economic environment for present and future generations. Improved technology and careful management can alter the carrying capacity of any area, but more often, environmental degradation as population increases results in decreased carrying capacity.

Ecological footprint

An "ecological footprint" is the amount of land needed to provide the resources that support a specific population or a human activity. The average "ecological footprint" of an American — who requires land to provide water, food, fiber, waste assimilation, and disposal — is about 12 acres. Five times the surface area of the earth would be needed to give every person in the world the lifestyle of an American. This is an obvious problem; highly developed nations must reduce their consumption to provide necessities for the entire world's population.

Environmentally Friendly/ Eco-friendly Materials and Practices

The terms "environmentally friendly" and "eco-friendly" refer to products, materials, buildings, and practices that cause little or no harm to the environment, minimally interfering with natural ecosystems. Straw bales, which are blocks of wheat, rice, oats, and other grain stalks, are an example of an eco-friendly building material because these are natural materials from left over from agriculture that do not require the use of nonrenewable resources for production.

Ecological design

Ecological design uses systems compatible with nature and modeled on natural systems, synergizing with the surrounding environment and minimizing damage to the landscape. Most conventional buildings are modeled after machines rather than nature and are designed to conform to industrial processes. Ecological design is sometimes referred to as "green design."

Ecological design faces a number of problems, including a dearth of knowledge about how to apply ecology to design. Ecologists understand ecology in different ways; some focus on energy usage while others focus on management processes. Building professionals typically only have a shallow understanding of ecology and follow a long tradition of machine-oriented design. Many natural processes, such as the growth of trees and the decomposition of materials, occur over periods that exceed a human life span, while man-made processes occur rapidly and at will.

Embodied energy

"Embodied energy" refers to the total amount of energy expended in acquiring and processing raw materials, transporting them to the building site, and installing them in a building. Products with greater embodied energy typically have a higher environmental impact because of emissions from the fossil fuels used to process and transport them. A highly durable product, though, has less environmental impact when you consider that it can remain in use for longer periods than another less durable material with less embodied energy. Also, some products have a much lower embodied energy when they are recycled, making them more environmentally sound than a product with less embodied energy that cannot be recycled.

Life cycle

The life cycle of a product, building, or material encompasses every phase of its existence, from its initial creation to its destruction. In green building, cost and sustainability is calculated over the life cycle of a building or material, not just when it is built or purchased.

The life cycle of wood floors would include harvesting wood from a forest, manufacturing the wood into a usable product, transportation to the job site, installation, use, and maintenance of the product, and ultimately, the disposal of the product when the building is demolished or the flooring is replaced.

High performance building

"High performance building" is commonly used as a synonym for green building. It refers to building practices that seek to maximize the efficiency of every aspect of the design and construction process, as well as the efficient use of energy and resources by the building itself and the creation of an optimal environment for the building occupants.

The Precautionary Principle

The Wingspread Statement on the Precautionary Principle, formulated during a January 1998 meeting of scientists, lawyers, policy makers, and environmentalists at Wingspread, headquarters of the Johnson Foundation, in Racine, Wisconsin, summarizes the Precautionary Principle:

"When an activity raises threats of harm to the environment or human health, precautionary measures should be taken even if some cause and effect relationships are not fully established scientifically."

Applied to green building, this means that no irreversible action should be undertaken in the face of scientific uncertainty, and alternatives should be sought for possibly harmful actions.

Recyclable materials

A large pavement-removing machine is tearing old asphalt off the road and loading it to a dump truck. The asphalt will be recycled again used to resurface roads.

Recyclable materials are made of various kinds of metal, plastics, glass, paper, or fibers that can be broken down and reused in the manufacture of a new product — ideally a new version of the same material. Recycling eliminates the use of energy and resources to create brand new materials.

Asphalt is one of the most recyclable construction materials available. Many forms of paper, metal, and plastic and glass bottles are also easily recyclable many times over.

Reclaimed materials

Reclaimed materials include discarded materials that can be salvaged and used in a new way. Wood from old furniture and buildings can be reused to create new furniture and new buildings. Reclaimed materials differ from recycled materials in that they have not been reprocessed and made into a new product but can be used in their original form for another purpose.

A charming, rustic garden shed made from reclaimed timber barn board

Transporting the oil used to make construction materials produces by-products.

Closed-loop material cycle

Closed-loop material cycle (CLMC) describes the concept of a construction made of materials and building elements that can be recovered from buildings and infinitely recycled through natural or industrial processes. Today, much of the debris from demolished buildings ends up in landfills, even though it contains some elements that could potentially be reused. One goal of the green building movement is to develop building materials that can be completely recycled when the building reaches the end of its life.

Deconstructability

The concept of deconstructability is being increasingly applied not only in the building industry but also in the manufacturing of automobiles and electronics. The goal is to make a product using components that can be removed and reused when the product becomes broken or obsolete. Instead of exploding an unwanted structure or smashing it with a wrecking ball and carting the rubble away, the building is dismantled piece by piece and its components are salvaged for reuse in another building or recycled into another product.

Energy efficiency

Energy-efficient design uses the least possible amount of energy to get the desired result. For example, south-facing windows, which allow sunlight to warm the interior of a building but prevent heat from escaping, will reduce the need for heating in the winter.

A building can be made more energy efficient by using insulation to help maintain the temperature inside the building, sealing cracks, and using materials that do not conduct heat and cold for window frames.

An energy-efficient product or appliance uses less energy than a conventional product of the same kind but provides the same service. For example, energy-efficient window air conditioners use up to 20 percent less energy than conventional air conditioners but still provide the same level and quality.

ENERGY STAR®

ENERGY STAR, a joint program of the U.S. Environmental Protection Agency and the U.S. Department of Energy, assigns energy performance ratings to buildings and appliances. A building or an appliance that meets EPA energy efficiency requirements is given an ENERGY STAR to let consumers know that they are saving resources when they purchase it.

Products that earn the ENERGY STAR prevent greenhouse gas emissions by meeting strict energy efficiency guidelines set by the U.S. Environmental Protection Agency and the U.S. Department of Energy.

Eco-efficiency

In 1992, the World Business Council on Sustainable Development (WBCSD) introduced the concept of including environmental impact and costs as a factor in calculating business efficiency. In other words, a company's goods and services should not only be competitively priced and satisfy human needs, they should also progressively reduce ecological impact and aim for sustainability. A number of corporations have begun including information on the sustainability and environmental impact of their products and business activities on their financial reports and statements to stockholders, in addition to the usual financial information.

The biophilia hypothesis

E. O. Wilson, a Harvard entomologist, coined the term "biophilia hypothesis" for the concept that human beings have a genetically based need to interact with nature. Numerous scientific studies have demonstrated that people experience less stress when they connect to nature in some way. Although the effect is difficult to quantify, there is conclusive evidence that workers in a building are healthier, more productive, and more content when they have access, even at a distance, to daylight and outside views.

Ecological rucksack and MIPS

"Ecological rucksack" refers to the total quantity of natural material (in pounds or kilos) that must be physically displaced to produce a particular product. It is a measure of the stress placed on the natural environment by a particular human activity. For example, 85 kilos of bauxite ore must be moved to produce a kilo of aluminum, so the ecological rucksack of aluminum is 85. Activities such as agriculture, mining, excavating, and dredging disrupt the environment. A material's biological rucksack can be used to compare its environmental impact to the disruption caused by other materials.

MIPS (materials intensity per unit service) is a measure of the amount of service delivered by a product. The greater the service, the lower its MIPS. Materials with low MIPS are considered the most eco-efficient.

The Natural Step

The Natural Step, developed by Swedish oncologist Karl Henrik Robert in 1989, provides a framework for evaluating the health effects of materials we create and use in our daily lives. He suggested that many health problems, especially in children, are caused by exposure to heavy metals, synthetic substances, and the carcinogens released by burning fossil fuels. Robert sets forth Four Principles of Sustainability that can be used in evaluating materials and products for use in green building.

The Four Principles of Sustainability

To become a sustainable society we must:

1. Eliminate our contribution to the progressive buildup of substances extracted from the earth's crust (for example, heavy metals and fossil fuels).

2. Eliminate our contribution to the progressive buildup of chemicals and compounds produced by society (for example, dioxins, PCBs, and DDT).

3. Eliminate our contribution to the progressive physical degradation and destruction of nature and natural processes (for example, over harvesting forests and paving over critical wildlife habitat).

4. Eliminate our contribution to conditions that undermine people's capacity to meet their basic human needs (for example, unsafe working conditions and not enough pay to live on, inequitable distribution of resources).

From the website of The Natural Step (**www.naturalstep.org/the-system-conditions**)

Principles of Green Building

Each green building project is unique. There is no single formula for greenness; every project employs a combination of strategies to achieve one or more green objectives. The scope of a green building project is determined by a number of factors, including the geographical location and physical characteristics of the building or building site, local materials and services, the priorities of the company, the needs of its employees, zoning laws and requirements, and the amount of financing available. Whether a project is large or small, green building is guided by a set of basic principles:

Build in a location that will maximize conservation and minimize destruction

A new building should be located on a site that will enable sustainability with minimal interference in the natural habitats and ecosystems that surround it.

Many local, state, and federal initiatives reward companies that choose to build on or redevelop a brownfield — a previously developed industrial site that has become vacant and run down — or a grayfield — a blighted urban site. By constructing a new facility on a previously developed site, the company avoids disturbing agricultural land or natural wilderness. Many brownfield sites are already served by existing infrastructure, such as roads, water and sewage systems, electrical power lines, and transportation routes, and are part of an existing tax base. You can find grayfield sites in the areas surrounding the downtown centers of many U.S. cities. As new suburbs are built, businesses relocate to more prosperous outlying areas, leaving behind wastelands of vacant shopping centers and abandoned factories. Erecting a new building on one of these sites reinvigorates a town's economy and improves the lives of the surrounding residents.

Greenfield refers to sites on previously undeveloped agricultural land or untouched wilderness.

The orientation of a building on the site also contributes to its sustainability. Ample southern exposure will maximize a building's potential to use solar energy for heating or electricity. The building's orientation also determines how much its interior temperature is affected by wind and external weather conditions, and how stormwater runoff is managed.

Reuse, refurbish, recycle

Reusing materials not only conserves resources, it saves money. If you will be demolishing part of your structure for a remodel, consider what you can salvage to reuse in your new office. Salvaged building materials such as broken concrete, used tile, and wood from old buildings can be used for flooring, wall facings, architectural features, and outdoor landscaping. Often, you can revamp, refinish, and transform items like desks, chairs, and other furniture into completely new-looking products. An interior designer experienced in green design can suggest ways to reuse existing materials.

Implement systems that will conserve energy and resources

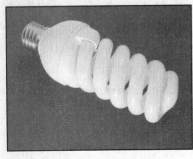

According to the Union of Concerned Scientists, 90 billion pounds of greenhouse emissions can be prevented if every U.S. household replaces just one regular light bulb with an energy efficient light bulb.

Many green buildings use natural resources like sunlight, wind, and water to provide heating, cooling, electricity, and interior lighting. Large south-facing windows, light shelves, skylights, sun tunnels, and mirrors direct natural light to the interior of a building. Water and energy conservation systems include dual flush and low-flow toilets, low-flow water fixtures, hot water recirculation, and heat recovery systems. Capturing and harvesting rainwater and using a gray water system reduces dependence on water from water treatment plants.

Implement systems that decrease waste

A variety of strategies can be employed to reduce waste. Using recycled paper or implementing a paperless policy for a portion of your office work will make an impact. Using energy-efficient light bulbs such as compact fluorescent bulbs and energy-efficient appliances and machines throughout your office will greatly reduce energy consumption and energy waste. More advanced methods for reducing waste include composting systems, recycling rainwater for water usage, and using recycled drywall instead of new drywall in new construction. Some companies have adopted a "zero landfill policy," meaning that all their waste, including manufacturing waste, is recycled in some manner.

Use natural, sustainable, nontoxic building materials.

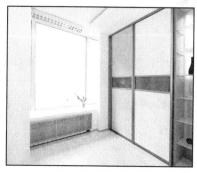

Using building materials that minimize harmful effects on the environment, such as deforestation or emission of high levels of greenhouse gases, is perhaps the easiest, most practical, and most affordable method of becoming green. For example, choosing bamboo flooring instead of traditional wood floors for your office lobby is an excellent way to green your building. Because bamboo is harvested from bamboo stalks that grow back very quickly and does not involve the destruction of forests, the impact on the environment is minimal.

Bamboo floors and closet doors were used in this contemporary office.

Create an environment that improves employee productivity and protects building occupants' health

You can green the interior of a building by making simple changes like switching to environmentally friendly cleaning products, optimizing natural light, and using non-toxic paints. Most paints give off volatile organic compounds (VOCs), harmful carbon-based toxins that cause long-term damage to the health of humans and animals. Using low- or no-VOC paints on all your walls will significantly improve the indoor air quality of your building and provide short- and long-term health benefits for employees, reducing the incidence of headaches and respiratory symptoms and the potential for more serious diseases such as cancer and asthma. Installing formaldehyde-free cabinets and natural wool carpets will also improve internal air quality and promote a healthy environment for building occupants.

Misconceptions About Green Building

As the green building industry has expanded, it has received considerable attention in the media. Though scientific studies have confirmed that green building is environmentally sound, financially viable, and results in fewer sick days and increased productivity among employees, critics continue to voice misgivings. Some of the critics' concerns are legitimate, but a number of misconceptions continue to influence the attitude of the public toward green building. *Some common misconceptions are explained in the following sections.*

Green building costs more

Recycled water collected from the air conditioning unit is used to water plants within the office.

In conventional building, costs are calculated in terms of initial investment in materials and construction. Green building considers the life cycle of each product, material, and process that goes into the construction and operation of the building must be considered. Though some green materials do cost more than conventional items — for instance, natural wool carpeting is more expensive than conventional synthetic carpeting — the cost of many green building materials is comparable to the cost of conventional materials.

A green project design considers the long-term budget for operating and maintaining a building as well as the initial cost of constructing it. Today, the initial cost of construction materials, permits, certification, and consultation averages 0 to 3 percent more for a green building than for a conventional building. However, using sustainable and durable building materials decreases maintenance costs over the lifetime of the building and will probably pay for the larger initial investment many times over. Over the lifetime of a building, the savings realized by installing rainwater systems and energy-efficient systems, such as solar panels or wind turbines, outweigh the costs of implementing them.

Green building is too involved

Green building can seem intimidating for someone who is unfamiliar with it. Green building designs, terminology, and ways of thinking about material usage deviate sharply from concepts of conventional building. In fact, the basic principle of green building is simple: Seek a cleaner and more efficient environment both inside and outside the building. Architects, consultants, attorneys, and engineers who specialize in green building can serve as resources for learning about the process.

Employees do not care about green building

This open atrium allows the use of natural light in the building and a man-made lawn to thrive. Another benefit is that the grass helps clean the air.

Research shows that many employees prefer to work for a green company. A 2008 Harris Poll study found that nearly 35 percent of prospective employees, which includes adults already in the workforce, would prefer to work for a company that is conscious about being environmentally friendly.

Employees in green buildings tend to be more satisfied with their jobs, healthier, and more productive. According to an April 2002 study conducted by the U.S. Green Building Council, the company VeriFone increased employee productivity by 5 to 7 percent and reduced absenteeism by 47 percent by installing skylights to increase natural light in workspaces and improve temperature control. The company also reduced its energy consumption by 59 percent. Small changes such as these can have enormous impact on productivity, health, and overall enthusiasm of employees.

If a building cannot conserve energy, it cannot be green

In this office, paper-recycling bins are placed throughout the building so employees can easily recycle.

Energy conservation is only one aspect of being green. If budget restrictions inhibit the installation of energy-saving systems, such as solar or wind power, there are many other things that can be done to make a building greener. Installation of bamboo flooring or formaldehyde-free countertops is considered a green practice that has little to do with energy conservation. Using less paper and initiating a recycling program will make your building greener.

Green buildings are always made from recycled material

Greenness is not determined solely by the extent to which recycled materials are used. Not all building materials are recyclable and using only material that has been recycled for a building would be almost impossible. Green building involves many considerations, including orientation of your building to make use of solar energy, choice of a location near a residential area so employees do not have to drive long distances to get to work, and sustainability of the overall building design. In some cases, using a new building material may prove to be greener than using a recycled one.

Green buildings are not attractive

Many people believe that green buildings look ultramodern and futuristic, but green buildings can also mirror conventional building designs. Architects and engineers can tailor a building design to meet just about any expectation. The external physical appearance of the Toyota Motor Sales headquarters building, constructed as a green building in 2003 in Torrance, California, gives no indication that the building is 30 percent more energy efficient than the requirements of local building codes, saves 11 million gallons of water a year by using recycled water for irrigation and plumbing, and is widely recognized in the state as a green building. The building itself looks very conventional.

Photos courtesy of Toyota Motor Sales, U.S.A., Inc.

There is nothing wrong with conventional materials

Many conventional building components have harmful environmental and health effects. Many paints contain high levels of VOCs. Most trim moldings and wood floors are coated with a chemical sealant that is hazardous to health. Vinyl tiles can emit harmful dioxins long after they are installed and some conventional countertops, wood products, and carpets are soaked in formaldehyde, a chemical proven hazardous to the environment, people, and animals.

The Evolution of Green Building

Anasazi Indian dwellings at Bandelier National Monument.

Some green building concepts are thousands of years old. Ancient builders used natural building materials to create comfortable and energy-efficient structures adapted to local climates. The Anasazi Indians, who inhabited what is now Arizona, Utah, Colorado, and New Mexico about 2,000 years ago, positioned their homes and villages to optimize natural light and heat from the sun. Their homes were built in tightly knit communities so that resources could be shared. The Anasazi captured rainwater and built using resources found in the immediate area, such as mud, earth bricks, sand, and wood. Green building today embodies many of these characteristics.

Ancient Romans positioned their bathhouse windows to face the sun and benefit from its warmth, and the Greeks positioned their dwellings to absorb the sun's warmth.

The rise of environmentalism

Human beings have had a negative impact on the environment for thousands of years as they cleared forests for agriculture, abandoned arable land after all the nutrients had been leached out of it by farming, overhunted and overgrazed, started forest fires, and in some cases, built large cities that depleted water supplies. The Industrial Revolution, which began with the establishment of the first large factories during the second half of the 18th century, rapidly accelerated the impact of human activity. World population mushroomed from about 500 million in 1550 to 2 billion in 1930, 3 billion in 1960, and 6.6 billion in 2007. For a century and a half, the opportunity for growth seemed limitless, as one new technology led to another, transportation became more efficient, buildings became taller, and cities grew larger. There was a general attitude that wilderness existed to be conquered and developed, and that progress could be measured by growth in the number of cities and factories.

During the second half of the 19th century, social activists in the United States and Europe began to agitate against unhealthy working and living conditions in cities and industrial areas, and laws were passed to protect workers and to ensure clean drinking water and adequate sanitation. In the United States, where timber barons had made fortunes cutting down large tracts of forest and selling the wood, a few conservationists began to speak out about the need to preserve wilderness areas for future generations. Ralph Waldo Emerson and Henry David Thoreau wrote about the appreciation of nature. In 1851, a California businessman named George Gale inadvertently drew international media attention to the issue of conservation when he cut down a 2,500-year-old sequoia tree known as "Mother of the Forest," to display a section of its bark in a traveling sideshow. The ensuing public outrage resulted in the establishment of the first federal state park in Yosemite Valley in 1864, followed by Yellowstone National Park eight years later.

In 1892, Henry Senger, Warren Olney, and John Muir established the Sierra Club to promote the preservation of wilderness areas. Today, the Sierra Club strives, as part of its mission, "to practice and promote the responsible use of the earth's ecosystems and resources."

The Forest Reserve Act of 1891 established a U.S. Forest Service and gave the president authority to designate forested public lands as protected areas. During his term in office, Theodore Roosevelt increased federal land reserves to almost 200 million acres and established federal control over the building of dams

Relict sequoia trees in Redwood National Park. The Sierra Club played a role in getting this park established.

and irrigation projects. In 1916, The National Park Service Organic Act established a National Park Service in the United States.

Edwin Drake drilled the first successful experimental oil well in 1859 in Pennsylvania. In 1882, Thomas Edison opened the first electric light and power plant, Pearl Street station, serving one square mile of New York City with steam-driven dynamos. In the early 1900s, Henry Ford revolutionized transportation when he introduced an automobile that was affordable to ordinary working people. In 1913, the first electric refrigerator was produced.

Growth of Energy Consumption in the United States

The introduction of affordable automobiles and electric power caused energy use in the United States to jump from **100 million Btu per person** at end of 19th century to **214 million Btu per person** in 1949.

Energy consumption increased steadily to a peak of **359 million Btu per person** in 1978 and 1979.

In 2009, people in the United States consumed **308 million Btu of energy per person**, 44 percent above the 1949 rate.

In 2009, total U.S. energy consumption was **94,578,267 billion Btu**; 7,743,759 billion Btu of that was from renewable energy sources.

During the era of prosperity that followed the Great Depression and World War II, suburbs and urban sprawl arose around U.S. cities. Fertilizers and pesticides came into widespread use, and air conditioning made it possible to live and work comfortably even in hot and humid climates. However, there were alarming signs of an environmental crisis. A suffocating blanket of smog covered Los Angeles in 1954. In 1952, a "London fog" killed 4,000 people in four days. In 1948, an atmospheric inversion temporarily raised the death rate in Donora, Pennsylvania, by 400 percent. In 1953, smog killed between 170 and 260 people in New York. In response, the National Air Pollution Control Administration (NAPCA) was established in 1955 under the Department of Health, Education, and Welfare (HEW). A predecessor to the Department of the Interior's Water Quality Administration (FWQA) was established in 1948 to deal with severe water pollution problems, including untreated sewage and industrial waste, dying rivers and lakes, and scalding water poured directly into streams and rivers.

Environmentalists began to predict a global disaster unless public attitudes toward natural resources changed. In *A Sand County Almanac,* published posthumously in 1949, ecologist Aldo Leopold suggested that human beings have an ethical responsibility to live in harmony with the natural world. *Silent Spring*, published by Rachel Carson in 1962, carefully documented the dangers of the pesticide DDT and led to its use being banned in the United States in 1972. This book made the public aware that toxins and pesticides are health hazards.

In 1968, biologist Paul Ehrlich published *The Population Bomb*, which discussed the effects of an expanding population on the environment. In 1972, a group of scientists published *The Limits to Growth*, which discussed the effects of human activity on the environment. In May 1969, Secretary General U Thant of the United Nations declared that the earth had only ten years to avert environmental disaster; the next month, he placed most of the responsibility for this catastrophe on the United States.

Environmental Protection Agency in Washington, D.C.

On New Year's Day, 1970, President Nixon signed The National Environmental Policy Act (NEPA) establishing a Council on Environmental Quality (CEQ) and requiring federal agencies to prepare Environmental Impact Statements for any major project that might potentially have environmental consequences. Later that year, the Environmental Protection Agency (**www.epa.gov**) was established to police air, water, and solid waste pollution.

"A thing is right when it tends to preserve the integrity, stability, and beauty of the biotic community. It is wrong when it tends otherwise."

ALDO LEOPOLD, *A Sand County Almanac*

Energy crisis of the 1970s

The United States experienced a wake-up call when worldwide oil shortages led to two energy crises during the 1970s. Suddenly, it became apparent that the United States would be competing with other large economies for a limited and dwindling resource. In response to the crisis, Congress passed the National Energy Act (NEA) in 1978 to reorganize a disjointed national energy policy. The NEA established energy efficiency programs, tax incentives, tax disincentives, energy conservation programs, alternative fuel programs, and regulatory and market-based initiatives. Many of the regulatory initiatives have since been abandoned, but the NEA included important components that became the basis for today's clean energy incentives. Part of the NEA, The Public Utility Regulatory Policy Act (PURPA), mandated local utilities to pay their customers for excess electricity generated by their solar and wind systems.

In the late 1970s, President Jimmy Carter announced a plan to conserve energy and pursue renewable energy sources such as solar power. The U.S. government became increasingly involved in the green building and energy conservation movement, motivated by the compelling need to reduce dependence on fossil fuels and the carbon emissions resulting from their use.

Emergence of green building guidelines and regulations

In 1989, the American Institute of Architects founded the Committee on the Environment (COTE) to advocate for environmentally responsible buildings. The establishment of the COTE pushed the green building movement into the forefront. In 1992, the federal government established the ENERGY STAR program to promote energy efficiency among individual consumers as well as businesses and organizations. The following year the U.S. Green Building Council (USGBC) was founded, and in 1998, the USGBC established a green building rating system known as Leadership in Energy and Environmental Design (LEED).

Environmentalism and Green Building Milestones	
1875	Establishment of the American Forestry Association to protect the nation's forests
Late 19th century	Yosemite National Park, Yellowstone National Park, and Sequoia National Park are established.
1891	The Forest Reserve Act of 1891 establishes a U.S. Forest Service.
1892	Foundation of the Sierra Club
1916	The National Park Service Organic Act establishes a National Park Service in the United States.
1935	Foundation of the Wilderness Society
1960	Foundation of the Alaska Conservation Society
1962	Writer Rachel Carson publishes *Silent Spring*, alerting the public to the dangers of pesticides.
1970	The first Earth Day is celebrated on April 22.

Environmentalism and Green Building Milestones	
1970	Foundation of the Environmental Protection Agency (EPA)
1972	The United Nations Conference on the Human Environment takes place in Stockholm, Sweden.
1974	Foundation of the Solar Energy Research Institute.
1977	President Carter initiates an energy conservation plan that emphasizes renewable energy.
1978	Passage of the National Energy Act (NEA) and Public Utility Regulatory Policy Act (PURPA)
1978	World's first renewable energy village at Schuchuli, Arizona
1980	National Bridges National Monument installs the (then) largest photovoltaic system in the world to supply 90 percent of its energy needs.
1985	Architect William McDonough designs the New York offices of the Environmental Defense Fund, incorporating natural materials, daylighting, and excellent indoor air quality.
1987	Publication of *Our Common Future*, often referred to as the *Bruntland Report*, placing environmental concerns on the political agenda and calling for the active participation of all sectors of society in decisions relating to sustainable development
1989	Croxton Collaborative designs the offices of the Natural Resources Defense Council to use only $1/3$ of the energy consumed by conventional buildings.
1989	Foundation of the Committee on the Environment (COTE) by the American Institute of Architects
1992	Establishment of the U.S. government ENERGY STAR program
1992	United Nations Conference on Sustainable Development (Rio Conference)

Environmentalism and Green Building Milestones	
1992	*Environmental Building News* began publication.
1992	The BREEAM green building rating system is developed in the U.K.
1993	"Architecture at the Crossroads," a joint meeting of the American Institute of Architects (AIA) and the International Union of Architects (IUA), releases the Declaration of Interdependence for a Sustainable Future, a code of sustainable principles and practices.
1993	The U.S. Green Building Council (USGBC) is formed.
1993	The Clinton administration initiates "Greening of the White House." The Old Executive Office Building renovation results in energy cost savings of $300,000 per year and reduces carbon emissions by 845 tons of carbon per year. Many federal agencies followed suit with energy-saving initiatives.
1994	The National Park Services publishes *Guiding Principles for Sustainable Design*.
1995	The Rocky Mountain Institute publishes *A Primer on Sustainable Building*.
1998	The Leadership in Energy and Environmental Design (LEED) system is established by the USGBC.
2000	LEED 2.0
2003	LEED 2.1
2007	The Energy Independence and Security Act, which outlines specifications and requirements for green federal buildings, is signed into law.
2009	LEED-NC 2009
2009	Research published in a book titled *Green Outlook 2009: Trends Driving Change* predicts that green building will double by 2013, making green building (residential and commercial combined) a nearly $150 billion market.

CHAPTER 2:
Why Build Green?

Each year, according to the EPA, almost 170,000 new commercial buildings are constructed in the United States and nearly 45,000 are torn down. The commercial construction industry has an unparalleled opportunity to create a safer, healthier, and more sustainable living environment, and to contribute significantly to solving the global environmental crisis. Building green is not a luxury; it is a necessity. Many green building practices will become standard for all commercial buildings. The United States, which has been the world's largest consumer of energy and resources for more than a century, may soon be supplanted by the growing economies of China and India. Global demand for fossil fuels, clean water, energy, and building materials such as concrete and steel increases every year. We can no longer afford to waste or discard precious resources. It makes sense to design and construct energy-efficient buildings that minimize waste and environmental damage.

Concern for the environment is not the only motivation for building green. Building green has significant financial rewards, including the savings realized on the cost of energy and maintenance, improved employee retention and productivity, and increased resale value of the property. A green building supports the perception that a company or organization is environmentally responsible and concerned about the well-being of its employees. This chapter explains why building green is a good idea.

The Cost of Not Building Green

There is now widespread acceptance of the fact that our resources will soon be exhausted if we continue our current rate of consumption. These statistics help to put the problem in perspective:

Consumption and waste:

- Commercial buildings in the U.S. account for:
  - 39 percent of total energy use
  - 12 percent of total water consumption
  - 68 percent of total electricity consumption
  - 38 percent of carbon dioxide emissions

- Nearly 10 percent of energy used in the United States goes to heating, pumping, and treating water, according to the EPA. Implementing alternative, greener, and more sustainable systems to treat, pump, and heat water alone could have a significant impact on energy consumption.

- Debris and waste from the construction and demolition of buildings equals approximately 160 million tons per year. This accounts for more than 25 percent of waste from non-industrial sources in the entire country. The construction, demolition, renovation, and use, of buildings generates about two-thirds of all non-industrial solid waste in the United States.

- In the United States, impervious surfaces, such as roofs and paved parking lots that prevent rainwater and melted snow from soaking into the ground, make up an area nearly as big as the state of Ohio. Thirty-five percent of rainwater runoff is due to roofs of offices, homes, stores, and patios, according to the EPA. The result of excessive runoff is flooding, erosion, and water contamination from pesticides and other chemicals.

- On average, more than 200 million tons of garbage and waste, including construction waste, is generated in the United States each year. Most of this goes to landfills and is not recyclable.

Health and environment:

- Indoor air quality is much lower than outdoor air quality, and Americans spend nearly 90 percent of their time indoors. The air quality inside an office building where people spend at least 40 hours a week affects their health. Though pollution levels inside a building are typically two to five times higher than the level of pollutants in the air outside the building, in some buildings they are as much as 100 times higher. These indoor pollutants come from a variety of sources including debris from construction and combustion; manufacturing and production activities that could include toxins and dust produced during on-site construction; volatile organic compounds (VOCs) from paints and furniture; toxic cleaning supplies; and heating and cooling systems. Toxins, including lead, radon, asbestos, and pesticides, also contribute to poor indoor air quality.

- According to a 2008 study, *Assumptions to the Annual Energy Outlook,* by the Energy Information Administration (EIA), buildings are responsible for nearly half of the harmful greenhouse gases, particularly carbon dioxide, that exist in the atmosphere today.

- A December 2009 finding released by the EPA officially recognized that certain greenhouse gases, such as carbon dioxide, lead to serious short- and long-term illness, including respiratory problems and cancer, and are hazardous to people's health.

Fossil fuels

Many traditional building practices consume resources that are finite and nonrenewable, like the fossil fuels coal and oil. Coal, which provides more than a quarter of the world's energy, was formed as accumulated plant remains deposited 286 to 360 million years ago during the Carboniferous Period were buried and subjected to intense heat and pressure. Oil generates 40 percent of the world's commercial energy. Oil and natural gas formed when the remains of marine organisms that lived about 300 million years ago were trapped under sediments on the ocean floor and subjected to similar heat and pressure. Fuels that formed over hundreds of millions of years cannot be replenished once they are used up. Scientists estimate that the world's coal reserves will be depleted in 155 years. Over the past 50 years, rapid population growth and industrial expansion has caused a seven-fold increase in the global demand for oil. The demand for oil is generally expected to continue growing at an average annual rate of 1 to 2 percent. The world has already consumed almost half the total amount of conventional oil that most experts estimate will ever be available. It is generally predicted that world oil production will begin to decline by 2020, and even the most conservative scientists believe the decline will begin before 2030.

Traditional buildings not only use energy generated by burning fossil fuels, but also incorporate materials that are either made of petroleum products or that are manufactured using energy from fossil fuels. Green building practices reduce or eliminate dependence on energy from fossil fuels and use building components made from renewable materials.

Greenhouse gases

Greenhouse gases are chemical compounds that trap heat in the earth's atmosphere by absorbing the energy radiated when sunlight striking the earth's surface is reflected back into space. Some greenhouse gases, including carbon dioxide, water vapor, nitrous oxide, and methane, occur naturally and are emitted by both natural processes and human activity. Others, such as hydrofluorocarbons, perfluorocarbons, and sulfur hexafluoride, are synthetic greenhouse gases emitted from a variety of industrial processes. These are sometimes referred to as high global warming potential gases ("High GWP gases").

If some greenhouse gases did not exist, the earth would be very cold. Without them, temperatures on the earth's surface would be about 60° F lower than they are now, and life as we know it would not be possible. Over time, if atmospheric concentrations of greenhouse gases remained relatively stable, the temperature of the earth's surface would stay roughly constant. Scientific evidence indicates, however, that human activity during the past century has exponentially increased the presence of greenhouse gases in the atmosphere, contributing to a rise in global average temperature and related climate change. Most of these greenhouse gases, primarily carbon dioxide and methane, have been emitted through the burning of fossil fuels.

Green building seeks to harvest energy in a responsible manner and create sustainable products without emitting environmentally harmful greenhouse gases or other by-products. At the end of their life cycle, sustainable products can be recycled and used to manufacture new versions of themselves, eliminating the need to use further resources to create the same product.

Global warming and climate change

Coal plants contribute to pollution and global warming.

Global warming is the slow rise of the earth's average surface, air, and water temperatures. Though global warming has been naturally occurring for thousands of years, it has increased at an alarming rate over the last 100 years. It is now universally accepted that human activities, such as burning fossil fuels, which releases greenhouse gases into the atmosphere; manufacturing; cutting down forests; and interfering with waterways have hastened the process. The National Oceanic and Atmospheric Administration's (NOAA) *State of the Climate Report* and the National Aeronautics and Space Administration's (NASA) *Surface Temperature Analysis* indicate that the average temperature of the earth's surface has increased by about 1.2° F to 1.4° F since 1900. The resulting changes to our ecosystems threaten our world food supply and the continued existence of many species of organisms.

Scientists warn that unless we cut greenhouse gas emissions in half by 2050, the risk to quality of life and the environment is significant.

Evidence that suggests global warming is a significant threat:

- The rapid melting of glaciers due to rising temperatures is causing a decrease in populations of animals like polar bears who depend on these glaciers for food, water, and survival. According to "Global Warming Fast Facts" by *National Geographic*, Glacier National Park in Montana now has only 20 percent of the glaciers it had 100 years ago.

Antarctic glacier from the melting Larsen B ice shelf on the Antarctic Peninsula. There are impressive crevasses. This ice shelf totally collapsed in 2002.

- An increase in the occurrence and intensity of natural disasters, including wildfires and hurricanes, in recent years may be attributed to changes in temperature, which create idiosyncratic weather patterns.

- According to a September 2008 study published by the *Proceedings of the National Academy of Sciences*, rising sea temperatures have a devastating effect on coral reefs. Coral reef destruction and death increased tremendously in 1998, possibly because of harsh weather conditions prompted by rising core temperatures. This included El Niño, a strong, warm ocean current that was very powerful in 1997 to 1998 and was responsible for droughts and higher temperatures in the Pacific, Mexico, and Central America during those years.

Reaction to Global Warming Heats Up

The Kyoto Protocol, a document initially introduced and adopted in Kyoto, Japan in 1997, seeks to minimize global warming by imposing regulations on greenhouse gas emissions and fossil fuel burning. Nearly 40 countries have signed the protocol and have committed to addressing global warming.

Although there is scientific evidence of accelerated global warming and its potentially disastrous effects on human life and the environment, significant numbers of people still do not believe global warming poses a threat to human life and to the environment. Some of the arguments against the existence of a global warming threat include:

- The urge to reduce consumption goes against the natural development of the human race and the rate at which it is growing and modernizing.

- Global warming is taking place, but it is a natural, non-threatening event that has been occurring for thousands of years and poses no significant risk to human, plant, and animal life.

- There is little evidence to support the theory that rising temperatures have contributed to severe weather conditions such as hurricanes.

- Even if temperatures do rise, human beings will adjust. There is no evidence to support the theory that increased temperatures will lead to a higher mortality rate.

CASE STUDY: IF WE GET PEOPLE EDUCATED, GREEN WILL CATCH ON

Mike McNatt, attorney
Roetzel & Andress LPA; Orlando, FL
www.ralaw.com

Mike McNatt became involved with green building virtually by accident. McNatt is an attorney with Roetzel & Andress LPA, where he works with clients to address issues unique to green building that arise during site selection, acquisition, construction, financing, and leasing. He also serves as the lead counsel for a commercial office development in Florida — the first one to achieve LEED certification in the state — and was the first attorney in central Florida to become a LEED AP. "I thought green was for hippies," he jokes, "until I started seeing the facts, and that is how it won me over."

McNatt began his career as a banker and later became a real estate attorney. Around 2002, he began working with a client who was seeking LEED certification, something he had never even heard of before. At that time, LEED and green building were not nearly as well known as they are today. McNatt was new to the concept of sustainable development.

"I think there was a reluctance [from the industry] to try anything new. There was a fear that green was a passing fad, but there was a slow inertia of movement," he explains.

However, by the time the project was over, McNatt was so enthralled with the process that he eventually became a LEED AP and made a career out of serving as a legal advisor on green projects.

"The passion was contagious," McNatt said. "I became a true believer. I thought, 'This makes sense.' From a rational business perspective not only does it help environmentally, but also it adds to the bottom line."

McNatt now works to help clients meet this bottom line in their green building initiatives by working with commercial office building developers to ensure all the legal aspects of building, leasing, or selling an office building or space are sound. He is now a prominent member of the green building industry in central Florida, as well as a member of the Florida Green Building Coalition. He also serves as chairman to the National Sustainable Development Forum. "Green building went from fad to trend," he said.

Legally speaking, a variety of issues unique to green building projects must be acknowledged and considered — from the site selection, building, and construction phase through to the leasing process. McNatt emphasizes the importance of working with the municipality to let them know about your green project and ensuring that the property does not inhibit or contaminate the surrounding environment during the site-selection phase. During the leasing phase, McNatt explains the importance of creating a clause in a lease that ensures tenants will not counteract the greenness of the building from a developer's or landlord's standpoint. This counteraction could be achieved if a tenant uses regular paint instead of low-VOC paint or chooses not to recycle, for instance. From a tenant's standpoint, this means understanding the regulations and instituting systems to follow them as a company or corporation.

McNatt also sees the importance of working with the right green building team. Having a sustainability or LEED consultant on the project can help because he or she can correspond with the local municipality and understand the building codes, permits, and the incentives offered. Today, incentives for building green can reap big cost savings. "It used to be about bringing jobs to the area or increasing taxes," he said. These days, incentives center on the total impact your building will have on the city, including its water and energy usage. Municipalities allow greater intensity of development because your green building will have less of impact on the local environment, which means less impact on the city sewer system and less emissions from employees traveling to work. "Most local governments have a LEED AP on staff who is able to negotiate incentives," McNatt said. "Which is why it helps to have a LEED AP or sustainability consultant on your own side to identify the incentives on your behalf. Many incentives exist that people are not even aware of."

McNatt believes that choosing the right contractor is one of the most important decisions in pursuing LEED certification. Contractors are ultimately responsible for overseeing the entire project, which includes ensuring that all specifications and requirements are met to achieve certification. This includes everything from ensuring the specified products are used to ensuring construction materials are recycled during the construction process. If products are switched out for less expensive ones during the construction process, which happens often so the contractor can pocket the difference between the costs of the products, the building may risk its certification without the developer even knowing it. This underlines the importance of working with a trustworthy contractor. "They are the ones held liable if they switch out products," McNatt said. "But you, as the developer, company, or corporation, are the one to lose out in the end if this happens."

As far as green building has developed, its relative infancy poses another interesting challenge when it comes to construction liability, which poses a risk to the developer. However, McNatt predicts that green building will predominate in the future. "Green requirements are raising the standards. Anything that is not green will be obsolete in five years," he said. "The future requirements of green building may include carbon neutral or off the grid, reducing energy so [buildings] are not on the grid anymore."

As for getting corporations, businesses, companies, and individuals on board with the concept of green building, McNatt says, "If we can get people educated, it will catch on."

Problems with Conventional Building Materials

Green building encompasses a variety of objectives: sustainability, energy efficiency, conservation of the natural environment, recycling, and the creation of a wholesome work environment. Many of the materials and products used in the construction of conventional buildings have characteristics that violate one or more principles of green building. To evaluate the greenness of a particular product, it is necessary to examine every aspect of it: its source, the process used to manufacture it, its chemical content, the transportation required to bring it to the building site, and whether the material can be recycled after demolition. Some building products are harmful to the environment because they are made from nonrenewable materials, such as petroleum or hardwood harvested from a rainforest. Others are manufactured using large amounts of energy generated by burning fossil fuels or giving off harmful emissions during the manufacturing process.

Many conventional building materials are made with harmful chemicals that pose a significant health threat to construction workers and the building occupants. Over the years, dozens of chemicals and building materials previously thought to be harmless, like asbestos, formaldehyde, and lead-based paints, have been declared public health hazards. As research has revealed more information about such threats to human health, green building has become increasingly popular.

The manufacturing processes for some conventional building products use or emit cancer-causing chemicals, known as carcinogens that could end up in our air or water, or sicken the workers who are exposed to them. In addition, the environmental impact of using certain materials must be considered. This includes the energy used and the pollution generated by transporting them for thousands of miles to the building site.

Sometimes it is necessary to compare the relative environmental impact of using two materials to decide which one is greener. For example, the amount of fossil fuel needed to produce a local product might be less than the amount of fuel that would be consumed transporting a greener product from a faraway manufacturing plant to your building site.

By-products

By-products are secondary products created as a result of manufacturing. Most by-products are created unintentionally or as a consequence of production. Pollution created during the transportation of construction material over long distances is an example of a by-product. Another example is toxic gases given off during chemical reactions in a manufacturing process, such as the phosphine given off when solar panels are manufactured.

Off-gassing

Off-gassing is the slow release of toxins, chemicals, and gases from a material. Off-gassing can cause severe allergies and respiratory problems, as well as other long-term health issues. Many paints used on interior walls continue to release chemicals long after they have dried. "New paint smell" (or the "new carpet smell" when new carpeting is installed) is actually the off-gassing of a product.

Volatile organic compounds (VOCs)

Volatile organic compounds (VOCs) are natural or synthetic chemical compounds found in many conventional building materials. Some VOCs pose significant health risks. The EPA regulates certain VOCs through the Clean Air Act and Clean Water Act, but many that are not regulated are found in the materials most commonly used in construction.

Follow your Nose

The best way to determine the presence of a VOC is by using your nose. The smell that accompanies new materials like carpeting, paint, and car interiors, often referred to as "new-carpet smell," "new-car smell," or "new-paint smell," is indicative of the presence of high levels of VOCs that may be toxic.

VOCs found in paint, carpeting, cleaning products, furniture, and even toner for printers and photocopiers contribute significantly to indoor air pollution. Studies from the EPA have shown that VOCs can be up to 1,000 times more concentrated indoors than outdoors because of lack of ventilation. Most people spend a lot of time indoors and are consequently exposed to potentially toxic chemicals that can seriously affect their health. Some of the short-term health effects of VOCs include:

- Headaches, dizziness, and nausea
- Fatigue
- Nosebleeds
- Skin irritation

Another effect of exposure to high levels of VOCs is sick building syndrome (SBS), an illness directly related to poor air and environmental qualities of the building in which the sufferer works or has worked. The term is used to describe both general symptoms and acute health problems that can be directly correlated to a specific area of a building, such as a cubicle or office, and cannot be attributed to any other specific illness or cause.

Building-related illnesses (BRIs) are more advanced forms of SBS diagnosed when the air quality of a building and its contaminants can be directly linked to specific illnesses. Symptoms of BRIs include fever, headaches, nausea, and coughing. BRIs not only undermine employees' well-being but also result in loss of revenue due to absenteeism, increased health care costs, and lower productivity.

☀ Formaldehyde

Formaldehyde, a toxic chemical compound, is used in the production of many materials found in the interior of buildings, such as cabinets and flooring. It is a known carcinogen and can cause respiratory, skin, and allergy problems. According to the U.S. Institute of Health, in 1987 the EPA recognized that formaldehyde could cause cancer in humans if they are exposed to it for long periods of time or in high doses. The International Agency for Research on Cancer (IARC) subsequently classified formaldehyde as a carcinogen. Multiple studies conducted on the role of formaldehyde exposure in the development of cancer have found that the chemical can be specifically linked to the development of certain types of cancer.

The EPA further recognizes the dangers of formaldehyde in manufacturing and building materials. Formaldehyde can be found in dozens of materials used in both the home and the office, including fuel-burning appliances that are not properly vented, such as gas stoves or kerosene space heaters; adhesives used for cabinets and furniture; drapes; floor finishes; paints; and other coating products. Formaldehyde can release dangerous gases for years after it has been initially used. It is used in a variety of ways and in a number of building materials including:

- Wood cabinetry
- Plywood
- Wood paneling

- Textiles
- Concrete
- Adhesives

Paints

Paint is one of the most common finishing products used throughout a home or commercial building. Traditional paints contain high amounts of VOCs, which can be toxic and cause short- and long-term health problems. The regulation of VOC amounts in common materials like paint vary by state, and some states do not have specific regulations. The nationwide limit on VOCs in paint is 250 grams per liter, but even at this concentration, they can be harmful. Paint manufacturers, including Behr, Sherwin-Williams, and Benjamin Moore, have started making low-VOC paints that have fewer than 50 grams per liter.

According to green architect Maia Gilman, the best way to ensure that a specific type of paint is low-VOC is to review a product's material safety data sheet (MSDS), which provides information on chemicals used in the product. Ask for the MSDS wherever you purchase your paint and supplies; many are available online. Look for VOC levels in the section that breaks down the characteristics of the paint.

New office buildings such as this one must be careful when choosing paint and carpet, since both are known to contain VOCs.

Constantly changing government regulations require companies to prepare an MSDS to provide information on any potential harm or side effects that each chemical in a product could cause, as well as an emergency course of action to take if someone is exposed to the chemical. The U.S Occupational Safety and Health Administration (OSHA) began requiring MSDS documentation for all hazardous substances in May 1986. The documentation includes instructions for the correct use and handling of products, health risks and side effects, substance evaluations, storage recommendations, and what should take place in an emergency arising from use of the products.

Material safety data sheets are used worldwide, but each country has its own laws regulating them. In the United States, a hazard communication regulation requires MSDS usage in any workplace where potentially hazardous substances are being handled. OSHA enforces these laws. Although consumer products, including household chemicals, are not required to carry MSDSs at this time, the documentation is available online for many products. For more specific information, check the manufacturer's website.

Carpeting

Carpeting, like paint, contains VOCs. Because most modern office buildings use wall-to-wall carpeting throughout the majority of the office space, with the exception of the bathrooms and kitchen, carpet is a major concern. Most conventional carpeting, particularly very inexpensive carpeting, is made from synthetic materials that incorporate vinyl, another dangerous compound. Other harmful chemicals, compounds, and products in carpets include:

- Antistatic sprays
- Petroleum by-products
- Artificial dyes
- Urethane

Some people report symptoms, including skin irritation, dizziness, headaches, and nausea, after a new carpet is installed — these are the symptoms of sick building syndrome. Carpets attract dust mites, mold, mildew, and other allergens that are difficult to control and can sicken employees who suffer from allergies. Carpeting is also highly unrecyclable, and about 4 billion pounds of carpet are wasted each year in the United States, making conventional carpeting one of the biggest offenders against sustainability.

Wood

Wood is used for a variety of building purposes. In commercial buildings, it is mostly used for flooring, molding and wall trimming, and furniture. Although wood is one of the most natural building materials, it is harmful to people and to the environment on a number of levels:

- The wood you purchase might have been harvested by clear-cutting forests, which involves the destruction of an entire forest and prevents its future growth. This has a significant negative effect on the environment. Clear-cutting diminishes future wood supplies,

This one-time forest in Washington State was clear-cut.

depletes oxygen in the earth's atmosphere, disrupts and kills ecosystems, and displaces thousands of animal, plant, and bird species. This is particularly true for tropical and exotic woods, which come from rain forests.

- The chemical sealants and floor finishes used to coat some wood products often contain dangerous VOCs that emit toxins throughout their lifetime and not just when they are initially applied to the wood.

- Wood is sometimes soaked in formaldehyde. Many wood cabinets and other pressed wood products, such as plywood, particleboard, and paneling, also use glue that contains formaldehyde.

A close-up of the texture of fiberboard

- Engineered wood, which is made out of smaller pieces of wood glued together, sometimes uses dangerous adhesives. The glue often contains formaldehyde. Examples of engineered wood include I-joists, plywood, fiberboard, glued laminated timber, insulation board, and cement board.

Insulation

Insulation is important in green building because it maintains the temperature inside a building and significantly reduces the costs of heating and cooling. Conventional insulation is made from fiberglass, a synthetic mineral fiber made from recycled glass and sand that can cause severe skin irritation and other allergy and respiratory issues. Inhalation of fiberglass insulation particles has also been linked to cancer. Most homes and buildings constructed prior to 1979 contain asbestos insulation, which has also been linked to significant health problems including cancer. If you are remodeling an older building (more than 50 years old), you will have to work with a hazardous materials specialist to remove the asbestos before you begin remodeling. You can start your search for reputable asbestos removal contractors and consultants using The Blue Book Building & Construction Network (**www.thebluebook.com**).

Some forms of insulation also use formaldehyde-based glues, similar to the adhesive used in engineered wood products, to bind the fiberglass together. The use of the formaldehyde in insulation can cause the same respiratory problems and skin, eye, and allergy irritations just as when the adhesive is used in wood products. These symptoms can also lead to sick building syndrome.

Fiberglass insulation being blown into a house. Fiberglass is known to have negative health effects.

Because insulation is a key component to energy conservation and green building, it cannot be left out of the building process simply because of its harmful effects.

Plastics

Plastics are perhaps the worst environmental offenders. Most plastic is made from oil. The production of plastic accounts for nearly 5 percent of oil consumption in the United States. Because the United States consumes more than a quarter of the world's oil supply but only has less than 3 percent as natural reserves, it must seek oil from other countries. This introduces a multitude of environmental and political problems, including pollution from the transportation of oil, the destructive effects of oil spills on marine life and marine ecosystems, dependence on oil from the Middle East, and competition with other oil-consuming economies.

Most plastics are polymers, chemical compounds composed of both natural and synthetic materials. Plastics in their most natural form are not generally harmful; the additives and fillers that are added to most plastics make them toxic. Bisphenol A (BPA) is the most common building block of plastics; it is the filler that makes plastic so versatile. BPA is a toxin associated with neurological problems, obesity, and multiple forms of cancer. Dozens of studies by the EPA, as well as organizations including the U.S. National Toxicology Program and the U.S. National Institute of Health, have reported these effects.

Plastics made from petroleum are not biodegradable, which means they do not naturally decompose and cannot ever serve as a useful resource again.

They will end up sitting in a landfill for decades. Recyclable plastics are most often made into a new plastic material that is not recyclable.

Animals and marine life are harmed when they unintentionally consume plastic products like bags, bottles, and bottle caps or become entrapped in plastic waste. The burning of plastic can pose significant health risks to humans.

The most hazardous of plastics is PVC (polyvinyl chloride), a synthetic plastic material used in thousands of building products that can cause serious health problems and creates environmental problems. PVC is used for things such as electrical wiring, piping, plumbing, and roofing. The fumes from burning vinyl are so toxic that inhaling them can be fatal, and exposure to the fumes can cause cancer.

Blue Vinyl: The Dangers of Vinyl Building Materials

A documentary titled *Blue Vinyl*, which won the Documentary Excellence in Cinematography Award at the Sundance Film Festival in 2002, details the dangers of vinyl. The documentary, comical and horrifying at the same time, chronicles one woman's quest to discover the dangers of vinyl after her parents decide to re-side their house with blue vinyl. The film shows representatives of the vinyl industry claiming that the main ingredient used in producing vinyl — chloride — is no more harmful than salt. The documentary also features vinyl factory workers from different parts of the world who are terminally ill with cancer and other diseases thought to be caused by exposure to vinyl.

Concrete

Although concrete is made from natural materials like sand and rock minerals, it cannot automatically be categorized as a sustainable building material. Concrete is made by mixing a variety of materials including water, sand, stone, and Portland cement. The production of Portland cement requires a significant amount of energy and generates large volumes of air pollutants, such as concrete dust and greenhouse gases.

To produce every ton of cement, 6,000 Btu (British thermal units) of energy are required. The environmental impact of using concrete becomes apparent when you consider that about 2.5 billion tons of concrete are produced each year. The burning of fossil fuels to produce this energy also produces greenhouse gases and other air pollutants, many of which are hazardous to the environment and to people, animals, plants, and ecosystems.

Concrete also contributes to nearly half of the waste produced by construction each year. Although concrete is recyclable because it is made from natural materials, it is rarely recycled.

Cleaning products

Your employees come into daily contact with the cleaning products you use in your building. Many common household cleaners like bleach, dishwasher detergents, and glass and wood cleaners contain chemicals that are toxic to the environment and to humans. In addition to containing environmental toxins, cleaning products are often packaged in containers made of harmful PVC and other plastics.

Common side effects of some cleaning products include eye and skin irritation, as well as respiratory problems. Cleaners that most often include toxins are:

- **Bleach-based products:** Bleach is one of the better-known toxic chemicals. Skin and eye irritation, asthma and other respiratory problems, allergies, and even poisoning are some of the negative health effects of bleach.

- **Dishwashing soap:** Some dishwashing soap contains phosphates, which are inorganic chemicals that can harm plant and marine life. Although phosphates are somewhat regulated now, they can still be found in soaps used for dishwashers.

- **Wood and furniture polish:** Many furniture pieces and wood polishes contain nitrobenzene — a chemical that can cause blood disorders, among other things.

- **Disinfectants:** Many disinfectants like Lysol® contain phenol, which, even in trace amounts, is extremely toxic and can cause serious respiratory, heart, and skin problems.

The Consequences of Using
Conventional Cleaning Materials

Six out of every 100 janitors are injured by working directly with chemicals found in cleaning supplies, according to the Janitorial Products Pollution Prevention Project, a collaborative investigation by the EPA and other local government organizations and commissions that studied the effects of cleaners on janitors. These products include toilet cleaners, glass cleaners, and general-purpose cleaners, among others. The study further reported that the janitors studied in the research lost significant time at work due to these injuries.

The toxic qualities of cleaning products in an office building are aggravated because most office buildings have very little natural ventilation. Using products every day in a confined space throughout an entire building can cause health problems and symptoms synonymous with sick building syndrome.

Asbestos, radon, and lead

Dangerous toxins, such as lead, asbestos, and radon, are found in many conventional building materials. These toxins are of particular concern during green renovation and remodeling because they can cause series illness such as cancer.

☀ Asbestos

During the late 19th century, asbestos became a popular component of building materials and many other products because of its flexibility; ability to absorb sound; and resistance to damage from heat, electricity, and chemicals. Though manufacturers became increasingly aware of the health risks associated with asbestos during the 1940s and 1950s, its use did not come under the regulation of the U.S. Occupational Health and Safety Administration (OSHA) until 1972. Asbestos is now banned in 60 countries, including the United States and the members of the European Union.

When crushed, asbestos separates into millions of tiny fibers that cause serious health problems when they are inhaled. Ripping or tearing of materials containing asbestos during demolition and construction can release asbestos fibers into the air. According to the EPA, asbestos causes the following health problems:

- **Asbestosis:** Asbestosis is a lung disease that involves scarring of lung tissue caused by inhaling asbestos fibers. The scarring makes it more difficult for the lungs to absorb oxygen. There is no cure for asbestosis.

- **Lung cancer:** Lung cancer is commonly attributed to asbestos exposure and is responsible for the largest number of deaths from exposure to asbestos. According to the Environmental Working Group, a nonprofit organization dedicated in part to exposing public health dangers, nearly 5,000 deaths a year can be attributed to asbestos, including lung cancer.

- **Mesothelioma:** Mesothelioma is a form of cancer directly linked to asbestos exposure. The rare form of cancer is found most often in the lining of the lungs, abdomen, and heart and can take years to develop after the initial exposure to asbestos. Efforts are being made by the government to prevent children from being exposed to asbestos in schools to decrease the likelihood they will develop a long-term illness such as mesothelioma.

In addition to insulation, asbestos was also used for roofing, flooring, piping, and shingling in buildings constructed before 1972. Asbestos is particularly harmful to those who work in the construction industry because they are most likely to work directly with it. Symptoms of asbestos-related diseases may not appear until 15 to 30 years after exposure. The EPA regulates the removal of asbestos because it can be so dangerous for those who handle it. For this reason, asbestos is referred to as an occupational health hazard.

Through the Clean Air Act and the Toxic Substances Control Act, the EPA bans asbestos in many building and consumer products including the following:

- Fireproofing material

- Insulations, including for boilers, hot water tanks, and pipes

- Spray-on applications "containing more than 1 percent asbestos to buildings, structures, pipes, and conduits unless the material is encapsulated with a bituminous or resinous binder during spraying and the materials are not friable after drying," according to the EPA

Asbestos roofing is removed from an old building.

- Corrugated paper, roll board, commercial paper, specialty paper, flooring felt, and any new asbestos product

Radon

Radon is a colorless, odorless, radioactive gas that can cause serious health problems, including lung cancer and other respiratory diseases, if inhaled in large amounts. Radon is a natural gas released by the breakdown of uranium and can be found in soil, rock, and water. It is not harmful in natural outdoor settings but can become extremely harmful in confined spaces with limited ventilation, such as buildings and homes. According to the EPA, radon exposure accounts for more than 20,000 lung cancer deaths per year.

Lead

Lead, a toxic metal most often found in paint, soil, and water, is poisonous in certain forms, particularly to children. In 1971, the Lead-Based Paint Poisoning Prevention Act (LBPPPA) established definitions for lead-based paint and lead poisoning and identified lead-based paint in federally funded housing as a potential hazard. The act was amended in 1973. In 1978, the Consumer Product Safety Commission banned the residential use of lead-based paint.

Demolition, as well as other renovation activities like sanding and cutting, can disrupt lead paints and create exposure to lead dust, which is toxic to vital organs like the lungs, heart, and liver. Exposure can lead to lead poisoning, which can cause serious neurological issues.

Your Company's Carbon Footprint

The goal of green and sustainable building is to minimize your carbon footprint. Your company's carbon footprint is the degree to which its activities negatively impact the environment. It is a calculation of the amount of carbon dioxide and other greenhouse gases generated by a specific product, company, country, or individual. Your carbon footprint can be minimized by adopting green building practices, instituting sustainable energy  systems in your building, and building with green materials that do not contribute to depletion of natural and nonrenewable resources. *The following sections detail some of the ways to reduce your company's carbon footprint.*

Installing renewable energy systems such as wind and solar power

Even if solar and wind systems cannot supply all of your company's energy needs, they reduce your reliance on conventional sources of energy, most of which comes from nonrenewable energy sources, such as coal and oil that emit greenhouse gases when they are burned.

Here you can see the solar power panels atop the Toyota Motor Sales Headquarters in Torrance, California. Photo courtesy of Toyota Motor Sales, U.S.A., Inc.

Recycling

Reducing the amount of energy needed to produce new products like plastic bottles, paper, and equipment is one of the easiest ways to reduce your company's carbon footprint and costs very little.

Installing energy-efficient light bulbs and appliances throughout your building

Even if you cannot install solar or wind energy systems, you can still reduce the amount of energy consumed by your building by using energy-efficient light bulbs and appliances.

Encouraging the use of public transportation or carpooling

Public transportation use reduces carbon dioxide emissions from employees driving to work in their cars. Choosing a site near public transportation for a new building reduces the number of employees who must drive their own vehicles to work every day.

Your total carbon footprint as a business can be calculated in metric tons using a formula that considers your transportation, energy use, and  infrastructure and the amount of carbon dioxide you are responsible for giving off. Knowing your carbon footprint can be very helpful, particularly if you are renovating or remodeling to make your building environmentally friendly. Knowing the size of your company's footprint will enable you to target specific areas such as energy consumption or transportation. Organizations such as The Climate Trust, which focuses on providing sustainable and green building solutions for businesses and large organizations, offer a carbon footprint calculator that will enable you to determine your average carbon footprint (**www.climatetrust.org/content/calculators/Business_&_Org_Calculator.pdf**). The EPA offers guidelines for calculating the carbon footprint of a small business on its website (**www.epa.gov/climateleaders/smallbiz/footprint. html**).

Carbon offsetting

"Carbon offsetting" is the process of financially investing in renewable energy, such as wind, solar, hydroelectric power, and other green systems, to offset carbon emissions and other greenhouse gases and to minimize your contribution to global warming. If you are not able to reduce your company's energy consumption or greenhouse gas emissions, you can compensate by purchasing carbon offsets to benefit the environment in general and reduce the amount of carbon emissions on a national level.

Carbon offsets are usually sold for specific projects, such as a windmill farm, methane combustion project, landfill reduction project, or animal waste management project, for instance. Many companies purchase carbon offsets to balance the amount of greenhouse gases they emit from actions such as construction, employee travel, and operations, and to meet annual caps on carbon emissions. The process of carbon offsetting is easy and can be done exclusively online. The typical process follows these general steps:

- Calculate your carbon footprint using an online calculator.

- Identify your biggest source of carbon emissions. For individuals, driving a car is typically one of the bigger sources of carbon emissions. For a business, it may be energy consumption to power a building or carbon emission from employees driving to work.

- Research what kind of carbon offset you want to purchase. There are many different kinds of carbon offsets that can be purchased from a variety of companies. Websites including Carbon Catalog (**www.carboncatalog.org**) and CarbonFund.org (**www.carbonfund.org**), make it very easy to purchase simply carbon offsets.

Make sure the offset you purchase is legitimate. The clean development mechanism (CDM) is a program that was established by the United Nations as part of the Kyoto Protocol, and it serves as a certification and verification program for green projects in developing countries. Purchasing a carbon offset that is CDM-certified is a way to ensure your offset is legitimate. The Environmental Defense Fund partners with businesses to reduce business's harmful effects on the environment, and their website (**www.innovation.edf.org**) lists certified green projects from various carbon offset "retailers" around the world.

The easiest way to purchase a carbon offset is online. Once you choose what kind of offset you want to buy — a wind energy, landfill reduction, or animal waste management project — you can make your purchase online. After you make a purchase, you will receive additional information about the project or system you invested in.

Although carbon offsetting provides an indirect way to reduce carbon dioxide emissions, it is not the ultimate solution to creating a more sustainable world.

Critics of carbon offsetting state that the method justifies carbon emissions by allowing individuals and companies to "pay off" their emissions. It presents the illusion that carbon emissions are somehow acceptable, as long as they can be compensated for in another way. Many scientists state that to significantly reduce global warming, carbon emissions must be significantly reduced and not just offset.

Consider carbon offsetting if you are remodeling or renovating your building, and your budget is limited. If you cannot renovate your energy system or install wind or solar power to power your entire building, you can purchase carbon offsets in addition to implementing simpler measures to reduce your emissions. These measures could include switching to energy-efficient light bulbs, encouraging employees to shut off computers and equipment at the day's end, installing sensor lights to minimize electricity use when no one is in a room, and using natural daylight to illuminate spaces.

Renewable Energy Credits (RECs)

Recent climate change legislation mandates that utilities, manufacturing plants, state and local governments, and certain industries reduce their carbon emissions and their consumption of fossil fuels by using renewable energy sources for a certain percentage of their energy needs. In addition, some manufacturers, industries, and organizations want to reduce air pollution and to publicize themselves as green industries selling green products.

To help in meeting these goals, a system of Renewable Energy Certificates (RECs) has been developed to track the source of energy and to differentiate between renewable energy and energy produced with fossil fuels. One REC represents 1,000 kilowatt-hours of clean, renewable energy, such as energy produced by solar panels or wind turbines. RECs can be bought and sold separately from the electricity they represent and are a sort of energy currency. A utility or industry that does not have access to clean, renewable energy can still meet its goals or declare itself green by purchasing RECs from an individual or a utility that produces renewable energy. The electricity represented by RECs is known as "green power."

RECs are registered, numbered, and tracked by regional tracking systems and any sale of RECs is accompanied by an affidavit that no one else can claim that energy as green.

Some utilities buy RECs from customers with solar or wind systems, and then sell them to customers who specifically want green power. An REC can be used only once. After a buyer has made an environmental claim based on a REC, that REC is considered permanently retired. Buyers can also have their RECs retired in their name by their supplier to ensure that no other entity can lay claim to the same environmental benefits.

Benefits of Going Green

Building a green office is a complex process that involves a serious commitment not only from the company or building owner, but also from the future occupants of the building. Everyone must be educated and motivated to think and act green. It is not a project to be undertaken lightly, but one that can reap rich rewards when it is carried out to its culmination. As a business, you are probably most concerned with both the immediate and long-term savings associated with green building, but other less measurable benefits will become evident over time. Costs for which savings can be clearly quantified and calculated are known as "hard costs;" costs associated with benefits that are not easily measured, such as improving employee morale and lowering absenteeism, are known as "soft costs."

Studies conducted on green building show that green building can improve your bottom line in several ways, including savings on energy bills, tax incentives, lower employee absenteeism, and increased productivity. It also helps create a positive public image for your company and is one of the ways in which the company can demonstrate its integrity and its commitment to sustainability.

Building green:

- Saves money on building materials, energy use, supplies, and long-term maintenance of your building.

- Attracts employees who are more inclined to stay with a company that is environmentally conscious and supports a healthy work environment.

- Reduces your carbon footprint and your negative impact on the environment.

Social benefits

Social benefits contribute to the betterment of society as a whole, as well as your internal society of employees. The social payoffs of building green include providing a healthy work environment, good indoor air quality, and a better way of life for employees.

☀ Attracting and retaining the best employees and increasing productivity

Employees spend about 23 percent of their lives, and 30 percent of their waking hours in the workplace. Over time, the conditions under which they work have a significant impact on their health and psychological well-being. Green companies tend to provide healthier and happier work environments for employees, which ultimately make them more productive, such as ergonomically designed workspaces with natural lighting.

Several studies have been conducted on the effects of going green on employee productivity. *Greening the Building and the Bottom Line*, published by the Rocky Mountain Institute in 1994, analyzed the impact of working in a green building on workers in eight different green companies. The study found significant improvement in productivity among employees when companies implemented green building practices, as well as better employee morale, a lower rate of illness among workers, and a decrease in the number of sick days taken.

Some of the highlights of the study:

- After installing an energy-efficient lighting system and undergoing a green makeover, productivity at the postal sorting facility in Reno, Nevada, increased by 6 percent. The rate of error also dropped to the lowest the post office had ever seen and the lowest rate in their geographical area.

- The airplane manufacturer Boeing saw significant improvement in worker productivity and general working environment after installing high-efficiency lighting systems in its manufacturing plants. Assembly line workers reported a 20 percent decrease in errors due to poor lighting — errors the company did not even know were occurring until much later in the manufacturing process when correcting them was expensive. Employees also reported a reduction in glare, which they experienced with the previous fluorescent lighting system.

- At insurance company West Bend's headquarters in Wisconsin, the company created individual workstations that allowed employees to control their own heat, air conditioning, and lighting. By allowing employees to control their own work environment on some level, productivity increased by nearly 3 percent.

- In 1978, ING Bank moved workspaces to a greener building, which operated on a green energy system and used natural light for illumination, among other things. Compared to the bank's previous building, absenteeism in the new building has been down more than 15 percent since the company moved locations.

Other interesting findings include:

- In a 1997 indoor air quality study, *Estimates of Improved Productivity and Health from Better Indoor Environments*, the authors found that improving the indoor air quality in buildings, thereby reducing illness among employees, could save the United States at least $18 billion in productivity alone in one year. They also found that increased productivity from improved lighting and temperature control could yield more than $100 billion.

- A 1991 study by Rachel Ulrich published in the *Journal of Environmental Psychology* found that exposure to natural light significantly reduces employee stress and sickness and has a positive effect on general attitude. Employees sitting near a window are likely to be happier, less stressed, suffer fewer illnesses, and have a more positive attitude.

☀ Public relations

A green building gives the impression that the company or corporation is concerned about its impact on the environment, cares about its employees, and is taking proactive steps to preserve and protect natural resources. Environmentally friendly buildings attract public notice and positive media attention. An organization or business with a green building not only will be attractive to potential employees, but also it will promote a positive public image.

Many buildings around the world have attracted widespread attention just for being green. The headquarters of the Ford Motor Company Premier Auto Group in southern California is LEED certified and incorporates a naturally insulated roof, a raised-floor air distribution system that reduces the company's energy use, and natural gas to provide 25 percent of the building's water and power. The Philip Merrill Environmental Center in Maryland is also LEED certified and incorporates a natural ventilation system, geothermal heat pumps to generate heat and air conditioning, and an energy management system that minimizes energy use throughout the building.

Buildings such as these are featured in news articles, TV programs, websites, and books about green building. One of the buildings of the World Trade Center complex generated worldwide media attention for being the first office building in the state of New York to receive LEED certification. When ING Bank moved to its new headquarters in Amsterdam in 1978, it was never the bank's intention to enhance its public image. But ING's business increased significantly because the green building gave the bank a new image.

According to *The E Factor: The Bottom Line Approach to Environmentally Responsible Business*, green buildings not only create a positive image among the public but also with building regulators, who are more likely to ease restrictions for a building that is working toward complying with the law by maintaining a healthy working environment and reducing waste.

☀ Green PR

Many companies actively seek to portray themselves as acting responsibly to protect and preserve the environment. Manufacturers are increasingly implementing programs to recycle their products when their customers are ready to discard them and creating products with parts that can be extracted and reused in new products. Some companies have "zero landfill" policies, meaning that all of their waste is recycled in some way, and nothing ends up in a landfill. Housing your company in a green building sends the message that it is genuinely committed to improving the lives not only of employees and customers but also of people in the community at large.

Greenwashing

Public relations efforts that make a company or product appear to be environmentally responsible without actually accomplishing anything are called "greenwashing." Examples include using words like "organic" and "natural" in packaging and descriptions, using images of plants and earthy colors in a company logo or offering environmental education on a company website.

☀ CSR: Corporate social responsibility

Corporate social responsibility (CSR) is a corporation's commitment to positive and ethical business practices that support not only the well-being of its employees but also of society as a whole. The essence of CSR is being a responsible member of society as a corporation by exceeding standards of operation and becoming a positive force in the community.

Examples of CSR include:

- The development of philanthropic programs to give back to society and the local community

- Commitment to avoid deceptive advertising

- Commitment to accurately reporting holdings and earnings

- Providing employees with excellent benefits and additional perks, such as tuition reimbursement and morale-focused retreats

- Building green to reduce energy consumption, waste, and harm to the environment

Innovative CSR practices receive attention and coverage from the media, attract new business, and boost investor confidence. Socially responsible investors and investment funds want assurance that their money is not supporting unethical or environmentally harmful business activities.

Green buildings fulfill CSR on several levels. They promote the health and well-being of their employees by providing a healthy and positive work environment, and they give back to society and the environment by reducing carbon emissions and other greenhouse gas emissions, conserving resources, and supporting overall sustainable living.

The financial benefits of green building

Misconceptions and concerns about the cost of green building prevent many building professionals from pursuing sustainable development. Building green costs only slightly more initially and realizes substantial savings over the lifetime of the building. Studies conducted on existing buildings to analyze cost savings and benefits of building green have found that:

- A 2 percent initial investment in a green building project will return nearly 10 times that amount over the lifetime of the building according to *The Costs and Financial Benefits of Green Buildings: A Report to California's Sustainable Building Task Force* by Greg Kats.

- Green buildings have a higher resale value than conventional buildings. *Energy Efficiency in Buildings* by the World Business Council for Sustainable Development.

- Green buildings save an average of 36 percent on energy use each year. Considering that the average cost per building for energy use is $1.50 per square foot, this translates into a savings of more than $27,000 per year for a 50,000-square-foot building. USGBC.

- Green buildings save on average nearly 10 percent on operating costs. The *2006 Green Building SmartMarket Report* published by McGraw-Hill Construction also states that the value of a green building increases by nearly 8 percent and the return on investment improves by nearly 7 percent.

After studying different companies and their increased productivity from integrating green building designs and practices, The Rocky Mountain Institute's study *Greening the Building and the Bottom Line* reported that:

- Lockheed Missiles and Space Company's commercial office building in California saved an estimated $500,000 a year in energy costs by designing the building to use natural daylight instead of synthetic light to illuminate a majority of the space.

- Airline manufacturer Boeing saw more than a 50-percent return on investment each year from the energy-efficient lighting system it installed in its manufacturing plant, which meant that the system paid for itself in just two years.

- West Bend Mutual Insurance Company's headquarters in Wisconsin reduced its energy cost per square foot by 40 percent by installing an energy-efficient HVAC system and lighting system, and a thermal-storage system that cools the building during the day from ice produced over the previous night. Increased worker productivity from installing individualized, climate-controlled workstations equated to $364,000 annually.

- Manufacturer Hyde Tools saw more than $25,000 in increased sales that could be correlated to the installation of an energy-efficient lighting system.

These studies show that green building construction has a high return on investment and that many projects requiring an increased initial investment paid for themselves after just a few years. The cost of managing and repairing equipment, HVAC systems, and plumbing, water, and energy systems in a green building is less than the cost for similar maintenance in a conventional building.

❋ Attracting investors and securing future funding

As the benefits of green building have been documented and publicized, investors have become increasingly willing to support the concept of green building. A number of federal, state, and local government incentives provide funding for green building projects.

❋ Tax benefits

National and state governments offer significant tax breaks for residential and commercial green homes and buildings. This can mean additional cost savings over the lifetime of your building and can provide further incentive to go green.

Growth in the green building industry

- According to *2009 Green Outlook: Trends Driving Change*, published by McGraw-Hill Construction, the market for green building is forecasted to grow to nearly 25 percent of the total construction market by 2013.

- According to the same report, the green construction market grew from 2 percent of the total construction market in 2005 to more than 10 percent in 2008.

- According to a U.S. Green Building Council study on green jobs, green building is projected to sustain nearly 8 million jobs from 2009 to 2013.

Environmental and health benefits

Buildings, which consume nearly half of all energy, play a significant role in global warming and climate change. National governments and international bodies now recognize that we are in the midst of an environmental crisis and are acting quickly to impose regulations on energy produced by burning fossil fuels. Building practices that conserve energy will soon become the norm.

The primary environmental benefits of building green are:

- **Enhancing and protecting biodiversity and ecosystems.** Using green energy reduces carbon emissions drastically and helps slow global warming. Global warming threatens many species, including marine life affected by rising sea levels and melting ice caps and plant species in desert areas. Using wood that is responsibly harvested, such as that certified by the Forest Stewardship Council (**www.fscus.org**), helps protect forest ecosystems. Many green buildings preserve as much as possible of the native habitat surrounding them.

- **Improving air quality, both indoors and outdoors.** Green energy from solar power systems and wind turbines reduces air pollution. Using sustainable building materials that can be manufactured without using large amounts of energy also reduces air pollution. Interior air quality in a building can be improved by using low-VOC paints, carpets, and wood materials, as well as non-toxic cleaning products.

Window and solar power are a great way to reduce air pollution.

- **Improving water quality.** Buildings are responsible for about 25 percent of water use, according to the EPA. Installing low-flow toilets and faucets, using a rain capturing or gray water irrigation system, and planting native plants for landscaping reduces consumption of water.

- **Reducing waste.** Construction materials are responsible for nearly a quarter of all waste generated in the United States. By using recycled or reclaimed material or renovating with existing materials that can be reused, green buildings can significantly reduce the overall waste.

- **Conserving and restoring natural resources.** Green buildings reduce the use of nonrenewable sources of energy and building materials. Many green buildings have pioneered systems that are self-sustaining or that generate resources, such as composting or planting trees on the building site.

Why You Might Not Want to Build Green

Some aspects of green building, such as higher initial costs for construction and materials, property valuation, and the additional time it may take to order and receive supplies, might deter a developer or a management committee from going green.

Higher initial investment

Some green building projects will cost more initially than conventional projects. If you are building in an area where green building supplies are not readily available, you may have to increase your budget for the purchase of materials. Unless you are thoroughly knowledgeable about green construction, you will have to hire professionals, such as architects, engineers, or consultants who are experienced in green building. If you are seeking LEED certification, depending on the size of your project, you will need an additional $2,000 to $25,000.

Energy efficiency does not always increase the value of a building

Building appraisers who provide valuation services do not always see energy efficiency as an added value to the building. The appraisal process is subjective in some ways and can vary from appraiser to appraiser. Appraisers may recognize the importance of energy efficiency, but they may not have the necessary tools and data to verify that their calculations are accurate. As more builders adopt green building practices, the appraisal process will become more structured, just as the process of LEED certification has done.

Green building may require more planning

There is no specific way to go green. You will have to consult an architect and possibly an engineer to evaluate what design strategies will work best for you and what materials you will be able to use. You may not be familiar with green manufacturers in your area or know what kinds of materials you can get to fit your budget. Green building can be like putting together the pieces of a puzzle. If this is your first experience with green building, it will probably take longer to create a plan and determine projected costs than it would for a conventional building project. Construction of a green building can take significantly longer if you are seeking LEED certification and do not familiarize yourself with the requirements prior to beginning the process.

For its occupants, a green building may be a significant departure from conventional buildings. For instance, if you incorporate natural daylight in workstations, employees will have to adjust to the change, which may include increased glare and a temperature change at certain points of the day. Implementing a paperless policy will mean creating office procedures to make it easy for employees to adopt this policy.

Remodeling while occupants are still in the building can be complicated

Though you are making the building more environmentally friendly, managing a remodel or renovation while occupants are still in the building can be a headache. An old building may contain asbestos, lead, or other toxins. Maintaining indoor air quality will be a primary concern, and you will be required to hire licensed professionals to manage the removal of any toxins, which can be costly and time consuming. Redesigning floor space to implement new design concepts, such as daylighting, may be disruptive to employees. Ripping up toxic carpets, repainting with low-VOC paints, replacing appliances, and redoing bathrooms to integrate low-flow toilets and faucets can also be inconvenient and disrupt workflow.

It can be difficult to determine the best green policies

It can sometimes be difficult to determine which of several possible strategies is truly greener. An action that advances one objective on your green agenda might have negative effects that cancel out another objective. For example:

- Is it greener to renovate an existing building and keep all of the previous furniture, carpeting, and flooring — all of which have high levels of volatile organic compounds and other toxins — or to throw these materials away, adding more waste to landfills, and purchase all new earth-friendly materials that will last much longer and protect building occupants' health?

- Is it better to buy bamboo flooring that must be shipped all the way from Asia, using a significant amount of fuel and contributing to global warming, or to purchase local wood that requires minimal transportation but has been harvested by clear-cutting a forest?

- Is it better to throw out old appliances and equipment, such as refrigerators, copiers, and fax machines that are not energy efficient, and replace them with new, energy efficient models to reduce energy consumption, or is it better to keep the old appliances and equipment and reduce waste?

Evaluate your current building, your budget, your future needs as a company, and the materials and resources available to you on a local level. If, for example, you have access to a local wood manufacturer who can supply you with low-cost salvaged and reclaimed wood for flooring, this would be a more effective choice than shipping in bamboo from Asia. A local business might recycle old appliances, carpeting, or flooring so that they do not have to be taken to a landfill. Green building consultants, such as interior and building designers, can help you determine which strategies are most cost-effective for you.

Challenges of Building Green

A green building project involves different commitments and priorities from those associated with the construction of a conventional building. *Someone building green for the first time will face additional challenges and should pay special attention to the aspects of the building process that are described in the following sections.*

Hiring the right team

Team integration is crucial to a green building project. Unlike a traditional building project in which members of the building team work separately at different stages of the process, green building requires a collaborative approach. Everyone from the architect and contractor to the day laborers and construction workers on your job site must work cohesively to accomplish the same goals. Hiring a trustworthy contractor who is experienced in green building is a priority. An experienced green contractor understands the importance of using certain materials, products, and procedures. If your contractor subcontracts construction workers who have no experience with green building, and they are not informed that they need to follow specific procedures, their actions may undermine your efforts and cost you points in the LEED certification process. An experienced contractor understands this and will make sure that all subcontractors and laborers are trained to follow LEED requirements.

An investment in concepts, systems, and materials you may not be familiar with

If you are new to the concepts of green building, they could be overwhelming and difficult to understand at first. Hiring a LEED consultant or a sustainability consultant at the beginning of the design process can be very helpful. Even if you hire a consultant, however, you should have a firm understanding of the concepts, systems, and materials you will be incorporating and implementing into your building. You might have to spend extra time studying and doing research.

Seeing the project through to certification

The process of getting LEED certification can take longer than the construction process. It could be six months or a year after construction is finished before your building achieves certification. Throughout the entire building process and the process of moving people into the building (this includes leasing the space if you are a developer), you must remain committed to adhering to the LEED guidelines or you will risk not getting certified. This includes ensuring the right materials are used, recycling construction debris, and implementing water, electrical, and HVAC systems that adhere to the LEED requirements.

Ensuring the building remains a green facility

You must ensure that your green office building stays green as it ages. If you are not the property owner, pay close attention to your commitments to maintaining a green building, which will be detailed in your lease agreement with the developer or landlord. This includes requirements like making sure your employees recycle. Core and shell buildings where tenants will build the interiors will have stricter and more specific requirements, such as installation of light sensors to minimize light use when a space is not occupied, installation of low-flow water fixtures in bathrooms, and the use of low-VOC and low-emitting paints and sealers. All the stipulations of occupancy should be clearly outlined in your lease contract with the developer.

Overseeing every detail

Products get switched out during the construction phase all the time. In conventional building, the consequences may not be as significant as in green building. If you specify that the paint to be used on the walls should be Benjamin Moore Aura, a pricey, high quality low-VOC paint that sells for about $60 a gallon. The contractor switches the paint out for a conventional paint with a high-VOC content; you will lose points during the certification process and end up exposing the building occupants to unhealthy toxins.

CHAPTER 3:

Planning and Designing Your Green Building Project

The design process is one of the elements that sets green building apart from conventional building practices. Green building uses an integrated design process (IDP) that involves getting input from a wide variety of sources before the designing even begins. Everyone involved in the project must be educated to understand its green objectives and the essential concepts of green building. Because green building is relatively new and because each project is unique, it may be necessary to call in specialists and consultants for various phases. Throughout the project, there must be a high degree of teamwork.

One of the characteristics of high performance building is efficiency and a minimum of waste, and this applies to the design and building process as well as to the building itself. The design and planning methods used in green building are now being adopted by conventional building projects because they are so effective in eliminating errors, delays, and cost overruns.

Building Delivery Systems

The procedure for designing and then constructing a building is called a construction delivery system. Conventional contemporary construction delivery systems are generally of three types: design-bid-build (hard-bid), construction management-at-risk (negotiated work), and design-build. In a hard-bid process, the building owner selects a design team to define and describe the project. Contractors are then asked to bid on the project, and the lowest qualified bid gets the job. Under the negotiated work system, the building owner contracts a design team and a separate construction manager who works with the design team and hires subcontractors to do the work. The construction manager typically guarantees that the cost will not exceed a maximum price, the guaranteed maximum price (GMP). In both of these systems, there are often tensions, conflicts, and miscommunications between the designer and the construction team that result in the original design not being carried out, or in delays, alterations, and even repairs. In the design-build, a single entity is contracted to do everything from design to the finished building. This eliminates much of the conflict and confusion because the design-build firm controls all aspects of the building process and can facilitate communication between the design team and the construction team.

The high-performance green building delivery system is a variation of the negotiated work system, with a much higher level of communication among the project team members. It requires the inclusion of end-users from the beginning of the project and education of the entire team so everyone understands the goals and objectives. A number of specialists, such as solar contractors or thermal engineers, might be called in at various times to advise the design team or to carry out certain portions of the project.

Design-build can also work well for green building. A single firm takes responsibility for the entire project and establishes a close collaboration between the design team and the subcontractors. A number of green building projects have been carried out using this system. In a conventional design-build project, the design-build firm makes many decisions without consulting the building owner, and the focus is on the finished product. In a green build project, however, the designer-builder must allow the owner and other participants in the project free access to information and decision making on all aspects of the building process, so they can confirm that their green building objectives are being followed.

The main steps in a green building delivery system are:

1. The building owner identifies the project's green priorities.

2. The building owner selects a project team: either a design team and a construction manager, or a design-build firm.

3. The building owner briefs the project team on the project's objectives, the concept of IDP, and how IDP will be used during the design and construction process.

4. A charrette (a type of brainstorming session, described below) is conducted to gather input and ideas from a variety of participants.

5. A detailed design is developed using IDP, including schematic diagrams, a building schedule, and documentation for any certification being sought.

6. Construction of the building

7. Commissioning of the completed building

Establishing priorities

A green building project begins with the building owner determining the scope of the project and the green features that will be incorporated in its design. Every green project is unique and defined by a number of circumstances. The priorities for every project are not the same. In a hot, arid climate, the priorities would probably be minimal water usage, an energy-efficient cooling system, and use of a photovoltaic system to provide electricity. In a cold, wet climate, the priorities might be the use of geothermal energy for heating, stormwater management, and daylighting. Some companies are willing to spend more to be socially responsible.

☀ Where will the building be located?

Brownfield left from a demolished factory; it is slated for redevelopment.

The location of a building is one of the major considerations in sustainable development. The site and location of a building directly affect the ecosystems surrounding it, the way the building can use the sun for energy, how far employees will have to travel to get to work, and eligibility for various government incentives. Some federal, state, and municipal government incentives are contingent on where a building is developed. For example, an environmental remediation tax incentive signed into law by the federal government in October 2009 is available to buildings developed on brownfield sites.

LEED certification uses a point-rating system to evaluate building sites and gives extra points to a building developed on a brownfield site.

☀ What types of energy systems will be implemented?

Energy systems using solar panels and wind turbines provide clean and renewable energy and effectively reduce your carbon footprint, significantly decrease your energy costs, and conserve natural resources. However, these systems are not practical in every geographical location. You might not be able to power your entire building with solar or wind energy, but you can install a grid-tie system that supplements your power supply with electricity from a local utility. You can also use solar or wind energy for specific purposes, such as heating air or water, or operating a water pump or outdoor lighting system.

☀ What types of water, plumbing, and sewer systems will the building utilize?

Water conservation is an essential aspect of sustainable building, especially if you are seeking LEED certification. Local zoning laws may specify how sewage and stormwater runoff must be dealt with, and special permits may be required.

☀ What is the budget for the project?

How much capital is available to finance the project? Some green features may have to be eliminated during the design process or replaced with less expensive alternatives if they are too costly. Is the company willing to seek additional financing if necessary to achieve certain objectives?

☀ Will this building seek certification? What level of certification is desired?

If the building owner wants to seek LEED or Green Globe certification, the project team must consider LEED or Green Globe requirements at every level. If implementing these requirements will result in additional costs, the project team may need to prepare cost analyses for the building owner to use in making decisions.

☀ What design criteria will be used for the project?

Even if certification is not being sought, LEED and Green Globe standards still provide thorough guidelines for producing a green building. If LEED or Green Globe standards will not be used, the building owner must outline detailed design criteria for the project team.

☀ How will the day-to-day operations of the company be organized?

The building is being constructed to house the daily business activities of its occupants. What types of spaces will be needed — an attractive reception area and meeting rooms to impress clients and visitors, a loading dock and staging area, a manufacturing floor, work studios that inspire creativity and collaboration among employees, or private work areas?

☀ What type of interior layout will the building have?

Consider what the layout of each floor will look like, whether the design will incorporate daylighting, and whether there will be an open floor plan with cubicles, or separate offices (or a combination of both). Pay attention to acoustics, noise levels, and possible noise travel in the building.

☀ What elements will the exterior of the building include?

 Outdoor space on the building site must be allocated for walkways, pathways, gardens, seating areas, and parking lots. Incorporating gardens and common areas outside the building provides employees with areas to enjoy during breaks and contributes to increased productivity. If you are incorporating a detention pond or other stormwater runoff system, you will also need space for these systems in your building layout.

☀ Will you be incorporating recycling or composting into your day-to-day operations?

Depending on your geographical location and what types of recycling and composting programs you incorporate, you may need to designate a space in your building for deposit, separation, storage, and pick-up of recycling and composting materials.

Selecting a Design and Construction Team

When the building owner's priorities and requirements have been established, it is time to select a design team and a construction team. A request for proposal (RFP) or request for qualifications (RFQ) is issued, specifying the goals of the project and the additional qualifications required for the professionals supporting the project design. The American Institute of Architects publication *Writing the Green RFP* (**www.aia.org/practicing/ groups/kc/AIAS074658?dvid=&recspec=AIAS074658**) offers advice on how to word a green RFP.

The building owner selects three to five design firms and construction management companies from among the submissions and invites them to give presentations. A final selection is made based on professional qualifications and previous experience with green building, work examples, and a demonstrated understanding of the building owner's goals. If the building is to be LEED- or Green Globe-certified, the candidates should have a thorough understanding of certification requirements, or a LEED AP (LEED accredited professional).

Integrated Design Process (IDP)

Integrated design process (IDP) or integrated design refers to the intense collaboration and communication that takes place among project team members during a green building project. According to the U.S. Department of Energy (DOE), the goal of integrated design is "to achieve high performance and multiple benefits at a lower cost than the total for all the components combined" by involving specialists in many design fields including architecture, HVAC, lighting and electrical, interior design, and landscape design throughout the design and building process.

Unlike conventional building design, in which experts are called in after the design team has already prepared the basic framework for the building, IDP involves the experts from the very beginning of the design process and repeatedly as construction is carried out. The input of these experts is crucial to creating integrated systems that complement each other to save energy, reduce waste, and maximize the natural advantages of the building site and orientation. For example, a solar engineer could run water from a gray water plumbing system through a mechanism to cool solar panels on the roof of the building and keep them operating efficiently on hot days. An HVAC engineer could use heat generated by the air conditioning system to produce hot water. A landscape architect could design an artificial wetland to collect gray water and purify it before it is discharged into the water table. An architect could design the building to be partially cooled by ocean breezes, and the HVAC engineer could then reduce the size of the cooling system. Various specialists combine their expertise to come up with innovative and efficient design features that complement each other.

Several other features of IDP contribute to its success. In IDP, the building owner and the designers are able to discuss alternative solutions whenever necessary and select those that best meet the building owner's objectives. An energy specialist evaluates various aspects of the design and tests them with simulation software to see if they perform as expected. Other specialists, such as lighting engineers or hydrologists, are called in when needed for short-term consultations. The goals and strategies of the project are constantly reviewed and updated. A design facilitator may be added to the team to organize communication, check that performance goals are being met, and call in experts when additional input is needed.

The Charrette

When the design and construction teams have been selected and briefed by the building owner, a brainstorming session, known as a charrette, is held. The purpose of the charrette is to obtain as much input as possible and create a complete plan for the building project. The size and extent of the charrette depends on the scope of the building project. A large project may employ additional smaller charrettes later on in the planning process to focus on specific aspects of the design. A nonprofit organization, the National Charrette Institute (NCI) provides guidance and training on how to hold a successful charrette. The basic procedure is:

1. The building owner and project team establish goals for the charrette, set a date and time, and invite the participants. The invitation should

include an explanation of the purpose and importance of the charrette. A typical green building charrette might take place over several days, in successive phases.

Who should participate in a charrette?

It is important to include representatives of all the stakeholders in a green building charrette. A stakeholder is anyone who is involved in the planning, design and construction of a building, the building owners, lenders, investors, future occupants of the building including employees and maintenance staff, customers and end-users, and anyone in the community who will be affected by the building. A building is a cultural symbol and will be in existence for decades, so its impact on the community is far-reaching. The stakeholders in a building vary according to its function, location, and ownership. A public building, such as a school, library, or city hall, is financed by taxpayers and used by all members of a community, so members of the community and civic leaders and officials should participate, as well as staff and future occupants. A retail center should involve tenants and residents from the surrounding community. A corporate office would require input from local officials and citizens, as well as from shareholders and employees. In addition, a charrette should include specialists and professionals who can provide instant feedback and offer suggestions for implementing ideas. If LEED certification is sought, a LEED specialist should be present.

2. The site of the charrette, typically a large room, must be prepared with whiteboards, projectors and screens, and large-paper display stands. The building owner and design team gather all the information needed for the charrette, including educational and research materials, preliminary plans, details of the site and zoning restrictions, data about local utilities, and information about specific technologies that might be employed in the building, such as solar energy or daylighting. The charrette will be most effective when as much information as possible is at hand, so questions can be resolved, and solutions can be worked out in detail during the discussion. It is a good idea to have contractors, engineers, and specialists present, who can suggest exactly how to implement proposed features, calculate the costs, and use simulation software to determine how the technology can be expected to perform.

Do not let financial miscalculations undermine your plans.

It is important to have an accountant and/or contractor present at the charrette to keep track of the budget and accurately estimate costs of proposed design features. Many building owners end up dropping key elements of their green project plan when they discover that the costs are higher than anticipated in the original plan.

3. The facilitator of a charrette should be someone who is very familiar with the green building process. Begin by educating everyone present about the concept of high-performance green building and the requirements of the building owner. Review the preliminary plans, the building site, the proposed budget, and proposed construction schedule. Explain the green objectives of the project, and if LEED or

other certification is sought, review the standards that must be met. Then the facilitator should conduct a brainstorming session to obtain input from the participants on every aspect of the green building project. The construction manager and other professionals should develop concepts as they are suggested and provide cost estimates. Put aside impractical features and ideas and gather more input on those that can be incorporated into the building design.

4. After the charrette, the building owner and design team review the results and prepare a report of the charrette. This document will serve as a guide during the rest of the design process and can be referred to whenever decisions are being made. A charrette often produces valuable suggestions from employees and future building occupants about how the building layout can improve workplace efficiency and increase the comfort of those who will be using the building.

5. Additional special-focus charrettes may be held at later stages of the design process to develop specific features of the building project.

CASE STUDY: THE ART OF GREEN DESIGN

Dan Perruzzi
Principal, Margulies Perruzzi
Architects
www.mp-architects.com

Boston-based design firm Margulies Perruzzi Architects, founded in 1988, is a leader in the field of green design. The full-service interior design and architectural firm specializes in green corporate building as well as health care. "Our projects include new shell and core construction, interior fit-ups, and full building renovations. We pride ourselves on our use of the latest technologies to streamline and enhance the design process," explains Dan Perruzzi, a principal at the firm. "More than 75 percent of our design staff is LEED accredited, which allows us to offer comprehensive sustainable design strategies to our clients. We have designed more than one million square feet of commercial office buildings, all Certified, Silver, or Gold under the LEED rating system."

Over the past 22 years, the company has lead the way in the green design process, incorporating a variety of design and materials selection processes that have helped them emerge as a leader in the field. "Our firm has made a major investment in the use of building information modeling, or BIM, resulting in a huge savings of time and cost for our clients," Perruzzi said. BIM is three-dimensional building software that enables designers to manage the building design process. Perruzzi explains, "We utilize BIM for all of our projects, regardless of size or complexity. BIM allows us to do a number of things that are of great value to our clients. First, all of our design work is in three dimensions, because BIM creates a digital model of the space or building. Drawings we use to present, document, and detail any design project are extracted from that model. Because all of the information is extracted from one model, the overall design is better coordinated, leading to fewer questions during construction and fewer costly change orders. More important, the design can be viewed in three dimensions from the very beginning, allowing for better collaboration during design and for a more informed design team. Because the model is three-dimensional, conflicts between building components (structure, ducts, piping, and cable trays) can be identified and solved before the work begins. Fabrication is more accurate using the digital model, allowing for greater prefabrication under controlled conditions. The overall result is a higher quality product for the client."

One of Peruzzi's clients, Blue Cross Blue Shield of Massachusetts, a health care company, recently hired the firm to renovate one of their commercial spaces to become more environmentally friendly. "The company was committed to creating an energy-efficient building because they viewed the project as a long-term investment," Perruzzi said. "The renovation included replacing the outdated exterior glazing with high-performance glass with better insulating value and special coatings to reduce solar heat gain. We added a white roof because of its reflectivity, meaning less heat build-up and lower cooling costs. We replaced plantings with drought-resistant plants to minimize the need for watering; we also removed the existing irrigation system."

The remodel also focused on water reduction; the firm created custom-designed pendant lighting fixtures throughout the offices and replaced all plumbing fixtures with low-flow hands-free fixtures. "The hands-free design reduces water usage while limiting the spread of germs," Perruzzi said. The renovation also included replacing materials, such as carpets, with low-VOC products. The HVAC system was also replaced with a new high-efficient system, which allowed more fresh air to flow through the building. The building ultimately received LEED certification.

Another project the firm worked on was Blue Cross Blue Shield's Hingham location, which received LEED Silver certification. Perruzzi describes this remodel: "We designed the site to use its existing contouring to minimize the grading and clearing of native trees. When we did clear, we made certain to use any excavated or cut material. All existing fill was reused elsewhere on the site. Trees were either harvested for timber or were ground on site into mulch. Rock that was blasted to make room for foundations was used either as fill or as the stone for retaining walls."

The location of the parking lot was also an important consideration in reducing the negative impact of the renovation on the surrounding environment and ecosystems. "Vehicles are housed on site in a structured garage, thereby reducing the heat island effect and minimizing clearing for parking lots. The net effect of all of these moves is a reduced impact on the site and a building that is well-nestled into the surrounding woods," Perruzzi explained.

In designing the exterior, the design team focused on heat retention and reducing energy use. "The building exterior features deep overhangs and sunshades above windows to keep the glass cool and reduce mechanical cooling costs," Perruzzi said. A white roof helps reflect solar heat gain and keep the building cool. Inside the building, the design incorporates Forest Stewardship Council (FSC) certified wood products, materials with low VOCs, and linoleum instead of vinyl tile. The company also chose to use local materials, reducing the need for transportation and shipping. "The HVAC system features a cooling tower filtration system utilizing electronics to clean system water, not chemicals, which can pollute the environment when these systems are flushed," explains Perruzzi, adding, "During construction, more than 90 percent of construction waste was recycled, and careful indoor air quality practices were employed. At the end of construction, a two-week air flush out of the building was performed prior to occupancy."

Margulies Perruzzi Architects' own headquarters, which is located in the Boston Children's Museum, is also LEED certified. The company specifically chose the building as its headquarters because the building was already LEED certified, and the company added features to the interior space to make a truly sustainable work environment. "The space is designed to maximize exposure to daylight. We used local materials with high levels of recycled content and carefully analyzed paints, carpet, sealants, and adhesives to be certain we were producing a space with low levels of indoor air contaminants. We provided areas for recycling of paper, plastic, and cardboard. More than 70 percent of the furniture in the space is reused from our previous location, lowering the demand for new resources. All of our office equipment (copiers, printers) are ENERGY

STAR-rated, meaning they use low levels of energy," Perruzzi said. The company also provided each workstation with individual lighting systems, enabling each employee to control his or her own lighting.

All of these features have greatly enhanced the company's output and increased productivity. "We have found that access to natural light has had a profound impact on the overall well-being of our staff," Perruzzi said. "Located next to the green roof of the building is our new roof deck, which enhances productivity. Holding meetings in the sun is a great way to get things done. As designers, we often looked with envy at the spaces that we created for clients. The new space gives us the sense that we have 'closed the loop' and are living and working in a way that is consistent with our design philosophy."

Hiring Your Green Team

The scope of your project will determine the professionals you need for your green project team: real estate agent or mortgage broker, architect, contractor, LEED consultant, commissioning agent, and green interior designer. You may need the expertise of specialists, such as lighting, acoustics and thermal engineers, landscape architects, and solar contractors. The most important consideration when hiring your green team is each professional's experience in sustainable development and commitment to the principles and objectives of green building and design.

Before you hire a professional

Because the systems, methods, and considerations for green building differ so much from conventional building, evaluate a professional's experience with green building before signing a hiring contract. Ask about:

☀ His or her experience with and general knowledge of green building

Many green building professionals get into the business because they truly care about the environment and are passionate about the overall process and what green buildings can attain. Talk with the professional about general green building concepts — after you have familiarized yourself with them — and get a sense of how familiar he or she is with low-VOC paints, subfloor ventilation systems, and other green design elements and processes.

☀ Samples of commercial office building projects he or she has worked on

A review of samples is the best way to gauge his or her experience and the kinds of processes, systems, and green building elements with which he or she is familiar.

☀ Familiarity with LEED

If you are seeking LEED certification, the contractor, designers, engineers, and other professionals you hire should at least be familiar with LEED and the various requirements for certification. Having an LEED AP to serve as a LEED consultant throughout the course of your project is the best way to ensure you are building in accordance with LEED requirements for certification.

☀ His or her involvement in the business of green building and knowledge of its future

Inquire whether the professional is a member of any local or national green building coalitions or associations and what his or her involvement is in the overall business of green building.

☀ Experience working on a green team

Green projects involve much more teamwork than traditional building projects. Experience working on a green project with other green professionals is important. Everyone should be able to work well together to meet the building's objectives.

☀ His or her recommendations for or comments on your project

The first time you speak with a green building professional, you should discuss your general needs and outline the goals of your project. Ask how the professional can achieve these goals for you, and what recommendations he or she has.

CASE STUDY: THE LEGAL ISSUES OF GREEN BUILDING

Melissa Collar, partner
Warner Norcross & Judd LLP
Grand Rapids, MI
www.wnj.com

As one of the largest firms in Michigan and one of the top 200 firms in the country, Warner Norcross & Judd LLP has experience in nearly every kind of law and has served a vast diversity of clients. The firm, which was founded in 1931, has more than 200 attorneys in Michigan who practice marketing and advertising law, health law, environmental law, trusts and estate law, corporate sustainability, and real estate law.

As chair of the Real Estate Services Group, Melissa Collar works extensively on construction issues specific to green and sustainable development. Collar regularly works with owners who are building green buildings to guide them through the legal issues that arise when negotiating a green construction agreement, a contract that greatly differs from a traditional construction agreement. "Green building starts from the moment you decide what you want to do with a property," she explains. From experience, Collar sees the necessity of a collaborative team approach from the very beginning of the process. This enables everyone on the team — designers, architects, engineers, lawyers, and contractors, to name a few — to be on the same page throughout the entire designing and building process.

An important part of establishing a monetary budget and a timeline for any green building project is determining whether you will build on a greenfield or a brownfield, and what state, municipal, and federal tax incentives are available to you. In Michigan, Collar's municipality is working on a new series tax incentives for green buildings, which include tax abatements and financing options under the Brownfield Act. The latter is a form of tax increment financing (TIF), a public funding method that uses future gains from taxes to fund development projects. The legislation being developed in Michigan is specifically designed to use tax increment financing to develop brownfield sites.

The type of land you will be developing will determine what federal, state, and municipal incentives are available to you. The next step is determining if you will seek LEED certification, which will require room in your budget. Next comes researching and selecting construction materials, some of which may cost more than conventional materials, and hiring an architect to design your building. If you are using low-flow fixtures in your bathrooms, for instance, you will need more equipment than a conventional bathroom fixture would require. "It costs more for design work and materials," Collar said, adding that, in the past, the cost of green building materials used to be more than a third higher than conventional materials, but they are now becoming increasingly affordable. Collar stressed that while green design and materials may require a slightly higher initial investment, the benefits from energy savings and long-term cost savings can make the investment well worthwhile.

From a developer's standpoint, there are many additional considerations when building green. "A developer needs to consider what kinds of tenants he will bring in," she said, in addition to determining what the operating costs will be and how the developer will work with tenants to ensure the tenants maintain the greenness of the building. Through a clause in the lease agreement, this can include things like creating or maintaining a recycling program and using low-VOC paints and finishes if a tenant is building the interior. From a tenant's perspective, green buildings are very attractive because of the cost savings, general quality of the indoor environment, and the appeal of the workspace to potential employees. "Tenants are looking at a different economy, so if someone is going to build new, they have to make it appealing," Collar said, "One of the ways to do this is to build green. It sets them apart."

If you are seeking LEED certification, you need a contractor whom you can trust to see the project through to certification. Some contractors are not familiar with green building. Among those who are, some are reluctant to commit to green building projects seeking LEED certification because of the additional requirements they are responsible for overseeing. If a contractor signs a contract to build a green building and then discovers that the developer does not want to commit to the specific design and construction requirements necessary to get LEED certification, that contractor could be in breach of contract. "If a building does not get certified, it is on the contractor. There is an elevated standard of care," Collar said. This is historically different from what contractors have been legally required to do.

Because a significant amount of time could pass between completion of construction and the determination of LEED certification — sometimes this takes a year or more — the contract must stipulate all the requirements for achieving certification. The contract should state that you have chosen a specific designer because of his or her experience. "[You] are depending on them for experience, and they have a standard of care to construct within the green building guidelines," Collar said.

At the end of the day, a successful green building project is the result of diligent and collaborative work by all parties. If a building does not get the LEED certification it is seeking, you as the business, corporation, or company are not the only one to be affected. Municipalities who provided financial and other incentives, lenders, and tenants also will be negatively affected. "If one part of it falls apart, then your green building may not be so green anymore," Collar said. "The key is proper management to ensure all parties are working together for the end result."

Sample Sustainable Building Designs

Although sustainable design strategies and building processes vary significantly, all green building projects have several common objectives: They seek to reduce their carbon footprint, provide a high-quality environment for workers, and save energy and money. Each project achieves this in a different way.

Here is a brief overview of the sustainable features incorporated in ten successful green commercial building projects:

Toyota Motor Sales USA, Torrance, California (LEED Gold Certified)

- Incorporates solar panels, high efficiency glass windows, and an ENERGY STAR roof that improves the energy efficiency of the building by more than 20 percent beyond the state's requirements.

- Structure is constructed of recycled steel. Recycled carpet backing, ceiling tiles, and wallboard were used for indoor materials.

- Low-VOC paints and finishes were used throughout the building.

- Building uses low-flow water fixtures, recycled water, and drip irrigation system to reduce potable water use by 80 percent.

- Outdoor pathways are made of recycled concrete generated from the construction process.

- Electric charging stations are available in parking lots.

Bank One Corporate Center, Chicago, Illinois

- The building's original foundation, along with some of the materials from the old building's structure, were recycled and restored, eliminating the need for demolition and new materials for a new foundation.

- Individual temperature controls incorporated into workspaces.

- Open floor plan allows for optimal access to daylight.

- Subfloor air distribution system increases energy efficiency of the building as well as air quality.

PNC Center, Pittsburgh, Pennsylvania (LEED Silver Certified)

- Building was built on a brownfield site.

- The building incorporates a hybrid air system that using a combination of forced air and natural ventilation to reduce energy consumption.

- Transportation to and from an on-site parking facility is provided to employees; employees also have easy access to public transportation.

- Oversized windows optimize daylighting; open floor plan encourages employee interaction.

- Sunshades prevent solar heat gain the summer.

- Interior materials, including carpets and flooring, are partially recycled.

- An extensive water purification system purifies all the potable water throughout the building.

Ford Motor Company North American Headquarters, Irvine, California (LEED Certified)

- Almost all employees have access to natural daylighting and windows.

- Electric charging stations for electric cars available in parking lots. Employees were given incentives to take public transportation, which is easily accessible.

- Subfloor air distribution system decreases energy consumption and increases air quality.

- The building's green roof controls stormwater, reduces the heat island effect on the building, and serves as a landscaped rooftop terrace for employees.

- Low-flow toilets and fixtures were installed in all restrooms.

- Light sensors and energy efficient bulbs control energy waste from lighting.

Tuthill Corporate Center, Burr Ridge, Illinois

- An efficient HVAC system reduces the building's energy consumption by more than 40 percent.

- Building was designed to incorporate a tight envelope that maintains indoor temperature more efficiently.

- Employees have access to daylight and windows.

- Subfloor air distribution system reduces energy use and increases indoor air quality.

- The outdoor landscaping is vast and includes a preserved prairie, ponds, waterfalls, and gardens.

Herman Miller International UK Headquarters, Chippenham, UK (LEED Gold Certified)

- Building is oriented to face south to optimize energy and heat from the sun.

- Overhangs keep the building cool in the warm months, and concrete terraces serve as natural heat blockers while also serving as recreation areas for employees.

- The building floor plan was designed to optimize natural ventilation through the building, improving air quality and reducing energy consumption from air systems.

- The open floor plan also leaves floors and ceilings exposed, eliminating the need for additional materials like drywall.

Buckeburg Gas and Water Company, Buckeburg, Germany

- The building uses solar hot water heaters and a solar panel system on the roof to generate most of the building's electricity.

- The building incorporates an integrated energy management system that uses natural air to balance the temperature of the building.

- Concrete walls work to reduce the building's heat in the summer and contain heat in colder months.

- A large multiple-story glass atrium encourages employee interaction, helps circulate the air inside the building, and offers access to daylight for most of the office space.

- Skylights and open floor plans provide access to daylight and help create an open, airy feel to the building.

Bank of America Tower, New York City (LEED Platinum Certified)

- The building uses a cogeneration system to generate nearly half of the building's electricity. The system uses recovered waste heat and a gas engine to generate electricity more efficiently.

- A green roof and waterless urinals reduce the building's water usage.

- Use of large windows and open spaces provides employees with access to natural daylight.

- Most of the materials used during construction are recycled and from renewable sources. Most of these materials were supplied from local manufacturers located less than 500 miles from the building.

- An innovative air filtration system filters out almost 100 percent of the toxins and pollutants from the indoor air.

San Francisco Civic Tower, San Francisco, California (LEED Silver Certified)

- Solar panels on the building's roof and wind turbines on the building's façade generate a significant portion of the building's electricity.

- A subfloor ventilation system helps to circulate the building's air.

- Light shelves reflect natural daylight to reduce the need for artificial lighting and give daylight access to more employees and office space.

- Mini greenhouses on each floor of the office incorporate green spaces for employees, and the plants in the greenhouses help circulate and improve indoor air quality.

- Use of demountable partitions in office spaces allow for the easy flexibility in office space and floor plan rearrangement without demolition and construction.

Manitoba Hydro Head Office, Winnepeg, Canada

- A geothermal heating and cooling system provides the building's energy. Heat energy recovered from exhausts in the building's parking garage is circulated back into the building and used to heat air.

- A subfloor ventilation system helps maintain the quality of the indoor air and improves the building's energy efficiency.

- A green roof helps control stormwater and the building's temperature.

- Outdoor gardens facing the south help to filter air before it enters the building, improving the indoor air quality.

- Large operable windows provide employees with access to daylight.

- A natural ventilation system, incorporating outdoor gardens, a solar chimney, and a subfloor air system, works to pump fresh air into the building at all times.

CASE STUDY: GREEN
BUILDING IS ABOUT PEOPLE,
PROFIT, AND THE PLANET

Mary Tappouni, president
Breaking Ground Contracting
Jacksonville, FL
www.breakinggroundcontracting.com

Mary Tappouni founded her company Breaking Ground Contracting, a commercial general contracting company, in 1997. Although the first few years of her business did not involve much green building, Tappouni came to a stark realization in 2004 and has been committed to green building ever since. "We were not consciously involved in green building," she explains, "but I saw numbers on the impact the construction industry has on the planet, and I thought 'I need to infuse this into my business and do something more positive than just building buildings.'"

Today, Breaking Ground Contracting not only works on sustainable building projects, but also under Tappouni's leadership, the company has created a system of sustainable building practices. It is currently constructing a new green office building, which it hopes to move into soon. The new building incorporates a number of innovative green systems and features, including a vegetated roof and living walls that capture, treat, and control stormwater right on the property. "The vegetated roof works by reducing the water coming off the roof and cleaning the water so it goes into the river clean," Tappouni said.

Breaking Ground Contracting also built a rain garden on its property to address water pollution. The rain garden is a system that captures polluted rainwater and prevents it from flowing into drains and sewers.

The construction materials used for both the interior and exterior of the building are mostly recycled and reclaimed materials, further adding to the building's greenness. "There is a huge amount of reuse," Tappouni said. For instance, she is converting old doors, which would have been thrown out, into desks. She is also reusing old glass for cubicle partitions and reusing hardware from cabinets and desks, as well as ceiling tiles and light fixtures. Breaking Ground even used reclaimed wood for framing, as well as for other exterior features. Daylighting was incorporated into the building by expanding the existing windows on the top and the bottom floors to bring in much more light, and all low-VOC and low-emitting paints, sealers, and adhesives were used on the building's interior. Additionally, each employee has his or her own heat and cooling controls. "People being comfortable at work is so important," Tappouni said.

The company has put much thought into integrating processes within its office environment to reduce waste, conserve energy and money, and reduce its impact on the environment. Tappouni has taken this initiative in her own hands and sought solutions to roadblocks along the way. For instance, because the city does not offer a recycling program for commercial construction materials, Tappouni pays a local vendor to recycle her company's construction debris. She also offers her employees cash incentives for using fuel-efficient vehicles and other incentives that reach beyond the employees' office life. The point is to encourage employees to incorporate green practices into both their home and work life to create a green way of life that does not stop when the employee goes home for the day. "The big thing is conservation, reducing the amount of waste produced in the first place. We want to incorporate composting in the new building, and we have a goal of going paperless," Tappouni explains.

Tappouni takes this same passion and commitment to creating, not just a green building, but also a green environment for her clients. "Our goal is to have 80 percent waste management," she said. This means that the company commits itself to reusing, recycling, or donating 80 percent of waste generated from construction and demolition. The company either reuses materials for other projects or donates the materials to a thrift store operated by the local Habitat for Humanity. Tappouni also reaches out to local suppliers to see if they are interested in purchasing the material, in addition to using highly recyclable materials like concrete, metals, and wood.

Beyond construction services, Breaking Ground Contracting offers an array of additional services as part of the community outreach program LEED Lunch and Learns to educate the public and other professionals in the building industry about sustainable development. The company also has an education division to educate realtors, developers, and even city officials about green building practices. About the green building momentum and interest in Jacksonville, Tappouni said, "We have seen a major shift in the past one to two years." Even the traditional building professionals who were skeptical of green building have begun to see the significant benefits it can offer.

Tappouni and her team are so passionate about green building that they have actually trained their competitors in green building techniques. "Our vision is for everyone to understand what sustainability is and what their impact is," Tappouni said. That dedication continues to make Breaking Ground Contracting a leader in the green construction industry.

Building Commissioning

Building commissioning is the systematic and documented process of making sure the building functions as intended, building systems perform efficiently, and building operators are properly trained. It is carried out by a third-party commissioning agent (CA) who is typically involved in the building project from the beginning of the design phase until the building is occupied. Commissioning is a standard practice of high-performance green building and is so effective that it is has also become standard for many conventional building projects. Many federal and state government building projects make commissioning an official requirement.

Building commissioning grew out of testing and balancing (TAB), the traditional procedure for verifying that a building's HVAC system is operating as it was designed to. An independent organization is hired to check that the pumps, dampers, hot water heating units, and other components are working properly, measure the flows of hot and cold water, and ensure that the airflows in each area of the building are properly adjusted. The Associated Air Balance Council (AABC) (**www.aabc.com**) is the governing authority of

TAB in the United States and has gradually shifted its activities from HVAC systems to commissioning whole buildings.

The Building Commissioning Association (**www.bcxa.org**), an international nonprofit organization, serves as the recognized authority and resource on commissioning. It develops technical resources, holds an annual conference on the latest innovations in the industry, and manages a certification program for credentialed commissioning professionals.

The CA acts as an advocate for the building owner during the construction process and can perform a variety of functions. The CA should be present on the project team from the very beginning to document how various features and systems are expected to perform. At each stage of the project, the CA reviews construction documentation for compliance with design criteria, checks over installations, ensures that the proper products and components are selected, that conditions for warranties are met, and watches out for potential problems in operating or maintaining the finished building. The building commissioning contract should define the scope of the CA's responsibilities, identify the systems that need to be tested and checked, and specify how their performance will be measured. The commissioning process should include all aspects of the building:

- HVAC systems
- Gray water systems
- Rain harvesting systems
- Plumbing fixtures
- Electronic water controls
- Irrigation systems
- Security systems
- Electrical and telecommunications systems
- Electrical appliances and equipment
- Solar or wind systems
- Ceiling tiles
- Floor coverings
- Windows
- Doors
- Locks
- Hardware
- Windows
- Millwork
- Lighting
- Any other component included in the building specifications

The CA also confirms schedules for starting up systems, makes sure the operating staff is trained, and prepares operation and maintenance (O&M) manuals for all the building systems. When construction is complete, the CA conducts a complete review of the building and verifies that everything is working as it is supposed to. After the building is occupied, it should be recommissioned at regular intervals to make sure it continues to perform as intended and that the indoor environmental quality (IEQ) remains at an acceptable level. The CA also conducts tests just before the warranties expire on various building components, so any malfunctions will be corrected under warranty.

A new building is commissioned to make sure it meets or exceeds the energy savings standards expected from its design. Commissioning an existing building identifies and corrects malfunctions and flaws that waste energy, such as simultaneous heating and cooling, air leaks, inadequate insulation, oversized equipment, and miscalibrated sensors. Data collected since 2004 shows that commissioning existing buildings is more effective in reducing CO_2 emissions than any other energy-saving measure undertaken to date.

Because building commissioning is an additional service, it adds to the cost of the building project. The cost of commissioning is determined by the scale of the building project and the complexity of the services involved. The average cost increase ranges from .05 to 1 percent more for a large building project (more than $50 million) and 2 to 4 percent for a project costing less than $5 million. In addition to the CA's fees, it may be necessary to pay the architects for the additional time required to prepare documentation for the CA. When a building project is looking for ways to cut costs, omitting commissioning is one of the most apparent choices. However, a 2004 study funded by the U.S. DOE of 224 commercial buildings concluded that commissioning is cost effective for both new and existing buildings. Commissioning existing buildings achieved median energy cost savings of 15 percent, with payback periods of 0.7 years. The median payback time for new buildings was 4.8 years, but when savings from improved equipment lifetimes, reduced operation and maintenance costs, fewer contractor callbacks, and improved indoor environment were considered, the payback period was almost eliminated.

Building commissioning also ensures that a building continues to meet its green objectives over time, as its components age.

The Importance of Insurance

Melissa Collar of Michigan-based law firm Warner Norcross & Judd LLP discusses the various types of insurance needed for a green building project and the importance of obtaining the right insurance:

Risks on the job site ran the gamut of everything from damage to construction improvements to worker injuries. There are a host of insurance policies that building owners will want to make sure they safeguard their investment.

Insurance policies generally fall under two types: occurrence-based policies or claims-based policies. Generally, occurrence-based policies are preferable, because claims made against a project may occur long after the initial insurance policy expires. An example of this would be a personal injury on the site. The claim may not be made for months or years after the policy expires and possibly after the construction is complete and/or the owner no longer owns the property. Nevertheless, if the injury occurs during the policy term, the owner's insurance will remain in effect no matter how long it takes the injured person to file a claim against the owner. On the other hand, a claims-based policy only covers an event within the policy period time and requires the claim to be made at that time.

It is not enough to get a declaration page (often referred to as a dec page) or certificate of insurance, which are customarily furnished to an owner who desires to be named as additional insured to a policy carried by third parties, such as a contractor or tenant. These certificates are not binding contracts, nor do they go into detail on what the specific policy and its endorsements cover. Endorsements are carve-outs or add-ins to the standard policy and will not necessarily be spelled out on either the dec page or the certificate of insurance.

The certificate of insurance is prepared by the agent, not the insurance company, and may not accurately reflect the terms of the actual policy. Owners may not contractually hold the insurance company to a certificate of insurance. Though an owner may have a claim against the insurance agent in such a case, the claim may not be collectible, depending on the amount of damages at stake.

It is critical for owners to read each policy thoroughly at the beginning of the process to ensure they know explicitly what is — and is not — covered. It is best to have an experienced risk advisor or insurance attorney review the policy.

According to Collar, in addition to workers' compensation, which is required in most jurisdictions, common insurance policies include:

- **Builders risk insurance** in the amount of the replacement value of the work. Either the owner or the contractor may obtain the policy, which covers the actual damage to any improvements being made during the construction process. It is preferable, though, for the owner to hold the policy, rather than the general contractor, to control the receipt of insurance proceeds and ensure they are used to replace or repair the damaged area. However, sometimes the contractor will carry the insurance if it can get a better rate to pass through to the owner.

- **Professional liability insurance**, which covers the professional errors and omissions of design work by designers. Only licensed designers, and in limited cases, contractors who are performing design/build contracts are entitled to purchase professional liability insurance. This insurance protects the designer from liability arising from claims of negligent design errors or omissions raised by owners. The owner cannot be named as an additional insured, and it is only available as a claims-made policy. Therefore, it is important for an owner to require that a "tail" of three to six years of professional liability insurance be carried by the designer after the designer's work is completed. The owner should remain diligent in assuring the tail insurance is maintained in effect for the period agreed to by the parties.

- **Subcontractor default insurance** gives construction contractors a single, comprehensive policy to manage subcontractor or supplier default. This insurance covers the costs of replacing subcontractors, accelerating a project, settling damages, and preparing claims to step in and complete a project if a subcontractor or supplier defaults on his or her obligations. Some owners are using this insurance in place of obtaining bonds.

- **Commercial general liability insurance**, which is also known as protective liability, covers damages or injuries on site to people and property other than the property that is under construction.

- **Auto liability insurance**, which generally covers vehicles being driven to, from, and on the construction site.

- **An umbrella policy**, which is increasingly required by owners to provide additional coverage to the policies mentioned above.

- **Additional specialized policies.** Depending on the nature of the project or location, an owner might want to have special insurance to cover such things as the use of explosives, if they are being used in the demolition process. Other specialized policies could cover projects that require working on or near the water using certain types of materials.

Collar adds, "Owners should require that they be named as additional insured on the policy, although as mentioned above, this is not possible for professional liability insurance."

It is also important for owners and contractors to protect stakeholders, including investors, lenders, and subcontractors, by securing bonds. According to Collar, there are five main types of bonds:

- **Bid bonds.** Although not very common, bid bonds guarantee that the contractor or subcontractor who is the successful bidder for a construction project will enter into the contract awarded to the contractor or subcontractor. Bid bonds protect the project owner. For example, if the winning low bidder on the job does not contract with the owner, the bid bond covers the increased cost to go to the next lowest-cost bidder.

- **Performance bonds.** These assure the owner and lender that the project will be completed in accordance with the contract and that the contractor and all subcontractors will meet their contractual obligations. If this does not happen, the surety company will come in and perform in place of the contractor (although sometimes the surety will make a monetary payment to the stakeholder who is the "insured" instead). Performance bonds can also be invoked for correcting any defects that arise during the warranty period if the contract provides a warranty.

- **Payment bonds.** Also known as labor and materials payment bonds, this type of bond ensures that all those companies that furnish material or labor on a construction project will be paid so that no construction liens are filed against the project. Payment bonds protect both lenders and owners, who may otherwise be at risk to pay for the work twice if the contractor and subcontractors do not pay the lower-tier parties who have performed work and are legally entitled to place a lien on the property if they are not paid. In the current economy, the credit worthiness of construction companies is becoming more questionable, so payment and performance bonds have increased in popularity.

- **Penal bonds.** These bonds discharge a construction lien and are purchased at the time a lien is asserted against a project. Penal bonds allow the owner to keep moving on a construction project while the validity of the lien is being questioned.

- **Maintenance bonds.** If owners have a long-term obligation for maintenance, such as under a warranty, they may ensure those maintenance obligations with bonds. Though maintenance bonds may be issued at the time of other performance and payment bonds, they do not take effect until after the project is completed.

"A final note of caution for all insurance policies and bonds: Keep them," Collar said. "Some claims may not surface for years, and if owners and contractors no longer have copies of the insurance documents, they may be declined coverage."

CHAPTER 4:
Building Site and Orientation

The building location and the outdoor environment play an important role in the overall sustainability of a green building. A site must be practical not only for the building project but also for the municipality in which the site is situated. You must be able to build on the site while maintaining the ecosystems and surrounding natural environment. Surrounding waterways, protected wetlands, and nearby farmland must be considered during site selection. Even if you are not going to seek LEED certification, the LEED requirements are an excellent guideline for creating a sustainable project.

LEED gives up to 26 credits for sustainable site projects, which include projects that:

- Restore and protect natural habitats
- Connect to the community and add to the community's overall development goals
- Are developed on brownfield sites
- Maximize open space

- Provide bicycle storage to encourage occupants to bicycle to work
- Provide primary space for low-emission and energy efficient vehicles like electric cars
- Provide convenient access to public transportation
- Incorporate a stormwater control system, such as a green roof
- Reduce heat island effects

The goal is not only to minimize interference in the community and the surrounding environment, but also to improve it and become a positive addition.

Factors to Consider When Choosing a Location

Most projects do not achieve all of the goals outlined by LEED for site selection. Identify the goals that are achievable for your project and that match your organization's objectives. *The following sections describe factors to be considered when choosing a location for your project.*

Environmental impact

A project's environmental impact is defined as the effect of its buildings, parking structures, outdoor gardens, roadways, and any associated development on land, soil, waterways, and ecosystems. In the LEED rating system, one point is attainable for projects that are not:

- Built on land that has been deemed prime farmland by the U.S. Department of Agriculture
- Built on land that serves as a natural habitat for endangered species
- Built on undeveloped land less than 50 feet from waterways that serve as a natural habitat for fish and that serve recreational purposes
- Built on land that was previously public parkland

To gain these points, the project must be designed to avoid any potential negative impacts on the surrounding environment.

Connectivity to the community

Under this category, LEED stipulates that a sustainable project should protect greenfields and use existing infrastructure by building on a brownfield or grayfield site located in an urban area. Overall, the project should contribute to the positive development of the surrounding community. LEED gives points for projects that are:

- Developed within a half a mile of a populated neighborhood or residential area
- Developed on a previously occupied site that is in an urban neighborhood
- Renovations to existing buildings
- Within a half a mile of amenities, including stores, places of worship, parks, restaurants, post offices, libraries, and medical care facilities. The site also must provide access to these places via sidewalks or roadways so pedestrians may easily reach them.

The goal is to add to the development or restructuring of an existing community and to have a positive impact on the community's growth.

Limiting new development

One LEED point is available for projects that are built on brownfield sites and that make use of previously abandoned or run-down land. This includes sites that are contaminated, as well as sites that have been officially classified by the government as brownfield sites. The goal is to minimize development on new land and recycle abandoned brownfield sites.

LEED also gives one point to projects that protect greenfields by limiting the size of the building's perimeter, which is achieved by:

- Building a parking garage underneath the building instead of on outside land
- Incorporating low-maintenance plants and shrubs that are native to the local area, which minimizes water use and impact on the soil and prevents the spread of invasive plants
- Keeping the construction/demolition site within a limited boundary to avoid unnecessary disturbance to the surrounding environment

Proximity to transportation

This is an important category for LEED. A maximum of six points are given to projects situated near mass public transportation, which includes a bus station, a train station, or subway station. The site must be within a quarter of a mile walking distance of at least one

stop for two methods of public transportation. The goal is to encourage future occupants to take public transportation to and from work instead of driving, which greatly reduces carbon emissions and its negative effects on the environment.

Availability of amenities for public transportation and carpooling commuters

One point is available for projects that dedicate room for bicycle racks and storage rooms, as well as changing rooms, showers, and storage lockers for workers who commute to work by bicycle. The racks must be within 200 yards of the building and be sufficient to serve 5 percent of the building's occupants. The showers and changing areas must be large enough to serve 0.5 percent of the occupants.

LEED gives three points to facilities that provide primary parking spaces for low-emission vehicles, such as electric cars. These parking spots must be discounted by 20 percent (if the company charges for parking). The point can also be achieved by making alternative fuel stations available on site or by providing employees with the opportunity to carpool or ride-share in a low-emitting vehicle. The commitment to ride-share must be for at least two years.

LEED gives two points for projects that dedicate primary parking spaces for carpools and that provide shuttle service to mass transportation stops nearby. The goal is to minimize available parking to encourage employees to carpool or to take mass transit.

Use of open space

One LEED point is available for projects that have a good ratio of open space to footprint of the building. Besides preserving the surrounding natural habitats and the environment, open spaces serve as outdoor areas for employees and improves the overall work environment.

These points can be achieved several ways, including:

- By providing open space that exceeds local zoning requirements by 25 percent in areas that also have open space requirements

- By providing open space that is 20 percent of the building footprint in areas that have no open space requirements

LEED suggests these goals can be achieved by using underground parking, instead of open parking lots, and by sharing parking space with neighboring buildings or facilities.

Stormwater control

One LEED point is designated for projects that reduce pollution from stormwater by at least 25 percent and incorporate irrigation techniques to control stormwater and prevent runoff. This can be done through vegetated roofs and the use of pervious paving — a specialty pavement that enables water absorption and prevents runoff. This point is also subject to a building's use of non-potable stormwater for landscape irrigation and toilet flushing. Another point is available for the projects that demonstrate the ability to capture and treat 90 percent of this stormwater runoff.

Reduction of heat islands

One point is available to projects that actively reduce heat islands by reducing heat-absorbing structures, like a black roof. This can be achieved by shading with trees or artificial sun blockers and by minimizing open parking lots, which draw heat. This can also be achieved by a vegetated roof or a roof painted a light color and by the incorporation of vegetation on the exterior landscape of the building.

Conducting a Site Analysis

A site analysis can help you develop a plan for land use, determine how well a site will fit your project's objectives, and enable you to meet LEED guidelines. A site analysis identifies the positive and negative effects of natural elements like the surrounding environment, the wind, the sun, and the trees on your project.

A site analysis:

- Identifies existing vegetation, natural habitats, and ecosystems, and measures the location and topography of trees and other landscaping

- Identifies areas that need to be preserved, such as waterways and wooded areas

- Assesses how compatible the site is with a project's space needs

- Assesses how the building could be oriented to protect the surrounding environment while optimizing the sun's use and the use of the land's space

- Identifies any other features that are located on the site, such as existing buildings, sheds, parking structures, or roadways

- Identifies the best way to incorporate these existing features into the new project's design or manage them with minimal destruction to the environment

- Assesses the local zoning regulations and how they will affect development

- Identifies neighboring structures that may affect your development

CASE STUDY: BUILDINGS ARE THE NEW SHELTERS FOR OUR EMERGING SELVES

Maia Gilman, owner and founder
Maia Gilman Architect
www.maiagilman.com

Sustainable design firm Maia Gilman Architect is a New York-based architectural firm that specializes in green building. Founded by architect Maia Gilman, the company works on a variety of green building projects throughout the New York area. "Maia Gilman Architect incorporates environmentally healthy solutions into all its projects, whether new construction or renovation," Gilman said. "The company takes a broad view of environmentalism and approaches each project holistically so that no influence on the building's health, and the occupants' well-being is overlooked. For example, the subtle energies of electromagnetism and the impacts of underground streams are considered as high a priority in our planning and design, as are the more visible material choices like reclaimed wood flooring or solar panels."

With more than 15 years of experience in green design and architecture, Gilman is a LEED accredited professional (AP) who leads her team on design projects for schools, businesses, and cultural buildings. Here is her firm's take on green building:

One of the most important considerations in developing an approach to green building is the long-term function of the building. Green building means considering longevity, both of the building itself and of the ecosystems that provide the materials for building and that are impacted by the building's use. Building in the industrial age and the new technology age has become toxic with chemicals, additives, and lack of awareness and respect for surroundings.

Green building can address these issues. By stripping away these unhealthy aspects of industry that have migrated into our buildings and by introducing sound advances in eco-technology, we can produce and re-habilitate buildings that are friendlier to the earth and to our own bodies.

We take a broad view of environmental design that comes from the belief that the earth is a living organism and that we are an essential part of that living system. This leads us to create design solutions holistically, rather than following a specific list of products or systems to include. We always consider climate, solar data, and the impact of geology. We map under-ground streams; source locations of nearby electromagnetic energy; the proximity of trees, hills, automobiles, industry; and sources of noise and light pollution. With this information, we can come up with a series of de-signs for our clients that reflect an appropriate response to the local and larger environmental stimuli.

The firm also incorporates innovative and unique design techniques that help meet each client's goal. We use traditional spatial planning systems like Feng Shui (a Chinese method of planning and design) and Vaastu (an Indian method of planning and design)," she said. "By looking at all of these factors, we are able to provide our clients with environmentally and consciously created spaces that support them and their goals."

There is no one approach to green building and to meeting clients' needs. There are countless decisions to be made in a green building project, and they require current knowledge of the building industry. The best way to start is to hire an architect to coordinate the project. The LEED designa-tion after a professional's name indicates that they are trained in navigat-ing the procedures for LEED certification offered by the U.S. Green Build-ing Council. Even if you do not choose to pursue LEED certification, which can add to the value of your property, a LEED-designated professional is trained to understand the ins and outs of green building, which will be an asset to you in the project.

A good way to start with your architect is to sit down with a standard list, like the LEED project categories, and begin to take note of the ways in which your project can be structured to be the healthiest that it can, Gil-man said. If you outline your goals early on in the process, you will be much more likely to end up with an environmentally conscious building in the long run, because critical decisions about building systems (site location, heating, cooling, and power) are made at the beginning of the process. Though it can be tempting to zoom in right away on your favorite green material choices (bamboo floor, recycled glass countertop), it is best to keep an open mind at the beginning of the process to see what unfolds as being best for the project overall. Rather than recommending particular building systems or products, we choose products based on the specific needs of the projects, which always vary.

You can bring your green building wish list to the table, but it is best to keep a broad perspective on the project and consider all your options. For example, you may love the idea of solar panels, but geothermal energy might be a better choice for your project. You might want a specific group of brand-name products, but by focusing on them exclusively, you might be missing out on a locally made, custom option that is still affordable. Talk with your architect about the overall feel and look you are aiming for, and be open to suggestions for ways of reaching your goal.

The result is a customized space designed to meet the specific needs of each client. But be aware of greenwashing — the process of falsely advertising products to be environmentally friendly when they are not — because it can be a stumbling block in the building process. It is easy to be blindsided by green marketing or greenwashing, so have your architect take a deeper look at your wish list items to make sure they really fit with the environmentally healthy goals of the project.

You also need to be aware of how to measure accurately how cost effective a green building will be. This all comes down to the life cycle of the building, and how the owner fits into that cycle. It can be tremendously economical and energy efficient in the long run to install new double glazed windows with low-E coatings, for example, but if the owner is only occupying the property for three years, he or she is not likely to see the cost saving. It will boost employee morale and health immediately to create a day-lit space with low-allergenic materials and with a high fresh-air exchange rate, which for a short-term or long-term owner will result in fewer sick days and increased productivity during the workday.

Green buildings will provide much more than just a space in which to work. Buildings provide shelter and inspiration, and they house our most intimate and expressive selves. Imagine how much clearer and finer our daily work would be if we could carry out our activities in spaces of full environmental integrity. The new green buildings allow us to be more illuminated and healthy in our every living moment. They are the new shelter for our emerging selves.

Building Shape and Orientation

New York City skyline at sunset overlooking the Hudson River.

Orientation refers to the position of the building on a plot of land and its location in relation to roadways, sidewalks, and landscaping. Shape refers to the physical shape of the building's structure. The most common building shapes for large commercial office buildings and structures are rectangles, squares, and triangles, because these shapes offer the strongest support systems. The orientation of a building is often determined by the most logical positioning. In New York City, for instance, there is not much room to contemplate orientation because most buildings are tall, slim high-rises with main entrances facing the main streets. In green building, however, the orientation and shape contribute significantly to the overall efficient function of the building.

The most efficient orientation for a new construction building uses and manages natural elements, including the sun and wind. Orienting the largest part of a building toward the sun maximizes the use of natural daylight. In hot and arid locations, exposure to the sun must be minimized or managed at certain times during the day. Although it varies slightly with geographical location, in the Northern Hemisphere, orienting a building toward the sun means facing the largest sides of the building with the most windows toward the south. The sun is strongest for the longest period on the southern walls of a structure. This allows for maximum exposure to the sun for the longest period of the day without direct exposure in any one direction. Windows facing directly to the east or west can cause excessive heat when light streams directly in during hotter months, making the air conditioner work harder and causing glare problems.

The Thinner, the Better

Tall, thin buildings are more efficient than wider, shorter buildings because taller buildings occupy less space on the ground and therefore have less impact on the surrounding ecosystems and environment. Narrower buildings also leave more square footage for landscaping and outdoor areas, and they have a smaller surface on which rain and stormwater can run off and cause pollution.

If a building is orientated to maximize exposure to the sun, solar radiation will provide not only daylight but also heat and energy that can greatly reduce dependence on an HVAC system.

It is also important to consider wind during the design phase, especially if you plan to use wind turbines for power. Wind puts additional stress on a structure and is a significant factor in heating or cooling a building. For example, The Jie Fang Daily News and Media building, located in Shanghai, China, incorporates a circular arch or indentation that extends through the length of the building. The design of the indentation reduces wind production that circulates into the building and reduces the impact the wind has on the building. The Shanghai Tower in Shanghai, China, also incorporates this concept by using a curved shape to minimize the lateral load on the building from strong winds.

Building shape and orientation go hand in hand. The shape and design plan of a building must support its orientation. A building will not automatically generate immediate cost savings just because it is oriented to receive full exposure to the sun. If the building design does not incorporate windows on the correct sides of the building to absorb natural daylight, the orientation will not have as strong an effect on energy efficiency. The building must be designed to function optimally within its orientation.

Green building also gives more consideration to the needs of the building occupants and how the shape of the building will support a green work environment, which often includes things like larger open spaces, more access to windows, and use of daylighting.

The Building Envelope

The building envelope is the space between the interior and exterior of a building. This space determines how well a building retains heat and cool air, which defines how much energy is needed for forced-air systems. The building's foundation, structure, roof, doors, and windows comprise a building envelope. All of these interact to determine how tight or loose this space is. The tighter the building envelope, the better the building will be able to control moisture and retain heat and cool air. The more efficient the envelope is in controlling moisture and preventing mold and mildew, the better the indoor air quality. The materials used to create a building structure play a significant role in the overall energy efficiency of the building envelope.

The structure of the building, and particularly the method and materials used to build it, plays a very important role in green building. Factors to consider when designing the architectural structure and design of a building include:

- The materials that will be used to frame the building

- How the structure will enable the building to use the natural resources (the sun, water, trees) without depleting, harming, or disturbing them
- The exterior needs of the building, such as space for wind turbines, solar panels, stormwater management systems, and outdoor landscaping and seating areas
- The interior needs of the building, such as interior layout of cubicle spaces, offices, conference rooms, and occupancy levels
- The amount of space you have available to build upon
- The available building materials, products, and resources
- Your project's budget

Foundations, floors, and roofing

Steel and concrete are two of the most popular materials used to structure a commercial office building and to serve as a foundation. Concrete has a high thermal mass, meaning it retains heat and cool temperatures well, and it is durable and can be made at the job site. There are many sustainable alternatives to traditional flooring materials.

Many green commercial buildings incorporate the concept of open, organic, and natural space. One popular feature is the use of exposed concrete floors that eliminate pollutants, such as VOCs, from carpeting and the use of wood flooring that might not be responsibly harvested.

Exposed concrete is not only aesthetically pleasing, but also its practicality makes it a natural choice for green builders. It not

Polished concrete floors in a commercial building.

only has a high thermal mass to retain heat, but it is also mold-resistant, low-maintenance, and highly flexible when it comes to colors and patterns.

Concrete can be made to look like granite or marble or can be customized to meet specific design needs.

If the use of exposed concrete is not a viable option, many alternatives including bamboo, linoleum, cork, ceramic, porcelain, and rubber are more

This floor was stained to resemble granite.

environmentally friendly than traditional flooring products and enhance the indoor air quality. All of these materials have a lower VOC content than traditional carpet or wood floors sealed with a chemical sealant. They also are manufactured more responsibly and have less negative impact on the environment. For instance, the prime ingredient in vinyl is polyvinyl chloride (PVC), which is primarily manufactured using petroleum, or oil. Linoleum, on the other hand, is made with natural materials, including linseed oil, pine resins, and cork.

Framing and structuring

Framing and structuring refer to the interior support system of the core and shell of a building. In green building, as in traditional building, steel and concrete are popular materials because they are durable. They are also environmentally friendly materials; steel is highly recyclable, and concrete can be made on site, reducing environmental impact from transportation.

Green building places significant emphasis on establishing systems that integrate to reduce energy use and increase indoor air quality. This means building a more efficient structure and using more efficient framing methods to create a tighter

Cast-in-place concrete system is being utilized here.

building envelope which, will achieve these goals while extending the life span of a building.

A building structure is typically composed of both vertical and horizontal, or lateral, framing to provide optimal support. Lateral framing provides resistance to wind and can be composed of a number of different systems or materials, depending on the building type. A common material used in green-building framing and foundation is cast-in-place concrete, which is made and poured on site into its final form.

In contrast, precast concrete is made from standard molds off site and then transported on site. Cast-in-place concrete enables more flexibility because the concrete is physically being poured into the actual design and structure of the building instead of being poured into molds off site and then fitted into the building later. Besides flexibility and convenience, cast-in-place concrete has a high thermal mass and works very well to reduce heat islands and maintain the temperature of a building.

Insulated concrete forms (ICFs) are blocks of expanded polystyrene — a form of recyclable plastic — that incorporate bars of reinforced steel. These blocks are filled with concrete, stacked and interlocked to form a highly durable and lightweight structure that retains heat and cool air, reduces energy use, and regulates noise within the building. The incorporation of ICFs in a commercial office building can earn more than 25 LEED points in the certification process.

Building Block LLC, an Oklahoma-based company specializing in ICFs, breaks down the points that can be achieved by the incorporation of ICFs into a variety of categories. (**www.buildblock.com/greenbuilding.asp**). These criteria can be used to assess the efficiency of other building materials:

- **Minimize impact on surrounding environment:** Because ICFs are constructed on site, construction that disturbs the environment on the surrounding site is limited.

- **Reduce the effects of heat islands:** ICFs are adaptable to many eco-friendly exterior finishes and glosses. Proper selection of light-colored reflective glosses can significantly reduce heat islands and gain LEED points.

- **Meet minimum energy requirements:** ICFs exceed minimum energy requirements designated by LEED because they have a very high thermal mass and serve as good insulators.

- **Create on site renewable energy and support green energy:** Given the ICFs' high thermal mass and natural ability to insulate, energy consumption to control indoor air temperatures is drastically reduced.

- **Reuse materials:** Although concrete is recyclable, it is not always reused every time. However, ICFs are easier to reuse because they are already in large blocks that have been measured.

- **Reduce waste from construction:** The waste factor of ICFs is 2 to 5 percent, which is lower than the waste factor of traditional construction methods. Waste factor measures the amount of waste that will be generated from the installation of a material.

- **Incorporate recycled content:** Some companies like Building Block incorporate recycled materials in the concrete, steel, and plastic in ICFs. To achieve the LEED point in this category, 20 percent of the materials must be recycled. These companies incorporate more than this percentage in their ICF products, exceeding the standards for LEED.

- **Use regional materials:** Materials cannot travel more than 500 miles to a job site to gain LEED credit for using regional materials.

- **Reduce use of uncertified and irresponsibly harvested wood:** ICFs greatly reduce the need for wood as a building material.

According to Building Block, ICFs reduce the need for large amounts of wood in the framing and structuring of a building, so the increased cost of certified wood can be justified and budget friendly because the amount is so much less.

- **Meet minimum indoor air quality standards:** ICF units release no VOCs after they are installed.

- **Increase indoor air ventilation:** ICFs prevent drafts from leaks in the envelope. ICFs have a high thermal mass, so heat and cool air are retained much easier, and the HVAC system does not have to work so hard to ventilate a space.

- **Reduce indoor air quality contamination during construction:** The materials used in ICFs emit low to no VOCs or other contaminants and prevent mold and mildew, which are both threats to indoor air quality.

- **Improve the energy performance of a building:** ICFs retain heat, cool air well, and reduce the need for forced-air systems to compensate for temperature variance.

- **Increase daylighting use of natural light and occupants' access to windows:** ICFs do not directly achieve this, but because of their ability to retain heat and air well, their use gives designers more flexibility on where to place windows.

The Pros and Cons of Steel and Concrete

Concrete

Pros: Concrete is very strong and can withstand significant impact. It can also be more affordable than steel, which has seen its cost increase significantly over the past 10 years. Concrete is very flexible and can be used for a variety of different shapes and structures. It can also be easier to work with than steel and can accommodate a shorter construction schedule because it can be mixed and installed quickly. Concrete also has a low VOC content.

Cons: Despite relatively low costs, concrete has at times been in shorter supply than steel. The reduced availability has led to a fluctuation in cost.

Steel

Pros: Steel is very durable, lightweight, non-toxic, fire retardant, mold- and pest-resistant, does not rot, and stands up well to high winds. It is also highly recyclable — 100 percent can be recycled after use — and the use of recycled steel for structuring new buildings can earn LEED points.

Cons: Steel does not maintain heat well and is not a great insulator. This may cause thermal bridging, which is the process of heat loss or gain through a material. Additional layers of insulation must be added to steel-framed buildings to compensate for this heating and cooling loss. Like concrete, recycled steel can also be in short supply due to its increasing popularity among builders around the world. The short supply can lead to increased prices.

CHAPTER 5:
Energy Efficiency

One of the primary goals of green building is the
reduction of carbon emissions from the burning of fossil fuels that produces
much of our electricity. This is accomplished in two ways: by reducing
the overall consumption of energy in a building and by replacing energy
generated from fossil fuels with clean energy. Clean energy is generated
without giving off carbon emissions. Another primary goal of green building
is sustainability — the preservation of resources for future generations. The
use of renewable energy supports sustainability.

This chapter discusses renewable energy sources and design and building
practices that minimize the amount of energy required to operate a building.
Other aspects of energy efficiency must also be considered during a green
building project. The "embodied energy," or "embedded energy," of a
building is an assessment of the amount of energy consumed during the
manufacturing of all the building components and materials, transportation
of materials to the site, construction, maintenance of building components,
and deconstruction of the building at the end of its life. Embodied
energy includes the energy used to extract raw materials used in building
components and process them. It even includes the transportation and

disposal of the building components after the building is dismantled. As buildings become more energy-efficient and consume less energy during operation, the significance of embodied energy will become proportionally greater. Embodied energy is one of the considerations used to evaluate the greenness of potential building materials.

Renewable Energy

Traditional sources of power and electricity use fossil fuels such as oil and natural gas, which are nonrenewable resources and emit greenhouse gases when they are burned. Renewable green sources of energy that do not deplete natural resources include hydroelectric power, geothermal power, solar power, and wind power. Commercial buildings increasingly are incorporating these sources of power into their sustainable office building designs.

Hydroelectric power

Hydroelectric plant in the mountains of North Carolina.

Hydroelectric power, the most widely used renewable form of energy production, is electricity generated by moving water. Most hydroelectric power is generated using dams incorporating turbines operated by overflowing water.

Hydroelectric power accounts for less than 10 percent of the power produced by the United States, and its supply varies significantly from state to state. In Florida, for example, the relatively flat terrain makes the production of hydroelectric power almost impossible, whereas the mountainous terrain of Washington provides many sites where hydroelectric power can be generated. The availability of hydroelectric power therefore depends on geographic location.

The major advantage of using hydroelectric power is the elimination of fossil fuels, including oil and natural gas to produce electricity. Other advantages include:

- Elimination of pollution that accompanies fossil fuel-burning methods of power production

- The free availability of water

- Low operating and maintenance costs of dams

- Water is highly renewable.

- The elimination of drilling and other invasive methods that destroy the earth to reach fossil fuels

- Dams create reservoirs and recreational lakes.

Disadvantages include:

- The disturbance of natural habitats and waterways to build and operate dams

- Displacement of some species, and even populations of people at dam sites

- The reduction in water quality of these waterways

Hydroelectric power is considerably cheaper than electricity generated by power plants using fossil fuels or nuclear energy. VMware, a software company that applied for LEED Platinum certification in late 2009, built a data center in East Wenatchee, Washington, that uses only hydroelectric power. It is one of several large technology companies that have chosen to locate their enterprise data centers in Washington because of its mild climate and cheap and abundant hydroelectric power.

What is a Power Grid?

The power grid is the network of electricity and power distribution. It includes power plants, transformers, power stations and substations, and the power lines that carry electricity from power plants to homes, businesses, and facilities. Green building aims to reduce the dependence on the grid by incorporating alternative sources of electricity, such as geothermal, solar, wind, and hydroelectric power. "Off the grid" refers to the practice of being self-sustaining and not relying on public utilities.

Wind power

Wind power involves the conversion of kinetic energy from wind into electricity. Wind power is highly renewable because wind is free and abundant. Wind energy is captured and converted to electricity using wind turbines, mills, and pumps. Wind farms are large groups of turbines that generate enough electricity to supply a public utility company or a large building complex. Individual turbines can be installed on a commercial building or a residence to supplement other sources of electricity. Energy generated by wind turbines can be stored in batteries for use when the wind is not blowing.

The Capitol Building in Washington, D.C., with a wind turbine generating alternative clean power

Wind power contributes about 2 percent of electricity usage around the world, but that number is growing significantly. Europe, especially Germany, has led the way in successfully replacing nonrenewable forms of energy with wind power and significantly lowering consumers' electricity bills.

Who is Winning the Wind Race?

The states that use the most wind energy are California, Texas, Iowa, and Oregon because of their access to open, high terrain with high wind speeds.

Wind farm in California

The U.S. government offers subsidies and grants to support the development of wind energy projects by wind developers, utility companies, businesses, corporations, and individuals. Utility companies harvest energy from wind farms and sell it to their customers. A private company or corporation can establish a wind farm, use the energy to power and operate its own business, and sell the excess power to a utility company. The Public Utility Regulatory Policy Act (PURPA) requires local utilities to buy excess electricity generated by private wind farms. A wind turbine can be installed to provide electricity for a private residence and excess energy can be sold to a utility through a net-metering program.

Considerations for Developing a Wind Farm

- **Space and site selection:** Wind farms require land and space and are not practical in many urban areas. Local weather conditions and wind speeds must be conducive to producing wind energy. According to the American Wind Energy Association, wind speeds must be at least 11 to 13 miles per hour to produce energy. These wind speeds often occur at the tops of mountains and other natural heights and ridges where wind is abundant and consistent. A single wind turbine requires about one acre of land to operate efficiently.

- **Accessibility to power lines:** High-voltage transmission lines are necessary to transfer and delivering energy generated from wind. If a wind farm site is not located near existing power lines, it can be very expensive — upward of $5,000 per mile — to install.

- **Investment capital:** Wind farms typically cost $1 million per megawatt to develop. According to the American Wind Energy Association, wind farms should generate at least 20 megawatts of power to be economically feasible, which means a $20 million investment. To put this in perspective, 1 megawatt of power is enough to power up to 300 residential homes (on average) per year. Wind farms generally take one to two years to complete and require specific building permits.

- **An understanding of wind energy:** Wind energy has to be used immediately. Large amounts of electricity cannot be stored efficiently. A windmill's blade length and configuration, combined with the wind's movement and direction, determine the amount of energy that will be generated.

- **Leasing to a wind developer:** If you have a site suitable for a wind farm, but do not have the financial resources to build one, you can lease the site to a wind developer.

Solar power

Solar power involves converting solar radiation to usable energy. Although it is most commonly used to generate electricity, solar radiation can also be used to heat and distill water as well as to heat a building.

Solar electricity is generated using a series of solar panels, known as a photovoltaic system (PV). Solar panels are made up of photovoltaic cells containing silicon infused with tiny amounts of impurities. When sunlight hits these cells, a stream of electrons breaks free, creating an electric current. Solar power can be stored in batteries to be used when needed.

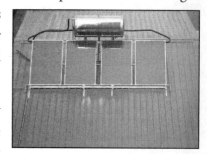

Rooftop solar-powered commercial water-heating system

Passive solar heating can be achieved by proper orientation of the building to the sun and does not require a photovoltaic system. Active solar heating and solar hot-water systems use solar panels to heat a fluid that is then pumped through a heating system or a hot-water heater. Some systems directly heat the water that is to be used. Most commercial buildings locate these solar panel systems on the roof.

A solar power system for a commercial office building can range from as little as $5,000 to upward of $50,000, depending on how large the system is, its capacity, and how many panels it includes. Although the initial costs of installing a solar panel system are high, the long-term cost savings from reduced energy use are very significant. Like wind power, it is also possible to sell excess solar electricity to a local utility.

The effectiveness of a solar panel system in providing electricity is determined by geographic location. A solar system is much more practical in an area where there is abundant sunlight (not necessarily heat). Not every builder has the space or the capital to purchase and install a solar system large enough to provide all of a building's energy. Although some solar systems are capable of generating enough electricity to power an entire commercial building, they often are used in conjunction with electricity provided by a utility. A solar system connected to a local utility is called a grid-tie system. An off-grid system is independent of any power grid and supplies all of a building's electricity. Off-grid systems require batteries to store electricity for use when the sun is not shining or when the solar panels are not producing enough power.

A typical solar panel is two- to four-feet wide and four- to six-feet long. Commercial systems can require thousands of square feet of roof space.

Using solar power to supplement electricity from a utility can realize substantial savings on energy bills. Reckson, the Connecticut-based real estate investment and management company featured as a Case Study in Chapter 9, installed a 100-kilowatt photovoltaic system on its corporate building in 2009 that generates 50 percent of

Solar panels on a living roof

the total electricity needed to power the building. Combining savings on electricity generated by the system with financial incentives like federal and state tax credits, the company expects to save thousands of dollars a year. Because Reckson is the landlord of this building, these savings are passed on to its tenants, making the property very attractive to them. The system is also projected to offset more than 6 million pounds of carbon emissions over the next 30 years.

Heating and cooling systems

Although lighting systems, electronics, and equipment use energy, the heating, ventilation, and air conditioning system (HVAC system) is the largest consumer of energy in a building. A variety of green heating and cooling systems that greatly reduce energy consumption can be incorporated into a building.

Subfloor systems

A subfloor air distribution system, or under-floor air distribution (UFAD), is a heating and cooling system installed beneath the flooring instead of in the ceiling like many traditional HVAC systems. Subfloor air distribution systems allow more targeted and widespread distribution of air throughout an office and better temperature control than an overhead system, reducing the use of energy. The system uses diffusers and linear air grills, which are similar to ducts on the ground, placed beneath the floor in work areas, offices, and workstations. Many systems allow the occupant of a particular space to control the duct or grill in his or her area, giving each employee a more comfortable work environment.

By providing more targeted air distribution at a controlled temperature, subfloor air distribution systems improve ventilation and contribute to overall indoor air quality. These systems also reduce HVAC energy consumption by as much as 20 percent, because they incorporate more efficient fans and other mechanical components than traditional ceiling air distribution systems. By moving air with natural convection currents instead of forced air currents, they can reduce the energy needed to force air by more than 30 percent. Many manufacturers, such as Tate Access Floors (**www.tateaccessfloors.com**), also incorporate low-VOC and recycled components, such as fans and plastic parts, in their products.

Subfloor air systems must be properly installed to avoid the growth of mold from excessive water retention and humidity. Though the long-term savings from subfloor air systems are significant, they can be more expensive than traditional HVAC systems to install. However, many systems require little maintenance if installed properly and can be easily adapted to new technologies.

Radiant heating systems

A radiant heating system is a type of subfloor system in which heat from warm water flowing through pipes installed below the floor rises to heat individual cubicle and office spaces in an office building. The advanced technologies of the system enable custom design and flexible, targeted zoning for different areas of an office space.

Radiant heating systems minimize exposure to the allergens and pollutants that are often blown into buildings by overhead forced air systems. A radiant heating system is also virtually invisible, with no exposed vents or ducts, and can allow for the individualized control of temperature by employees. Increased employee comfort leads to increased productivity. Radiant heat is also much quieter and less distracting than traditional forced-air systems.

Floor heating systems like these are more energy efficient than traditional HVAC systems because the heated air is directed to each space instead of blowing out of vents into a general area. These systems also enable more flexibility when interior space is reconfigured, because many subfloor systems can be easily adjusted.

The water used by radiant heating systems to provide heat can be heated using alternative energy sources, such as water pumps and solar energy.

Geothermal heat pump systems

Geothermal power is generated from the earth's natural heat and uses the earth's natural resources, such as decayed minerals and energy from the sun absorbed by the earth, to create electricity. The process eliminates the burning of nonrenewable fossil fuels for the production of electricity.

One of the most common and practical ways to incorporate geothermal power into a commercial office building is through a geothermal heat pump system — also referred to as a ground-source heat pump system — that extracts and transfers heat and cool air from the earth to the interior of a building. This transfer is achieved by pumping a refrigerant through the pipe system, which can either be an open- or closed-loop system.

Open-loop systems connect a water source, such as a well, pond, or lake, to a discharge area in the building. Water in open-looped systems is extracted from the source, delivered to the building, and circulated only once. In closed-looped systems, water continuously recirculates throughout the system, and no new water is introduced. Closed-loop systems are generally more cost-efficient and eliminate the need to maintain the water quality, which is a disadvantage of an open-looped system. Open-looped systems typically function better and last longer, but can be more costly to install.

Although they can be more expensive than traditional heating and cooling systems to install, return on investment for geothermal heat pumps can typically be realized in as little as three years. According to the EPA, geothermal heat pumps are the most energy efficient and environmentally responsible heating and cooling systems available. Combined with energy from renewable resources such as wind, solar, or hydroelectric, the potential for savings in energy and costs is very significant.

Passive solar heating and cooling

Passive solar design uses building components to maintain a comfortable indoor environment by harnessing and managing the natural effects of solar radiation, ambient breezes, and outdoor temperatures.

Passive solar heating reduces the demand for space heating by designing the building to collect, store, and distribute solar heat gains naturally. The thermal storage is the structure itself, and the heat flows by natural means (radiation, convection, and conductance). Mechanical equipment may not be necessary at all, though sometimes fans or blowers are incorporated to distribute the heat more efficiently. Passive solar heat systems assisted by fans and blowers are referred to as hybrid heating systems.

Passive solar heating should be incorporated during the initial design stage of a building because it requires the use of certain architectural design concepts. In climates where heat is needed, large south-facing windows allow sunlight to stream into the building for most of the day. This provides opportunities for daylighting and outdoor views. Buildings with passive heating usually have rectangular floor plans, elongated on an east-west axis; large windows in the south-facing wall; building materials with high heat capacity, such as concrete slabs, brick walls, or tile floors exposed to the solar radiation that comes through those south-facing windows; overhangs or other means of shading the south-facing windows from the summer sun; windows on the east and west walls; and preferably no windows on the north walls. Window design and the type of glass used in the windows determine how well the system performs.

The simplest passive solar heating systems, known as direct-gain systems, allow solar radiation to enter through windows and heat up a thermal mass inside the building. An indirect gain passive solar heating system, also called a Trombe wall or a thermal storage wall, is a south-facing glazed wall that absorbs sunlight and heats up slowly during the day. At night, as the wall cools, it slowly releases heat into the building interior. Thermal walls are usually made of heavy masonry, but sometimes contain tanks or pipes filled with water or phase change materials (materials that are capable of storing and releasing large amounts of energy as they freeze and melt). Isolated gain, or sunspace, heating collects heat from solar radiation in an area that can be shut off from the rest of the building. During the day, doors and windows from the sunspace into the rest of the building are opened, allowing the accumulated heat to circulate out into the building. At night when it cools, the area is closed off from the building.

Passive solar heating works best and yields the most energy savings in climates with clear skies during the winter heating season, when other heating sources are relatively expensive. It functions best in smaller buildings, where the demand for heating and cooling is regulated by the design of the building envelope. When using passive solar heating, be careful that the system does not overheat the building during the summer months, necessitating additional air conditioning. Reduce the size of the HVAC system to match the reduced heating needs.

Passive solar systems do not have a high initial cost or a long payback period like many active solar heating systems. Modest levels of passive solar heating, also called sun tempering, can reduce building auxiliary heating requirements from 5 percent to 25 percent at little or no extra cost. More aggressive passive solar heating can reduce a building's heating energy use by 25 to 75 percent over a comparable structure. A passive solar heating system requires little or no maintenance over its life cycle.

Passive cooling is achieved with a variety of techniques, including the use of reflective coatings on windows and exterior walls, shading, white roofs, vegetated roofs, living walls, strategically placed overhangs, and ventilation systems that use natural breezes to cool a building. In Germany, it is becoming standard practice to use natural ventilation to cool office buildings, even in the summer months. The San Francisco Federal Building uses a perforated metal exterior skin to control the flow of air and light through the building.

CASE STUDY: MORE THAN JUST SAVING SOME GREEN

Q&A with Gordon Holness, president
American Society of Heating,
Refrigerating, and Air Conditioning
Engineers (ASHRAE)
www.ashrae.org

ASHRAE is an international organization composed of more than 50,000 heating, ventilation, air conditioning, and refrigeration (HVAC&R) engineering professionals from around the world. The organization aims to promote sustainability by providing resources, information, and research on sustainable development.

What is the importance of HVAC&R systems in green building?

HVAC&R systems have a significant impact in buildings and environment, primarily because of the amount of energy used to operate them. In turn, when it comes to creating a truly green building, HVAC&R systems offer the greatest opportunity in reducing energy use (and the buildings' impact on the environment) while also ensuring comfort and good indoor environmental quality.

What is the best way — in terms of cost, time, and waste — to replace an HVAC&R system during a remodel project?

One of the key criteria in selecting replacements systems is the available vertical shaft space and horizontal ceiling space. Many older buildings lack available space for major duct distribution and lend themselves more toward unitary rather than central equipment. Another significant criterion may be whether the building is to remain in partial occupancy during renovation, which might also favor unitary systems. You should also consider if the total system replacement is necessary or if some parts of the distribution system(s) can be retained.

What kinds of energy-efficient HVAC&R systems are available for new construction commercial office buildings?

Every system selection must be tailored to the particular occupancy and operating characteristics of the building to be served. The building location and climate zone will also significantly impact system selection. For typical office occupancies, the ventilation and latent loads are not significant and can be met efficiently with a dedicated outside air unit, incorporating energy recovery from the exhaust systems. The internal sensible heat/cooling load can be met with a variety of highly efficient systems, such as by radiant heating/cooling or by a heat-pump system, which can be ground/water source heat pumps or variable refrigerant flow heat pump system.

What components, including design techniques and energy and water systems, did ASHRAE include in the renovation of its green office building?

One of the main goals in renovation of the existing headquarters was to demonstrate ASHRAE's commitment to sustainability — to create a sustainability showcase, so to speak. To achieve that, we focused on all areas of green design, including water and energy reduction, reuse of materials when possible, and recycling of those that could not be reused. A green roof is provided over the learning center while the main roof and parking lot have light reflective surfaces to reduce heat island effect. Low-VOC emitting materials and furnishings were used throughout. A full commissioning program was considered critical to achieve the design goals, reduce energy consumption, and improve occupant comfort and indoor air quality.

How is the new ASHRAE building more sustainable?

ASHRAE reduced its annual energy use by more than 32.5 percent through enhancements to the building envelope and use of systems such as a dedicated outside air supply with energy recovery, ground-source heat pumps, and mini-splits systems with heat recovery. It also reduced its estimated annual water consumption per year for bathrooms by 52.3

percent and its estimated annual water consumption by 46.3 percent by using low-flow fixtures. Lighting quality, use of daylighting, and good acoustical qualities were also key considerations. You can see a list of sustainable highlights at **www.ashrae.org/building**.

What benefits have you seen from the remodel?

ASHRAE had four goals in renovating its headquarters: to provide a healthy and productive workplace and meeting space for employees and members; to demonstrate a commitment to sustainability; to build a learning center to increase resource for on-site educational opportunities and meetings; and to create a "living lab" by heavily monitoring and metering the building to capture building performance data. We feel we have been successful in meeting the first three goals while continuing to work on a way to make the data more widely available for the fourth. The benefits can be seen in how we met each of the goals.

How can buildings use energy audits to measure energy use?

It is important to provide owners with information on how, where, and when building energy is used. Metering and submetering of systems, such as elevators, plug and process loads, lighting, and HVAC&R systems, can identify where major energy use or waste is occurring. Such metering, combined with audits with real-time tracking, can aid significantly in providing a starting point for making improvements or adding controls.

By going green, how can buildings save money?

Going green has far more implications than simply saving money. It relates to the long-term impact on the occupants of buildings, on our environment, and on what we leave for future generations. Eliminating or recycling construction waste can reduce the continued expansion of landfill sites. Installation of energy-efficient lighting and HVAC&R systems can reduce energy use and greenhouse gas emissions. If collectively designed and operated correctly, they can also save money.

What operational adjustments can buildings make that will yield significant results?

The single primary adjustment that has the greatest impact is that of occupancy control. Too often, we see lights left on in unoccupied spaces or air conditioning systems operating well after normal working hours. Studies have shown that 10 to 40 percent of energy savings can be achieved by changing operational strategies. So, simple tools like time clock controls, occupancy sensors, and demand control ventilation can have a big impact.

Describe the energy efficient systems that ASHRE seeks to promote.

ASHRAE does not necessarily promote one system type over the other. Instead, we strive to offer technical guidance to help in the design, construction, and operation of a variety of building types and systems. What we do advocate is integrated building design. It is only by all parties in the design and construction process working closely together that we can achieve the levels of system performance that we are all seeking. Our ultimate goal, along with that of the U.S. federal government and many leading building energy groups, is net-zero-energy buildings, those that use no more energy then they produce.

How can indoor air quality be improved during a renovation project?

The important elements here are: the selection of building materials with minimal off-gassing and VOC emission; the provision of adequate outside air ventilation properly distributed throughout the building; the installation and maintenance of air filtration at recommended efficiency levels; and the proper location of outdoor air intakes to prevent recycling of building or vehicle exhausts.

What is the importance of building green?

Today's buildings mortgage our energy and environmental future. To ASHRAE, building green calls for balancing environmental responsibility, resource efficiency, occupant comfort and well-being, and community sensitivity while supporting the goal of development that meets the needs of the present without compromising the ability of future generations to meet their own needs. It is ultimately about ensuring a world for future generations that inspires us to continue our mission of promoting a sustainable world.

Hot Water Heating Systems

Typical office buildings supply hot water from storage tanks to various parts of the building. Heating and storing gallons of hot water consumes significant amount of energy. In addition, thousands of gallons per person are wasted each year waiting for this hot water to reach the tap.

A Little Goes a Long Way

If you cannot install an alternative hot-water heating system, putting a conventional hot-water heater on a timer can also drastically reduce wasted energy and money by automatically shutting the heater off at night and on the weekends when the office is vacant.

Cost effective and environmentally friendly alternatives to conventional hot water tanks include on-demand hot water systems and solar hot water systems, both of which can significantly reduce the amount of energy needed to produce hot water and the amount of water wasted during the process.

On-demand hot water systems

On-demand hot water systems — also referred to as tankless water heaters — work by heating water only as it is being used. When a hot water tap is turned on, cold water travels through a pipe into the unit, where it is heated by either a gas burner or an electric element before passing out through the tap. On-demand systems typically produce two to five gallons of hot water per minute. Large office buildings may require multiple on-demand hot water systems to provide enough hot water for faucets, sinks, and dishwashers. On-demand hot water systems can be installed at each hot water site for optimal efficiency.

On-demand hot water heaters prevent cold water from being wasted while people wait for hot water to reach the tap. They also eliminate the use of energy to heat and store hot water that is never used. Although an on-demand system is more expensive to install than a conventional hot water heater, its life span is almost double that of a hot water tank. Tankless heaters can last up to 20 years, while water heaters typically last less than ten.

Solar hot water systems

Solar hot water systems use the sun to heat water and can provide up to 80 percent of a building's hot water needs. Solar hot water systems typically use solar panels to absorb energy from the sun and transfer that energy as heat to water stored in an insulated tank.

There are two types of solar hot water systems: active and passive. In an active system, also known as a heat exchange or an indirect exchange system, an electric pump circulates a transfer fluid, such as a non-toxic glycol solution, through copper pipes in a solar collector (solar panel), where it absorbs heat before traveling through pipes inside the water tank. In passive solar-heating systems, or direct-exchange systems, the hot water itself travels through the solar collector, or the water is heated in an insulated water tank painted a dark color that is exposed to the sun's rays.

Solar hot-water tanks are often combined with other means of heating water. Because the capacity to heat water is dependent on access to sunlight, a backup hot water tank typically provides hot water at night and on cloudy or rainy days when the system cannot work to its maximum potential.

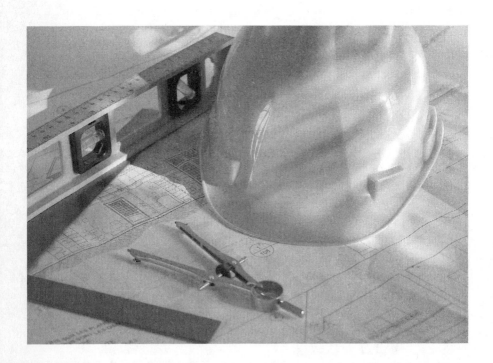

CHAPTER 6:

Water

Worldwide demand for water tripled over the past century and is currently doubling every 21 years. Scientists predict that by 2025, one-third of all humans will face severe and chronic water shortages. Environmental responsibility requires that we use water sparingly and efficiently.

Systems that minimize a building's water use and waste are a key element of green building. Effective water-efficiency planning seeks to use less water without sacrificing comfort or performance. There are a variety of ways to integrate water-saving methods — from installing a stormwater management system that captures and cleans rainwater to installing low-flow faucet fixtures to reduce water pressure.

Water Efficiency

CalRecycle (**www.calrecycle.ca.gov**) recommends these measures for efficient use of water in an office building:

- Install a dual plumbing system that uses recycled water for flushing toilets.

- Use a gray water system to recover non-potable water for landscape irrigation.

- Use ultra low-flow fixtures to reduce waste and conserve water.

- Use a recirculated or point-of-use hot water system to provide hot water for sinks, dishwashers, and showers.

- Use a low-pressure, micro-irrigation system to supply water to exterior areas of the building, like the landscape.

- Install a separate meter system for the landscape.

- Control water usage from hoses, sprinklers, and other water distribution systems with irrigation controllers.

Dual plumbing/gray water systems

A dual plumbing or gray water system has two sets of pipes — one that provides clean water for drinking and washing, and another that collects wastewater from sinks and showers, known as gray water, and recycles it for purposes like flushing a toilet or irrigating landscape. The system stores and treats gray water, often in a tank underground, and then makes it available for use.

Many states, like New York, offer tax credits for incorporating gray water systems into a building or residence, while other states such as Colorado only allow gray water to be used for cleaning and irrigation.

Just So You Know…

Toilet wastewater is referred to as "black water," and it is not used in gray water systems because it is unsanitary.

Public health concerns have generated controversy over the use of gray water systems, particularly in highly populated urban areas. Gray water systems are more common in rural farmland areas. Gray water systems have many advantages, including:

- The conservation of fresh water by using recycled water for land irrigation and watering. This is particularly beneficial in hot, arid areas of the country like Arizona, Nevada, and parts of California, where fresh water supplies are severely limited.

- Less wear and tear on a septic tank from non-toilet wastewater, which can translate to lower maintenance costs

- The recycling of natural nutrients from this wastewater that would otherwise be wasted, which enriches the quality of the soil in your landscape

The cost of gray water and dual plumbing systems varies depending on the size. A system is generally either a gravity system or a packaged system. The simpler gravity system treats and delivers gray water without using electricity; more advanced and efficient package systems require electric pumps and cost significantly more. In a typical residential household, a simple gray water system can save anywhere from 10,000 to 50,000 gallons of water a year, which yields less than $200 a year in savings.

How Low Can You Go?

Incorporating a gray water system into an office building can help earn LEED points in the "Innovative Wastewater Technologies" category. To earn water efficiency credits, an office building must reduce potable/fresh water use for sewage by 50 percent, which can be achieved in part through the combination of low-flow fixtures and gray water systems. Low-flow fixtures use high pressure to create a water flow very similar to what a traditional fixture would produce, but they use significantly less water. Aqua Pro Solutions, a company that manufactures and promotes gray water systems and other water conservation products, provides a very helpful breakdown of these LEED points and how their gray water system can help achieve these LEED points. The report can be found at **www.aquaprosolutions.com/product_specs/AQUS_ Water_Efficiency_LEED_Credit_Review.pdf.**

Despite costs and health concerns, many corporations and companies have incorporated gray water systems into their office buildings. Huber Technology Inc., a global technology company with a head office in Germany, incorporated a gray water system in 2003; the water is used to flush toilets and irrigate the company's outdoor park. The system is inspected annually and has required little maintenance per year since its installation in 2003.

Low-flow fixtures

In 1994, the government required that toilets use no more than 1.6 gallons per flush compared to 3.5 gallons per flush for toilets manufactured prior to that year. Since this guide was established, the use of low-flow fixtures for other water sources has become increasingly popular as a method of water conservation.

Low-flow fixtures reduce the amount of water flowing from water fixtures, such as showerheads, faucets, and toilets, without lowering the water pressure. They use much less water than conventional fixtures. Aerators, low-flow fixtures that mix air with water to slow down the water flow without affecting the pressure, can be attached to sinks and showerheads to significantly reduce water use by 30 to 70 percent.

What Does Low-Flow Mean?

Low-flow is defined as:

- 1.6 gallons per flush for toilets
- 2.5 gallons per minute or less for faucets
- 2.5 gallons per minute or less for showers

These are just minimums, however. It is possible to incorporate fixtures that use even less than these amounts of water.

Low-flow faucets, toilets, and showers installed at the Veterans Affairs Hospital in Portland, Oregon, have yielded more than $50,000 a year in water savings.

Sensors that control the amount of time water flows through a faucet and turn water off automatically are another low-cost way to reduce water consumption. Some sensors require that the user physically hold the water knob down to produce flow, and others allow water to flow

Sensor faucets help control water wastage.

through the faucet for five or ten seconds at a time. Sensors can also be used for outdoor landscaping.

Toilet and urinal flushing typically account for nearly one-third of a building's total water consumption. Dual-flush toilets, which have different flush volumes for liquid and solid waste, greatly reduce water usage for flushing toilets. Ultra-low flush (ULF) toilets and waterless urinals are coming into increasing use. Some local building codes have not been updated to allow waterless urinals.

Submetering

Installation of extra water meters in specific areas of the building allows the monitoring of water use for various purposes. Data collected from these meters can be used to analyze future water use and implement possible behavioral changes among employees to further reduce water waste.

Your Water Budget

Part of the building design process should be the creation of a water budget detailing the building's expected water use. The water system should be commissioned before the building becomes operational, and data regarding water flows should be recorded. If the water usage later exceeds the water budget by more than 10 percent, it is a sign that the water system is not performing as it should be. There could be a leak or faulty connection, or the designers could have miscalculated when they anticipated the behavior of the building occupants.

Stormwater control

Stormwater control entails a system to capture, treat, and release water from rain and melted snow. Stormwater can be damaging to the environment because water that does not soak immediately into the ground flows across parking lots, roads, and fertilized landscaping, collecting oils, toxins, and excess nutrients before running into drains and sewers and ultimately into waterways. A stormwater management system treats this water and removes pollutants before it reaches the waterways. Retention ponds, vegetated roofs, and exterior living walls are all excellent methods of controlling and treating stormwater.

Retention and detention ponds

Retention and detention ponds are an effective method for controlling stormwater. Retention ponds are designed to hold water permanently, while detention ponds are used to hold water temporarily and control runoff while it drains to a new location.

"Wet ponds" and "Dry ponds"

Retention ponds are also referred to "wet ponds" because they always hold a certain amount of water, like a regular pond. Detention ponds are also referred to as "dry ponds" because they do not hold any water when there is no storm.

Both pond types control stormwater runoff by preventing flooding and acting as holding tanks to interrupt the water's journey into the sewer system and waterways. In detention ponds, a control — also referred to as a "low-flow orifice" — located at the bottom of the pond regulates the release of water from the pond. During dry periods, there is no

Office building with a retention pond.

water in a detention pond; retention ponds have a permanent level of water. During storms, the low-flow orifice levels the pond and controls the water level.

Retention and detention ponds can be incorporated into your office building design if you have sufficient outdoor space. Both types of ponds can serve as outdoor spaces for employees in addition to controlling stormwater runoff. These ponds require routine maintenance to unclog filters and remove litter and natural debris.

Permeable pavement and concrete can also be used for stormwater management.

Under the Clean Water Act, the EPA has developed a stormwater prevention plan, and depending on your geographical location, you may be required to register for a discharge permit if you are conducting building activity. Stormwater runoff can be dealt with in numerous ways, including installing a vegetated roof, incorporating living walls, installing a rain garden, or creating a detention pond.

Vegetated roofs

Vegetated roofs — also referred to as eco-roofs, green roofs, and living roofs — capture and clean polluted stormwater from rain and snow that would otherwise run off the building and circulate back into the water system via drains and sewers. A vegetated roof is composed of multiple layers of soil and plants that act as barriers to storm runoff. The plants act as a natural filtration method that prevents polluted water from entering into potable drinking water sources, such as rivers.

A Helpful Site

4specs.com (**www.4specs.com/s/07/07-0870.html**) lists green roofing companies, as well as building products and manufacturers.

There are several components to a vegetated roof, and they can vary significantly depending on the building's capacity. An intensive vegetated roof is an integrated system of soil, plants, trees, and other shrubbery and greens, essentially a mini-garden that becomes part of the outdoor environment. These roofs are referred to as "intensive" because they require a significant amount of maintenance, feeding, and irrigation in the absence of precipitation.

An intensive vegetated roof requires an irrigation system, a soil bed, and the structural ability of the building to hold the increased weight of the roof. The weight of a green roof can vary significantly, but it can add as much as 150 pounds per square foot to the roof. The weight capacity of an existing building's roof should be determined by a professional engineer, who will inspect the roof and advise whether any additional structural support is needed to support the additional weight. The engineering standards for green roofs are different from the requirements for traditional roofs. An intensive roof can cost upward of $30 per square foot and requires a significant flat, open, growing space.

Green roof amongst a sea of skyscrapers.

An extensive green roof, on the other hand, is typically less than 6 inches deep and requires less maintenance. These are designed to be self-sustaining, intricate systems of plants and shrubbery that need very outside little care and nurturing.

177

Vegetated roofs also require a waterproof membrane — hot rubberized asphalt is often used in green roofs — that deflects water and prevents the roof from absorbing the water.

Another form of vegetated roof is a garden of plants placed in smaller sections around the roof, instead of covering the entire roof. These are sometimes referred to as modular block vegetated roofs and are a good alternative if a fully vegetated roof is not practical for cost or space reasons.

The industry term for the combination of plants, shrubbery, and greenery incorporated into a green roof is referred to as "growing media."

According to the Environmental & Water Resources Institute (**http://email.asce.org/ewri/VegetatedRoof.html**), green roofs can cost anywhere from $10 to upward of $30 per square foot, depending on the type of roof installed and the level of maintenance required. The cost varies according to the types of plants and the geographical climate. Plants that thrive in hot, dry climates, for instance, would be suitable for an office building in Arizona, but not for one in New York City. An experienced green roof company will be familiar with the types of plants and shrubbery that will work best in different climates. It is important to consider the climate in your geographical area and what plants are native to your area before incorporating a vegetated roof into your green building.

Extensive roofs tend to cost less than intensive roofs because they are less involved and require less maintenance. Intensive roofs cost more because they incorporate more features and plant types. These can serve as functional outdoor spaces for employees and can even incorporate waterfalls, rock walls, and small ponds. Think of an extensive roof as being more like a lawn or open green space, and an intensive roof as an interactive outdoor garden.

Green roof on a local real estate office.

Vegetated roofs not only prevent polluted rainwater from entering potable water sources, but also they can help minimize heat absorption, reducing the amount of energy needed to cool the building. Vegetated roofs can retain heat up to 20 percent more efficiently than traditional roofs because the layers of plants, soil, and shrubbery serve as a natural retention system to keep heat, as well as cool air, inside the building.

Vegetated roofs can last longer than traditional roofs if properly maintained. Because the vegetation covers the roof membrane, which is typically the exposed surface of a traditional roof, and protects it from harsh weather conditions and sunlight, a vegetated roof can last three times as long as a traditional roof. According to a study by the University of Michigan's horticulture department (**www.hrt.msu.edu/greenroof**), green roofs cost an average of $22.50 per square foot to install as opposed to less than $16 per square foot for a conventional roof. However, the long-term cost savings of a green roof make it more cost-effective even though it is more expensive to install. According to the University of Michigan horticulture department, a green roof can save more than $200,000 over the course of its life in energy conservation alone. This brings the cost per square footage of green roofs down from $22.10 to $12.57, yielding a savings of $3.38 per square foot in contrast to traditional roofs.

Maintaining a green roof — especially an intensive one — involves watering, fertilizing, weeding, and replacing and re-soiling plants. The degree of maintenance varies significantly between an intensive and extensive green roof. Extensive green roofs often are accessed only a few times a year to perform maintenance work, which can be done by a professional green roofing company. Because the soil levels on intensive roofs tend to be much deeper — anywhere from 12 to 20 feet deep — and incorporate more plant and tree varieties, the maintenance is more demanding and can cost more than maintenance of an extensive roof. Only green roofing professionals should perform maintenance work on a vegetated roof. Many green roof companies offer maintenance services for roofs they install.

The USGBC recognizes the use of vegetated roofs in the LEED system, and a variety of points may be achieved by the incorporation of a green roof in a commercial building project. Points can be earned across several categories, because green roofs serve a variety of positive functions. Points can be earned for optimizing energy performance, controlling stormwater, reducing energy, incorporating water efficient landscaping, and reducing site disturbance.

Living walls

A living wall is essentially the same concept as a vegetated roof, except it integrates plants on a vertical wall instead of a horizontal roof. Living walls, which can be used either outside the building or inside, clean and irrigate stormwater, and they help significantly with air filtration. Living walls that help with the circulation of air inside a building are often referred to as active living walls. These walls give off oxygen inside a space and absorb carbon dioxide, improving the air quality. Active living walls are typically incorporated into the building's air conditioning and filtration system and are used to clean and depollute the indoor air. Inactive or passive living walls do not contribute to air filtration and are typically not hooked up to the building's air filtration system.

Living ivy wall at Princeton University.

Living walls serve a variety of functions. Outdoor living walls clean and irrigate stormwater like a vegetated roof would. Exterior living walls reduce the overall energy use of a building by keeping the building cooler. Because insulation within a building retains heat, it can often lead to an excessive heat buildup during warmer times of the year or in warmer climates.

Living walls provide insulation for the building, and they help control excessive temperatures. Urban heat islands (UHIs) in city environments can cause a higher than average temperature within a building. UHIs are a result of the solar radiation absorbed by all the buildings, sidewalks, and rooftops in a city. Because these heat-absorbing surfaces are so dense in cities, the heat becomes trapped in the building's envelope, causing temperatures to rise. Living walls work to reduce temperatures from UHIs by evapotranspiration, the plant process of transferring water from a surface to the atmosphere. Energy from the sun that is absorbed by plants during the process of evapotranspiration is not rereleased into the building environment as heat. The result is a decrease in UHIs and an overall lower indoor air temperature, which conserves energy by eliminating the need to cool spaces.

What to Grow

Some plants that are particularly efficient at filtering toxins out of the air are bamboo palms, chrysanthemums, spider plants, and certain variations of ivy.

Buildings in cities or areas where space is limited can greatly benefit from living walls, because they allow the vertical integration of plants and vegetation and do not require any additional square footage. The aesthetics of living walls used inside an office, the incorporation of outdoor and more natural elements into the workspace, and the improved air quality help create a more wholesome indoor environment for employees. Some living walls include waterfalls, which add to the overall aesthetic and acoustic benefits in an office space. Waterfalls help drown out distracting noises from mechanical systems, outdoor noise pollutants, or noise pollution from employee conversation.

Irrigation systems

The next chapter discusses water-efficient landscaping that requires very little irrigation. Where irrigation is required, advanced irrigation systems deliver the water to where it is required more efficiently than traditional water sprinklers. Drip lines directly water the roots of plants or target each plant with a micro-spray. Rain sensors should be used to turn off the irrigation systems when they are not needed.

CHAPTER 7:

Green Interiors and Exteriors

Although utilizing day lighting for open floor spaces
is ideal because it gives employees access to natural light and ultimately lowers
your electric bill, it can also create glare issues and eliminate privacy.

Sustainable Floor Plans

One requirement of sustainable interior design is the minimization of
construction waste due to renovations. This means anticipating your needs
as accurately as possible and incorporating possible future alterations in your
plans.

**Will you need the ability to change your floor plan regularly, adding
and removing cubicle spaces, offices, conference rooms, and even floors?**
If your company will be expanding in the years to come, or you want the
ability to create new spaces without having to remodel, you can use a movable
office system with modular walls, such as DIRTT (Do It Right This Time,
www.dirtt.net) products that eliminate the need for rebuilding.

What kind of common areas will you need? Common areas include
conference rooms, reception areas, lobbies, restrooms, and kitchens.

Consider where these should be placed on each floor and how to best incorporate these spaces to increase space utilization. For instance: Can a conference room double as a break room for employees when it is not being used for meetings?

Evaluating Green Materials

One of the ongoing challenges of the green building movement is how to determine the relative greenness of a particular product or building material and how its use will affect the environment. There are many ways in which the use of a product might impact the environment, beginning with the energy used to produce it and the disturbance of the environment caused by extracting and moving raw materials. A product might use up an inequitable amount of resources, emit harmful substances during its use, consumer energy, generate waste, end up occupying space in a landfill, or leaching toxins into the soil or water table. In addition, there is no universal agreement on environmental priorities. One school of thought emphasizes recycling materials and keeping them in productive use, even if some additional energy must be expended to do so. Another viewpoint considers global warming as the greatest threat and uses energy consumption as the primary criterion in selecting green materials; if more energy is required to recycle a product than to use virgin materials, recycling should not be done.

A product that greatly increases the energy efficiency of a building, reducing overall carbon emissions, may be made of materials that cannot be recycled. An example is the energy recovery ventilators (ERVs) or heat recovery ventilators (HRVs) that are often used to meet LEED ventilation requirements. As heated air leaves the building, ERVs can transfer as much as 80 percent of its heat to the incoming outside air — heat that would otherwise have been lost continually and replaced by the heating system. However, the components of ERVs cannot be easily reused.

Use materials available from local manufacturers.

Although bamboo is an environmentally friendly alternative for wood flooring from clear-cut forests, most bamboo flooring is manufactured in Asia. Using bamboo, therefore, may require shipping it from Asia, which not only increases the cost to you but also contributes to carbon emissions from the transportation of the material. There may be a reclaimed wood manufacturer a mile from your construction site where you can source wood-flooring materials cheaper and eliminate the need for transportation, which eliminates the carbon emissions from transportation and, therefore, reduces your impact on the environment.

Green building materials are basic materials used directly in construction or as component of green building products that have low environmental impacts compared to their alternatives. Green building products are building components whose characteristics convey some kind of environmental benefit and make them preferable in some way to other building components with similar functions. A green building product could be an energy-saving device that does not contain any green materials.

Even green building materials may have a harmful environmental impact. For example, wood certified by the FSC comes from a sustainably managed forest that protects the biodiversity of local ecosystems. However, harvesting that wood, processing it, and transporting it to the building site consumes large amounts of water and energy.

The selection of materials for a green building project typically involves a trade-off. There is no one rule for deciding which product, material, or technology is best. Choices must be made based on the building owner's priorities, the site location, the availability of products and materials, and the project budget.

Green Construction Materials

The CalRecycle (**www.calrecycle.gov**) website for California's recycling and green building initiatives gives the following resource efficiency criteria for building materials:

- **Recycled content:** Products with identifiable recycled content, including postindustrial content with a preference for postconsumer content.

- **Natural, plentiful, or renewable:** Materials harvested from sustainably managed sources that preferably have an independent certification (certified wood) and are certified by an independent third party.

- **Resource-efficient manufacturing process:** Products manufactured with resource-efficient processes, including reducing energy consumption, minimizing waste (recycled, recyclable, or source-reduced product packaging), and reducing greenhouse gases.

- **Locally available:** Building materials, components, and systems found locally or regionally, saving energy and resources in transportation to the project site.

- **Salvaged, refurbished, or remanufactured:** Includes saving a material from disposal and renovating, repairing, restoring, or generally improving the appearance, performance, quality, functionality, or value of a product.

- **Reusable or recyclable:** Select materials that can be easily dismantled and reused or recycled at the end of their useful life.

- **Recycled or recyclable product packaging:** Products enclosed in recycled content or recyclable packaging.

- **Durable:** Materials that are longer lasting or are comparable to conventional products with long life expectancies.

Selecting Materials for the Interior of a Building

The materials used inside a building are just as important as the materials used for the foundation and structure. Cost-effective and manageable alternatives to many conventional building materials contribute significantly to the greenness of a building. A primary objective of green building is a high indoor environmental quality (IEQ) achieved through appropriate lighting, efficient temperature control, access to daylight and outdoor views, and good indoor air quality (IAQ). This objective serves as a guide for selecting materials for the inside of a building, alongside consideration of the possible impact of each material or product on the environment.

Wood

Much of the wood used for commercial and residential building has been harvested by clear-cutting forests, and many conventional wood products are treated with chemical finishes that can be toxic. When it is responsibly harvested and not treated with chemical sealants, wood is a very green product. For wood flooring, cabinetry, and office furniture, always choose products that are certified by a reputable third party, such as the Forest Stewardship Council (FSC) or the Sustainable Forestry Initiative (SFI). Certified wood should be accompanied by a certificate that provides detailed information on the wood's origin and processing. Always ensure that any finishing material applied to the wood is formaldehyde-free. For more information on wood guidelines, visit **www.fsc.org** and **www.sfiprogram.org**.

EPA Recommends Exterior-Grade Pressed Wood Products

According to the U.S. National Institute of Health, "the EPA recommends the use of exterior-grade pressed-wood products to limit formaldehyde exposure in the home. Before purchasing pressed-wood products, including building materials, cabinetry, and furniture, buyers should ask about the formaldehyde content of these products. Formaldehyde levels in homes can also be reduced by ensuring adequate ventilation, moderate temperatures, and reduced humidity levels through the use of air conditioners and dehumidifiers."

Carpeting and flooring

Traditional carpeting has very high levels of VOCs. These chemicals come mostly from the adhesives used in the carpet backing and other glues and materials to hold the carpet together. In the early 1990s, the Carpet and Rug Institute (CRI) launched its Green Label program to certify carpeting and other upholstery material. Their more recent Green Label Plus program certifies carpeting materials as low emitting (under 50 grams per liter). For more information on green carpeting, standards, and guidelines, visit **www.carpet-rug.org/index.cfm**.

For non-carpeted areas of a building, green options include bare concrete floors, bamboo, linoleum, cork, and rubber.

Cradle-to-Cradle

The concept "cradle-to-cradle" was introduced by William McDonough, an architect, and Michael Braungart, a chemist. "Cradle-to-cradle" refers to a method for evaluating the impact of a product on both human life and the environment, from the product's inception through the manufacturing process, use, demolition, recycling, and ultimately to its non-use. The method assesses the use of every synthetic and natural material and process associated with the product, such as the stormwater discharge during the manufacturing process, the potential reuse of the product, and the toxicity that each material in the product exudes to the environment.

Insulation and drywall

One of the best green alternatives to traditional fiberglass cut-to-fit insulation is blow-in insulation. Blow-in insulation conforms to fit a space more precisely, ensuring that all gaps are filled. This tightens the building's envelope, prevents air leaks, and helps to maintain the temperature in the building, reducing the energy required for heating and cooling. A good blow-in insulation is Green Fiber, made with 85 percent recyclable material, which is profiled later in this chapter. Look for products that contain cellulose, a product that is more than 75 percent recyclable. Products with boron or hemp are also good choices.

- There are few alternatives to traditional gypsum drywall. The best strategy is to minimize the use of drywall by keeping walls exposed. This is a growing trend in green building but may not be suitable or practical for your space. In that case, consider using a product like EcoRock. This product is made from 80 percent recyclable material, uses 80 percent less energy to produce it than traditional drywall, and is low-emitting. Incorporating EcoRock can also earn LEED points if you are seeking certification. The product is one of the first of its kind and is leading the way on the green drywall front. For more information, visit www.seriousmaterials.com/html/ecorock. html.

The Importance of R-value

R-value refers to the thermal resistance of a material, or how well the material resists heat flow. The higher the R-value of an insulation product, the more effective the insulation will be in protecting the building against heat loss.

Sealers

Traditional sealers have high levels of VOCs and other toxic chemicals. A variety of sealant products that are low emitting and contain low levels of VOCs and chemicals are available. Green building website Green Building Supply (**www.greenbuildingsupply.com/Public/Non-ToxicFinishes/ Sealers/index.cfm**) provides an extensive list of green alternatives to traditional sealers for cement, wood, stucco, stone, and other materials, as well as for grout and caulk.

Cleaning products

Cleaning products can have the most direct impact on the indoor air quality of your building and on the building occupants' health. Using cleaning products with natural ingredients and limited chemicals and toxins is an excellent, inexpensive way to drastically improve the indoor air quality of a building. Many companies make green cleaning products, including Method, Seventh Generation, and Simple Green.

Third-party certification

- The best way to ensure the materials you are using meet the low-emitting standards of green building is to choose certified products and materials. Institutes like the FSC and the CRI have their own guidelines and certification processes to ensure products in their industry are sustainable. Several other third-party organizations and watchdogs do the same thing for a variety of products and materials. These include Green Seal and BIFMA.

☀ Green Seal

Green Seal is a nonprofit organization created to ensure that standards of environmental sustainability are uniformly monitored for cleaning services claiming to be green. The organization maintains strict standards for its Green Seal stamp of approval. They consider the Green Seal as an indicator of environmental responsibility for products and services.

The group was founded in 1989 and maintains specific environmental standards for products and consumers. It first implemented product certifications in the early 1990s. Now, according to the Green Seal website, more than 30 categories of products can be certified by the organization. Green Seal tests and evaluates products based on their contents, how the materials were obtained, how the products are manufactured, what they are contained in, how they will be used, and what methods will be necessary for product and container disposal.

If a product has been approved by the Green Seal organization, the Green Seal logo will appear on the product's label. When researching and interviewing cleaning services, you can ask if their business and their products have received the Green Seal stamp of approval. Information is available on the Green Seal website.

If you wish to have a service or product certified, you can follow the evaluation procedure outlined on the Green Seal website (**www.greenseal.org**). The organization institutes standards based on requirements determined by the International Organization for Standardization (ISO). The standards for obtaining Green Seal certification are broken down into the following categories:

- Home products and services
- Personal care and consumer-packaged goods
- Construction materials, equipment, and systems
- Facility operations, maintenance, and services
- Hospitality, lodging, and food service
- Transportation and utilities

☀ BIFMA

The Business and Institutional Furniture Manufacturer's Association (BIFMA) is a nonprofit organization that establishes performance and manufacturing standards for office furniture and textiles, including office chairs, desks, storage units, panel systems, seating areas, and file cabinets. The organization follows the guidelines of the American National Standards Institute (ANSI) to provide builders with the information they need to evaluate a product's greenness, along with its durability and safety.

Products are reviewed for their materials use, manufacturing process, and overall sustainability on an environmental, social, and economical scale. The products that meet the BIFMA standards are certified and accredited. For more information on the specific standards applied to different products, visit **www.bifma.org/standards**.

Look for bargains at local Habitat for Humanity and liquidation stores.

Habitat for Humanity sells excess and donated building materials in its thrift stores. You may not find enough of the same material to complete a large project, but you might find enough tile, for instance, to use for your ground-floor bathroom. Liquidation stores also sell salvaged or leftover construction materials, fixtures, and appliances at deeply discounted prices.

☀ Finding green manufacturers and retailers

A Google search of green manufacturers and retailers in your state will yield myriad results for everything from insulation and concrete to window treatments and carpeting. There is almost always a green(er) alternative. Here are some websites with information on green building materials:

- **Building Research Establishment Environmental Assessment Method (BREEAM) ECD and the Building Research Establishment (BRE). (www.breeam.org)**

- **Green Manufacturer (www.greenmanufacturer.net/directory):** An online directory of green manufacturers around the United States. It also has an abundance of other information on green building.

- **Why Not Green? (www.whynotgreen.com):** This website includes a search for manufacturers and retailers of specific building materials and green alternatives. It also compares between green building products.

- **Green Builder (www.greenbuilder.com/general/greendbs.html):** This website lists sustainable sources as well as other green building information. It also has an extensive green building and design database.

Several trade shows and conferences around the country are excellent sources for finding green manufacturers and retailers and for learning more about the green building industry. These include the Green Manufacturing Expo (**www.canontradeshows.com/expo/gmx10**) that takes place around the country each year; Greenbuild (**www.greenbuildexpo.org**), an annual international expo and conference sponsored in part by the USGBC; and more regional conferences, such as the Lean to Green manufacturing conference (**www.sme.org/cgi-bin/get-event.pl?--001981-000007-home--SME-**) in Columbus, Ohio.

Resources to Assist in the Assessment of Building Materials

The Athena Institute (**www.athenasmi.org/about/index.html**). Using software including the ATHENA v.2.0, the institute helps professional architects, engineers, and builders assess the life cycle of different products.

***The Environmental Resource Guide* by the American Institute of Architects and the EPA.** This guide helps professionals assess the life cycle of different building products and materials, which determines what each product's impact is on the environment. The guide is a good resource for an introduction on green building materials and can be purchased at **www.wiley.com/WileyCDA/WileyTitle/productCd-0471183768.html**.

CASE STUDY: PERFORMANCE
DETERMINES SUSTAINABILITY

Bohdan Boyko, building science manager
at GreenFiber
www.greenfiber.com

Bohdan Boyko is a 25-year veteran in the green building industry who specializes in the field of blow-in insulation. "Blow-in insulation is any loose material that serves as a thermal barrier to restrict the transfer or flow of heat energy, from one location to another," he explains. "Blow-in insulation differs from cut-to-fit insulation in that loose fill blow-in insulation conforms to fit a space, ensuring that all gaps are filled. One issue with cut-to-fit insulation is that even what is deemed to be the most precise cut will leave gaps around pipes or wiring, creating a thermal bypass."

Boyko's career began with GreenFiber, a company specializing in green insulation, back in 1995 when he served as a quality control manager for the company to ensure builders used the best possible building products and practices. "In my current role with GreenFiber as a building science manager, my primary focus is on understanding the thermal material component in heat, air, and moisture transfer," Boyko said.

This concept is directly correlated to energy performance of a building, and GreenFiber provides homeowners, contractors, and builders with green insulation materials to achieve optimal thermal performance in a building. "GreenFiber is a natural fiber blow-in insulation that is made of 85 percent recycled materials," Boyko explains. "GreenFiber helps reduce heating and cooling costs by reducing the transfer of heated or cooled air through walls and ceilings. Also, because it is made from recycled paper products, GreenFiber not only helps the environment by reducing energy draws, it also helps divert materials from landfills."

In addition to being environmentally friendly, GreenFiber is also very efficient in controlling noise and is also fire resistant. "Our insulation is infused with a flame retardant treatment that can actually help prevent the spread of fire," Boyko said. "Though GreenFiber is made from 85 percent recycled paper fiber, the remaining 15 percent is composed of non-toxic additives for fire resistance. GreenFiber insulation undergoes a strict regimen of tests to ensure that it adheres to the required technical standards. GreenFiber is manufactured without any harmful chemicals, like formaldehyde or asbestos, and its sound control properties help block out outside noise from traffic, and inside noise like conversations."

How do green insulation products like GreenFiber compare to traditional non-green insulation products? "All types of insulation work present different types of challenges," Boyko said. "Because of the necessary equipment, potential health issues that can arise with harmful chemicals, and temperature and barometric restraints, open and closed cell foam insulation products require professional installation. A blown-in insulation product allows the greatest flexibility because of its ability to conform to the space and fill any cracks or voids."

Boyko recommends that contractors be informed about all the products they are choosing for a green building project because not every product that a manufacturer claims is green or eco-friendly really is. "Contractors should inquire about validity testing, certification, or verification from an independent, third-party organization. This is the best way to know that a product stands up to the claims behind it. GreenFiber recently received third-party certification from Scientific Certification Systems (SCS) that verifies our natural fiber insulation products are made from 85 percent recycled content. It was an arduous process, but it verifies our claims — specifically, 55 postconsumer / 30 pre-consumer recycled content." Pre-consumer waste refers to waste that is created during the product's manufacturing period before it reaches the consumer, and postconsumer refers to waste that is discarded after the consumer is done with it.

"Any material that claims to be green but requires thousands of gallons of fossil fuels to ship it halfway across the globe does not seem very green to me. I would encourage people to buy products that use local distribution models to help reduce dependency on fossil fuels. Bamboo flooring is sustainable because it is plentiful and has rapid growth. But if you are shipping it in from China, then what is the point? Also, the embodied energy — the energy required to produce a product — should also be taken into account. Is a product green if it requires a ton of energy to make it? By many accounts, it requires 10 times the energy to produce fiberglass insulation than it does to produce natural fiber insulation products like GreenFiber."

In terms of cost, "GreenFiber is comparable in price to other commercial insulation products. The cost per square foot varies greatly by region and by the scope of the project. Builders have an opportunity to realize cost efficiencies with a greater economy of scale with a larger insulation project versus a smaller one."

Hundreds of products besides insulation can be incorporated into a sustainability project. "The products that are built to last are the most sustainable to me," Boyko said. "One product that comes to mind is decking material that is made primarily of sawdust and resins, and it looks and performs exactly like wood except it lasts a very long time. Even though some plastics and resins are used in its manufacture, the fact that it lasts for such a long time is a good trade off." Similar factors can be considered for a variety of products. "The worst process is the one that gives the most emphasis to the green materials and not the results. It is not the recipe that is important; it is how the main dish tastes when it comes out of the oven. The ultimate sustainability and efficiency of the building is the measure of its performance."

When thinking about green building as a concept, it is important to think about the entire process and not simply the products used. "The whole issue of being sustainable or green is really not about the products specifically, but more a reflection of the building practices used. Namely, is this building constructed in a manner that will make it functional over the next 75 or 100 years and perform efficiently over that time? Someone could construct an office building made out of the most sustainable materials, by anyone's standards, but if it is inefficient and is bulldozed and dumped into a landfill in 50 years, then it does not seem sustainable to me. To me, building green means using the best practices to ensure that it will be around for a long time and perform well while it is here."

What makes green buildings truly sustainable, said Boyko, is their long-term performance across a variety of categories. "The best processes involve simply employing the best practices — buildings that are built to very demanding performance standards — and how they perform over time is the ultimate measure of green."

Acoustics

Acoustics are often an overlooked aspect of green building, but they have a tremendous impact on employees and occupants inside a building. Acoustics refers to controlling noise generated inside the building by conversation among employees, the operation of mechanical systems like the HVAC system, vibrations from construction and system operations, and any outside noises from street traffic or construction that can be heard inside the building. It is important to consider acoustics when choosing materials and designing the interior of your building.

Because building green emphasizes using less materials and creating more open spaces, acoustics are often compromised. With fewer materials like ceiling tiles and carpeting to absorb sound, the noise level inside the building may be higher in a green building than in a conventional one. These acoustical consequences can be addressed with a few simple techniques. Acentech, an acoustical consulting firm profiled later in this chapter, originated some of these techniques.

Choose materials that absorb sound well

In traditional office buildings, materials like carpets and ceiling tiles soak up noise and prevent it from traveling and bouncing off the walls, ceiling, and floors. In many green office buildings, floors are bare concrete or hardwood with a finish, and ceilings are kept open and exposed, a design mechanism that minimizes materials used and creates an open feeling inside the office. These trends pose an acoustical problem because there are no materials to absorb and control the sound. One of the solutions used by Acentech is rubber floors, which absorb sound well and still meet various green building and design objectives. Rubber floors are considered green because rubber trees are highly renewable, and rubber is recyclable. Recycled rubber flooring — available in a variety of textures, shades, and tones — is an even better alternative than new rubber flooring.

If you are incorporating open spaces, find a way to offset noise

Though incorporating natural daylight into an office space creates a greener environment, conserves energy, and minimizes costs, it can pose a problem acoustically because access to this light requires an open space plan and the use of low or no cubicle walls. Acentech advises clients using daylighting in an open floor plan to install glass cubicle walls, which help to control noise while also enabling access to sunlight from windows.

If you cannot control a noise, integrate a sound system to mask it

Acenetch integrated an artificial sound system in its corporate office building to mask noises from machinery operating in the building. Artificial sounds can be anything from music to sounds imitating mechanical systems like air conditioners. The steady background noise is barely noticeable, but it is effective in covering up some sounds that would otherwise be distracting.

CASE STUDY: THE ART OF GREEN ACOUSTICS

Jeff Fullerton and Ben Davenny,
architectural acoustic consultants
Acentech Inc. (www.acentech.com)

Jeff Fullerton and Ben Davenny are experts in the field of green acoustics. They are key personnel at Acentech, a prestigious consulting firm based in Cambridge, Massachusetts, which specializes in acoustical, audiovisual, noise, and vibration consulting. The company is the largest organization of its type in the country and is a valuable resource for engineers, architects, and developers, as well as companies, corporations, and businesses building a green commercial office building or remodeling an existing building to make it environmentally friendly.

As a specialized consulting firm, Acentech provides consultation on acoustics throughout the design and construction of a building. Both Fullerton and Davenny are LEED APs who work specifically on green projects to address noise control issues arising from green building. "We look at the acoustical consequences of building design," Fullerton explains. These consequences are unique to green building designs because of unique design features, such as open space and the use of fewer materials.

Acoustics are a very important factor during the course of green building design and construction, but they are often overlooked. Noises can include the sound of the heating and cooling system in the building and other mechanical systems, as well as noise produced by daily foot traffic and conversation. In green buildings, noise control is crucial to maintaining the daily operations of the office with minimal interference and distraction. "Acoustics relate to privacy of employees and provide freedom from distraction," Fullerton said.

"Too much noise can increase the barrier of distraction," Davenny added. When employees are distracted by noise, their level of productivity and level of happiness in their work environment may decrease.

In a traditional office building, noise is easier to control because the spaces tend to be more closed, and floor plans typically do not change significantly. One green building trend is the use of movable office equipment that can be taken down and moved very easily to create new cubicle, conference, and common spaces when needed. "More office spaces want to change things around and use demountable partitions, but these have cracks and gaps and tend to be leaky. They are not the greatest barrier, so there is a need to add more noise masking," Fullerton explains. "You can make the green design work, but you have to compensate for it." If developers and designers do not take the time to compensate for it, it can significantly affect business. Fullerton and Davenny point to recent post-occupancy studies completed by the Acoustical Society of America and the Architectural Record that found employees were unhappier about the acoustics in green buildings than they were in traditional buildings.

There are three ways of minimizing noise: absorbing, blocking, and covering it. This is of particular importance in open spaces. Absorbing noise is traditionally achieved by installing noise-absorbing ceiling tiles, while blocking is achieved by placing screens like high cubicle walls between cubicles to block out conversation and other noises. "Our office space has six-foot-tall barriers, which control some of the noise between work stations," Fullerton said. Covering is achieved by installing artificial noise systems to cover up background noise; something Acentech has done in its own offices. An airflow sound system that produces artificial sound over loud speakers embedded in the ceiling masks the noise created by mechanical systems, equipment, conversation, and other minor noises.

Some methods of absorbing, blocking, and covering are challenging to integrate in a green office building. Daylighting, for instance, requires an open space with low cubicle walls to optimize employees' access to the daylight. Although the use of daylighting is an excellent way to make an office building greener, it can increase the amount of noise between work-stations and distraction among employees. "We are seeing daylighting strive to push barriers shorter so employees can see outside, but it comes at an acoustical price," Fullerton said. Both he and Davenny find solutions to problems like these in green buildings. In this instance, they would advise clients to use transparent glass barriers to minimize noise while giving employees access to daylight.

Many designers want to use architectural light shelves to reflect natural sunlight throughout the office space. "There are plenty of absorbing acoustical materials like acoustical ceiling tiles, which can also help reflect light," Fullerton said. Because most of these tiles are white or off-white, they are a natural choice for addressing noise control while simultaneously reflecting light. Some manufacturers track and measure how well these products are reflecting light and how well they are performing.

Another acoustical issue in green buildings is flooring. One popular method of green design is leaving the floor bare instead of covering it with carpeting. "An alternative way to treat a floor is to use a non-porous surface like a rubber floor. Rubber is a rapidly renewable material and because carpet is a mediocre absorber of airborne sounds, you are not losing a lot going from carpet to a rubber floor," Davenny said.

According to Fullerton and Davenny, the lack of inclusion of acoustics points in the LEED green building rating system contributes to the challenge of getting people to realize just how important acoustics are to green building and how important it is to address acoustics during the design process. In 2000, Fullerton participated in a panel to develop criteria for acoustics in buildings seeking LEED certification, but the criteria have yet to be incorporated into the system. Fullerton and Davenny believe this is because the USGBC does not want to overwhelm designers. "Innovative design credits can be achieved, but [contractors and developers] do not have to address acoustics," Fullerton said. "Indoor environmental quality is not being considered in most LEED projects, but they are slowly coming about. These points are very important to incorporate."

After 60 years, Acentech continues its quest to create sound acoustical environments for the hundreds of green office buildings being constructed each year. As green building becomes and increasingly popular, it becomes more apparent just how valuable green buildings are and what they mean for the future.

"Green design means better for the community," Fullerton said.

Lighting

Because electric lighting accounts for about 20 percent of the energy consumed in office buildings, it is a primary focus in reducing energy consumption. Perhaps the most effective way to save energy on lighting is to install sensors and dimmers that prevent lights from being left on all day when no one is occupying a room. Occupancy sensors turn lights on automatically when someone enters a room, and automatically turn lights off when they detect no movement for an extended period. Sensors can be installed in a variety of common areas, including kitchens, bathrooms, storage and utility closets, and conference rooms.

Although lights on dimmers still use about half as much energy as when they are fully turned on, light dimmers can be used to reduce some energy use. Dimmers can provide building occupants with the ability to control the lighting in their workspaces, which greatly increases employees' level of comfort, happiness, and productivity at work. In common areas like hallways, the dimmer can be preset to prevent employees or other occupants from changing the setting.

Another way to conserve energy is to incorporate lamps at workstations (task lighting), so employees and can turn them on as needed instead of illuminating the entire room with overhead lighting (ambient lighting). Individual lamps can also be used in combination with reduced overhead lighting.

When designing a lighting system for a large building, make a plan for maintaining the lighting system and replacing bulbs. The easier it is to access the lighting system, the lower the cost of maintaining it. A professional lighting engineer can recommend cost-effective lighting components.

Daylighting

One way to reduce the energy consumed by electric lighting in a building is to reduce the demand for it. Daylighting brings indirect natural light into the building using windows, skylights, and reflective surfaces. Daylighting has other benefits, too. Electric lights give off heat, which raises the temperature in a building. Preliminary studies have shown that daylighting and outdoor views reduce absenteeism in the workplace. Employees have reported that they experience less stress and feel more positive when their offices have natural light.

Successful daylighting creates beautiful, appropriately lit spaces while saving energy. Metrics for successful daylighting have yet to be established, so good daylighting is a combination of art and science. It is achieved primarily through the placement of windows. Light shelves featuring glass partitions angled to reflect light further into the building can be attached to windows. Skylights and roof monitors (cupolas with vertical glass windows) can be used to extend daylighting into deep spaces and closed areas, but their use is typically limited to one-story buildings. Solar tubes, which capture light through domes on the roof and channel it into the building interior through reflective tunnels, can be used in some multistory buildings. Light-colored interior walls and furniture help to diffuse light throughout a room. External shading with landscaping, shades, or architectural features is used to prevent direct light and glare from causing discomfort.

Daylighting is typically used with supplementary electrical lighting operated by sensors that turn it on when the natural light drops below a certain intensity.

Climate and geographical region, building type and use, and building orientation determine the success of daylighting. Daylighting should be part of an integrated design process, because the windows will affect heat gain or loss in the building.

The Building Exterior

In addition to greening the inside of your office space, it is also important to pay attention to the landscaping and outdoor space surrounding your office building and to the paints and other materials used on the exterior.

Permeable pavement

Permeable pavement is a method of paving roads, walkways, parking lots, and other outdoor spaces to enable stormwater to drain properly. If you cannot incorporate a full stormwater control system to capture, treat, and reuse rainwater, this is an excellent, less expensive option. Installing permeable pavement involves using a pervious material, such as concrete, to create a design that enables water from storm runoff to drain through and between the concrete pavers to be absorbed into the soil beneath them. The concrete used in permeable pavement — pervious concrete — is carefully manufactured to allow water to pass through it and down into the soil. This is achieved mostly through the absence of sand in the concrete mixture for the pavers.

In addition to the environmental benefit of stormwater control and management, permeable pavement is made primarily of recyclable materials. Permeable pavement is also cooler and helps to control heat islands. Using permeable pavement can earn LEED points for its eco-friendly potential.

Landscaping

Creating a sustainable landscape in your outdoor space will contribute significantly to your building's greenness. Green landscape planning and design incorporates a multitude of factors, including climate, erosion control, maintenance, water usage, and the natural habitats in the surrounding area. Instead of intruding on any natural habitats or ecosystems, the objective is to landscape with plants, flowers, grass, and shrubbery that enhance the indigenous surroundings. You will also want to consider how you will encourage employees to use this outdoor space and what types of shade and sun areas you want to create.

It is always best to choose vegetation that is native to your local area. This is beneficial not only because it reduces transportation distance, but also because these plants, flowers, grass, and shrubbery have adapted to the geographic climate and the soil in your area and will flourish with a minimum of irrigation, pesticides, and fertilizers. Besides looking good, native vegetation can help control and treat stormwater by absorption and cleaning, just as a green roof would. Trees and shrubbery also help reduce air pollution by absorbing carbon dioxide given off by cars and releasing oxygen back into the air.

A properly designed landscape can also aid in controlling the building's temperature and provide a natural barrier to outdoor weather. Landscapes can be designed, for instance, to create breezes in certain areas of the space and to direct wind. This helps to lower the overall thermal temperature of the building and reduces the need for forced-air systems like air conditioning.

In general, your landscape should complement your building and help achieve your overall green goals. Consult a landscape designer who has experience with native vegetation in your area as well as green design.

☀ Xeriscaping

The word xeriscape is derived from the Greek words "xeros," meaning "dry," and "scape," meaning a kind of view or scene. Xeriscaping means to landscape with slow-growing, drought-tolerant plants that can thrive without regular maintenance in the climate conditions where they will be used. Though indigenous plants are a natural choice for water and waste-efficient landscapes, xeriscaping is not restricted to native plants. Plants from areas with similar climates can also thrive in a xeriscape.

The ideal xeriscape needs little or no irrigation and very little trimming or maintenance. Xeriscapes require less fertilizer and fewer pest control measures than traditional landscapes, reducing the release of excess nutrients and pesticides into local water systems. All of these benefits — reduced maintenance costs, no need for fertilizers and pesticides, and reduced water usage — translate into additional cost savings.

CHAPTER 8 :

Green Building Certification

Any product or building can claim to be green, but as the movement for sustainable building began to expand during the 1980s, it became clear that official standards are needed to certify that a building is truly energy-efficient and environmentally sound. The first certification system, the Building Research Establishment's Environmental Assessment Method (BREEAM), was established in 1990 in the United Kingdom to measure the sustainability of new commercial buildings. The Leadership in Energy and Environmental Design (LEED) program was introduced in the United States in 1994 by the U.S. Green Building Council (USGBC).

In 1996, the Canadian Standards Association published BREEAM Canada for Existing Buildings. In 1999, Canada implemented a more streamlined, question-based tool, the BREEAM Green Leaf eco-rating program. In 2000, BREEAM Green Leaf became an online assessment and rating tool called Green Globes for Existing Buildings. In 2002, Green Globes for Existing Buildings was introduced online in the United Kingdom as the Global Environmental Method (GEM). In 2004, the Green Building Initiative (GBI) acquired the rights to distribute Green Globes in the United States. In 2005, GBI was accredited as a standards developer by the American National Standards.

LEED and Green Globes are both used in the United States. Other building certification programs include CASBEE (Comprehensive Assessment System for Built Environment Efficiency, Japan), Green Star (Australia), BREEAM Gulf, Evaluation Standard for Green Building (China). SBTool, developed for the iiSBE Sustainable Building Challenge, is a comprehensive tool in the form of a spreadsheet that establishes benchmarks and compares a building's performance to other similar buildings. The 2010 version can be downloaded at **www.iisbe.org/sbtool-2010**.

Most green building assessment systems assign scores for a building's performance in different categories, such as energy efficiency, waste management, water use, and land use. Green certification programs are constantly being re-evaluated and updated to reflect new information and an increasingly global view of environmental impact. Though there is no requirement that a building must be certified to be officially considered a green building, many developers and companies choose to seek certification because it adds a level of credibility to their claims of building green. Certification may be required to qualify for certain financial incentives, and lenders, investors, tenants, and prospective buyers are willing to pay more if a building is officially certified. Certification increases market demand for sustainable building and fosters competition that will eventually result in the construction of more high-quality, high-performance buildings.

The Sustainable Building Challenge

Every two years since 1996, the International Initiative for a Sustainable Built Environment (iiSBE) has held an international Sustainable Building Challenge. High-performance buildings around the world are selected, assessed, and then presented with key performance indicators and discussed at World Sustainable Building Conferences. The last of these was in Melbourne in September 2008, and the next will be in Helsinki in October 2011.

The certification process adds to the cost of a green building project. Certain standards must be met when making decisions about design, building materials, and technologies. Additional work must be done to submit required documentation, conduct inspections, and verify that the building is meeting green objectives, and certification fees must be paid. Some building owners choose not to have their buildings certified, but still follow the certification guidelines to guarantee that they achieve the maximum in energy efficiency, water use reduction, and waste reduction.

Determine whether you are going to be seeking LEED certification or Green Globe certification before you begin building or remodeling. The certification process is lengthy and detailed, and points are earned for each recommendation that you implement, beginning with site selection and design. Correct documentation must be prepared and submitted at each stage. It is best to follow the process from the very beginning of your project, so you do not have to redo anything to earn additional LEED points.

To LEED or not to LEED?

Some developers and companies use the LEED guidelines during the building process but do not officially seek certification. By doing this, they ensure their buildings are operating just as those with LEED certification do, but they do not have to spend the extra time and money to seek the official LEED certification. However, the LEED certification credential is becoming increasingly recognized as desirable by employees, investors, clients, and customers.

LEED Certification

The U.S. Green Building Council (USGBC) is a nonprofit organization dedicated to pursuing and supporting a more sustainable world through green, sustainable building. The organization was founded in 1993 and today has more than 15,000 members through dozens of local chapters. In 1994, the USGBC recognized the need for specific guidelines and national standards of green building and formed the Leadership in Energy and Environmental Design (LEED) program, led by scientist Robert Watson, who served on the National Resources Defense Council. LEED was established to provide builders and other professionals with a specific framework for building green.

In 1998, the USGBC launched a building assessment program for new construction, now known as LEED-NC, with Platinum, Gold, Silver, and Certified ratings based on the number of points a building scored in several categories. Since the program was introduced to the marketplace in 2000, more than 36,000 commercial projects and 38,000 single-family homes have participated in LEED. In November 2010, the USGBC announced that the total footprint of commercial projects certified under the LEED Green Building Rating System had surpassed one billion square feet, and that projects totaling another six billion square feet are currently registered and working toward LEED certification around the world.

U.S. Green Building Council (USGBC)

The USGBC website (**www.usgbc.org**) provides valuable information on green building, including how to get your building certified as a green building and how to join a local chapter of USGBC. The website offers extensive resources, from courses and study guides on green building to articles and research on every area of sustainable building. The USGBC also hosts an international conference on green building each year, bringing together builders, architects, corporations, manufacturers, designers, and other professionals in the industry who are focused on green building and sustainable living.

LEED requirements

The LEED system provides minimum requirements and awards points in each of the following areas. Depending on which level of certification a building is seeking, points can be earned in the following categories:

- **Sustainable site development:** This category concerns the land, or site, on which a project is developed. LEED encourages the development of brownfield sites and discourages building on previously undeveloped land. This category is also concerned with the preservation of the surrounding ecosystems and waterways on the land.

- **Water savings:** This category encourages efficient use of water, which is often achieved in green buildings by incorporating a dual plumbing system, potable water supplies, and low-flow fixtures.

- **Energy efficiency:** This category rates the energy efficiency of the building and how well the building incorporates energy-saving practices, such as minimizing light use when the building is not occupied, and energy-saving systems to reduce energy consumption.

- **Materials selection:** This category is concerned with minimizing waste during the construction process and promotes the use of recycled materials. The credits offered in this category also encourage the use of locally grown and harvested materials that do not have to be transported over long distances.

- **Indoor environmental quality:** The credits concern the quality of the environment inside a building. Credits in this category encourage the use of natural light, improved acoustics, and low-VOC paints and furnishings.

- **Innovation of design:** This category encourages new and innovative structural design that improves a building's overall performance. This includes areas that have yet to be specifically addressed by LEED but contribute to the overall sustainability of a building.

- **Regional priority:** LEED recently began offering certification points in the regional priorities category for buildings that address critical issues specific to their local environment. For instance, in the southern and western United States, where water is scarce, a regional priority is water conservation. Buildings seeking LEED certification in the southern and western parts of the country can earn extra points for incorporating water conservation methods, which speaks to the specific environmental issues of that region. Regional priorities are listed at **www.usgbc.org/DisplayPage.aspx?CMSPageID=1984**.

LEED uses a point system to rate buildings in each of these categories. Buildings are scored on a 100-point scale and have the opportunity to earn points in each of the seven areas. Ten additional "bonus points" are available for innovative design and regional priority. Depending on a building's score, it will be certified on one of four levels:

- Certified: 40–49
- Silver: 50–59
- Gold: 60–79
- Platinum: 80 and above

Through LEED, the USGBC provides certifications for the following:

- **LEED-NC (new construction):** Builders of new buildings must meet requirements in the categories described in the previous section to become certified as Gold, Silver, or Platinum.

- **LEED-EB (existing buildings):** Existing buildings are ones that are being renovated. LEED evaluates renovations on existing buildings and looks for improvements in operations, maintenance, and function. It addresses specific renovations, such as implementing recycling programs and making system upgrades to increase energy efficiency.

- **LEED-CI (commercial interiors):** LEED measures commercial interiors by looking specifically at the internal (minus the core and shell of the building) construction of a space. Points are awarded based on the functionality of the space, how the different products used and systems installed decrease the company's carbon footprint, and how healthy the space is for employees.

- **LEED-CS (core and shell construction):** Core and shell construction refers to the structural aspects of a building, including the foundation, the building envelope, and the HVAC system. It refers specifically to the design of the building as a whole. Many times builders or developers will build a core and shell building and leave the tenants — companies, businesses, or corporations — to finish the interiors. It is possible to have LEED certification on the core and shell without having certification on the interiors. It is up to the tenant to pursue LEED certification for the interior.

- **LEED for schools:** LEED certification for schools involves addressing a variety of child health issues and the space layout that is unique to schools. It includes site selection based on environmental considerations, internal acoustics of the building, and mold prevention.

- **LEED for retail:** Retail buildings are rated on their design and how well they use space while limiting energy use and negative effects on the environment. The certification is further broken down into new construction retail stores and interiors, similar to commercial buildings.

- **LEED for health care:** As in many of the other categories of buildings, LEED certification for health care facilities is based on structural design. To achieve LEED certification, a facility must be high performing, meaning it provides an environment with limited chemicals, pollutants, and toxins. It also must address issues such as patients' access to natural spaces and minimizing the distance between parking lots and the facility.

- **LEED-H (homes):** LEED for homes measures the degree to which design and construction of a residence optimizes water and energy efficiency, sustainable waste management, and use of low-VOC products.

- **LEED-ND (neighborhood development):** Neighborhood development is the newest category to be added to the LEED system and refers to neighborhood and community development as a whole. It rates neighborhood designs for their site selection, consciousness of the environment surrounding the neighborhood, and incorporation of green building design and concepts that minimize waste and energy use and optimize function.

The Experts

The Green Building Certification Institute (GBCI), a third-party organization founded in 2008, is responsible for accrediting and credentialing LEED professionals, as well as providing certification for building projects. Professionals who have passed the Green Building Certification Institute exam are referred to as LEED accredited professionals (APs), which means they are fully knowledgeable about the LEED system and are considered LEED experts on some level.

The number of points offered in each category and further subcategory are determined based on the impact the process, material, or system has on the environment and on people. Each point system varies moderately for different structures. The system for new construction, which also applies to significant remodeling projects, was designed specifically for office buildings. Here is a quick look at some of the things a building can earn points for:

- Development on a brownfield site

- A light pollution reduction system

- An on-site renewable energy system

- Using recycled or reclaimed building material

- Using certified wood or rapidly renewable resources

- Using natural daylight to reduce dependence on energy for artificial lighting

The steps to getting certified

Step 1: Ensure you meet the LEED minimum requirements.

- Comply with environmental laws. You must comply with federal, state, and local laws and codes regulating construction.

- Build a permanent space on an existing site. Your building must be constructed on a permanent space and intended as a permanent structure on that space.

- Build or remodel the whole building. If you are remodeling, you will have to remodel the entire building to qualify for LEED certification, not just a portion of your building.

- Know the area boundaries of your project. You may be building a single structure, in which case the area boundaries are easy to determine. If you are constructing multiple buildings within a development, this becomes more complicated. You also cannot build on land that you do not own unless the land is part of the LEED project.

- Comply with square footage requirements. Buildings cannot be less than 1,000 square feet.

- Comply with occupancy rates. At least one full-time employee, or multiple people working part-time who are full-time equivalent, must use the building. Part-time employees' hours add up to the equivalent of one full-time employee.

- Provide the USGBC with information on energy and water use for five years. You will need to provide bills from your utility provider that outline your energy and water consumption and allow USGBC access to this information for a minimum of five years.

- Comply with building area requirements. Building a 1,000-square-foot office building on 100 acres of land is not acceptable. The floor size of a building must be at least 2 percent of the size of the entire site area.

Step 2: If you meet the above qualifications, register your project with the USGBC at **www.usgbc.org**.
- Click on "Certify Your Green Building" to get started. Registration fees are currently $1,200 for non-USGBC members and $900 for members.

Step 3: Begin your application.

- Through an innovative online system, you can manage the entire process exclusively online with LEED Online. The system allows you to document all the necessary requirements online and submit items for review throughout the building process.

Step 4: Ensure you meet all of the prerequisites. This is a requirement before submitting an application.

- Set up a construction activity pollution prevention plan. This requirement seeks to minimize pollution from the process of construction by reducing soil erosion, reducing dust and other allergens caused by construction, and preventing erosion of sewer systems and similar systems. Guidelines are available from the EPA's National Pollutant Discharge Elimination System (NPDES) stormwater program (**http://cfpub.epa.gov/npdes/stormwater/ cgp.cfm**), which regulates construction activities that disturb one or more acres, or smaller sites that are part of a larger common plan of development or sale.

- Design a water-use reduction plan. This incorporates practices such as using 1.6 gallons-per-flush toilets (which are now a widespread standard) and 2.2 gallons per minute (gpm) faucets in restrooms.

- Complete a review of energy systems. LEED requires you to hire a professional commissioning authority (CA) to confirm the proper installation of the heating, ventilation, air conditioning, and refrigeration (HVAC&R) system; the hot water system; the lighting system; and any solar or wind power system.

- Meet minimum energy standards. Review your energy systems to ensure a minimal impact on the environment from the building's energy use and adherence to the basic energy requirements and regulations of the New Buildings Institute or the American Society of Heating, Refrigerating, and Air-Conditioning Engineers (ASHRAE). The standards you will have to meet depend on the specifics of your building, such as size.

- Complete a review of HVAC systems. If you are remodeling, you must assess your heating, air conditioning, refrigeration systems, and appliances to make sure they do not use chlorofluorocarbon, which is prohibited.

- Have an established system to manage recyclables. You will need a recycling program in place and a designated area for collecting and managing the recyclables.

- Meet minimum indoor air quality requirements. These standards are outlined by ASHRAE.

- Meet smoking regulations. This means you must have a system to minimize the exposure of employees to tobacco smoke, and prevent smoking within 25 feet of entries to the building.

Step 5: Submit your application. The LEED program offers two different review methods for new construction and remodel structures.

- A building can be reviewed for its design and construction at the same time.

- The design and construction aspects can be reviewed separately. The benefit of the second choice is that review takes place throughout the process of designing and building, enabling you to meet prerequisites slowly and through each phase rather than all at once.

Step 6: Pay the certification fees. The fee — which is separate and in addition to the application fee of $900 to $1,200 — depends on a variety of factors, including:

- The size of your building

- The method of review (either with design and construction combined or each separately)

- Whether your structure is new or a remodel of an existing structure

- Certification fees range anywhere from $2,000 to upward of $25,000.

Step 7: Wait for a verdict.

- LEED will review your application and either certify you or deny certification. If you are denied certification, there is an appeals process, and you may appeal credits separately (for a fee).

Although LEED certification is not required for a building to be considered green, the system provides a very accurate guide to green building practices. Official certification ensures your building is operating according to current green standards, which means you are optimizing your cost savings in particular areas. If you are building new or doing a significant remodel and are considering becoming LEED certified, begin the process at the very start of your project.

CASE STUDY: GREEN IS GOOD BUSINESS

Peter Carey, founder
Streamline Material Resourcing
New York, NY
www.streamlinemr.com

In 2009, Peter Carey founded Streamline Material Resourcing, a company that specializes in materials sourcing and furnishings for architecture and interior design firms in New York City. Streamline is a consulting firm that helps companies and corporations design the interior of their green building space to coincide with the sustainable building practices incorporated in the exterior of the building. The company, which provides consulting either in person or as an online tool, was founded to meet the rising demands accompanying the trend of green building. The company selects, presents, and advises on materials and furniture for the interior design of a building, providing personalized solutions for each client.

Carey, who is a LEED AP and has worked and consulted on many green building projects, has experienced the evolution of green building firsthand during his more than 20 years in the architectural, design, and consulting business. "It has taken green so long to become so pervasive because it is such a complex web," Carey said. Green design is not defined by a specific set of guidelines but is instead an intricate combination of dozens of factors and considerations that may differ from building to building. Since the creation of LEED in 1994, the concept of green building has made significant strides because of the availability of specific guidelines for businesses constructing green spaces. LEED certification has also benefited businesses, companies, and corporations. "LEED certification gives the appearance of being green to their clientele," he said. This quality has become quite attractive to customers, employees, and clients.

Because green building is defined by what a client has access to, what he or she can work with, and what he or she wants and needs, Carey strives to provide the avenue through which to achieve this. "It is not about what I have to offer," he said. "It is about what the client wants." Carey also explains that green does not mean the same to everyone. One person or business, for instance, can be motivated to build green for environmental reasons, while another can be motivated by cost savings. "The main question you want to ask is: 'What is the most important thing to you?'" he said. Once a business, company, or corporation identifies what is important to them, the planning and design can begin. "The client has to first be committed and then find the space and the site. Site selection has a lot to do with what your LEED credits are going to be," Carey said.

In fact, site selection is one of three main areas of green building according to the LEED system. "Site selection is about reducing greenhouse gases and encouraging employees to use public transportation and to drive less," Carey said.

The second major focus of green building is managing and reusing stormwater, as well as reducing the stormwater pollution that a building generates. "In the next 50 years, water levels are expected to rise 10 feet. LEED anticipates that sort of thing," Carey said.

The system allots a significant number of points to water management and encourages buildings to measure how much they use. "Once you are aware of how much you use, you tend to use less," he said. This is an important concept in green building, because many buildings, companies, corporations, and individuals often do not realize how much they are wasting. Once they do, it is usually easier to use less and become more aware of the impact of this use on the environment.

The third important component of sustainable building is indoor air quality. Dozens of factors contribute to the air quality of a building, from the heating and air conditioning systems installed in the building to the paint used on the walls. Furniture and other products used inside an office space also play a significant role in the indoor air quality, because many of these products can be manufactured with dangerous volatile organic compounds (VOCs) that give off gas for years after their initial installation. Because of the increased awareness that products like desks, chairs, and workstations may be made with dangerous VOCs, several new manufacturer's standards established during the last few years address these issues. These standards include those of the Business and Institutional Furniture Manufacturer's Associate (BIFMA), which provides manufacturers with standards by which a product can be rated on multiple levels. There is also the SMaRT rating system developed by the Institute for Market Transformation to Sustainability that provides standards for flooring and textile.

These standards address what Carey refers to as the triple bottom line: "The standards are about how the manufacturer addresses the economic, social, and environmental aspects of a product." Streamline addresses the triple bottom line together with its clients to ensure that the materials and products used meet the building's objectives in a way that conserves the environment, protects the indoor air quality of the building, and ultimately saves money. "We have enough knowledge base to know that being green does not cost a lot," Carey said. As for the future of green building, Carey predicts that in five to ten years, green and sustainable building will be the standard.

"The marketplace is moving toward green. Soon, green is not going to be a buzzword," Carey said. "Green is good business. It does not take a lot to be green."

LEED professionals

LEED professional credentials and exams are administered by the Green Building Certification Institute (GBCI). There are two levels of LEED credentials:

LEED green associate: Has demonstrated a basic knowledge of green building and LEED concepts through testing and maintains his or her credential either through continuing education and practical experience or by retaking the test every two years

LEED accredited professional (AP) with specialty credentials: Has demonstrated an advanced level of green building knowledge and LEED practices through testing and maintains his or her credential either through continuing education and practical experience or retaking the test every two years

A recently introduced credential, **LEED fellow**, is awarded to LEED professionals who are nominated by their peers and have demonstrated technical mastery and an outstanding level of commitment to sustainable building by educating others and advocating for green building practices.

You can find LEED professionals in your area by searching the GBCI LEED Professionals Directory online (**http://gbci.cyzap.net/gbcicertonline/onlinedirectory/**).

Green Globes

The Green Globes rating system is administered by the Green Building Initiative (GBI) (**www.thegbi.org/green-globes/**).

Green Globes awards a building a rating of one to four Green Globes, depending on what percentage of the available 1,000 points the building achieves. The program includes a building assessment protocol, a rating system, and a guide for integrating environmentally friendly design into commercial buildings. It is designed to be interactive, flexible, and affordable.

The Green Globe system is organized as a series of online questionnaires to be filled out at various stages of the project. A project is registered online, and a preliminary questionnaire is submitted. Based on their answers to the questions, users receive a report after each questionnaire advising them what steps to take next. If a building achieves at least 35 percent of the available points, it is eligible for verification. An independent, trained verifier then visits the site, physically examines the building, and interviews the project team.

Unlike LEED, which rates all buildings using a fixed number of points, Green Globes adjusts the number of available points according to the project's location and bases its rating on the percentage of available points achieved.

Green Globes Categories and Points for New Construction

Assessment Category	Points	Description
Energy	360	Performance, efficiency, demand reduction, energy efficient features, use of renewable energy, transportation
Indoor environment	200	Ventilation, lighting, thermal and acoustical comfort, ventilation system
Site	115	Ecological impact, development area, watershed features, enhancement
Resources	100	Low-impact materials (LCA), reuse, demolition, durability, recycling
Water	100	Performance, conservation, treatment
Emissions and effluents	75	Air emissions (boilers), ozone depletion, water and sewer protection, pollution controls
Project management	50	Design process, environmental purchasing, commissioning
Total	**1000**	

Green Globes professionals

The Green Building Initiative (GBI) certifies two types of Green Globe professionals:

- **Green Globe assessor (GGA):** A highly experienced industry professional who has received extensive training and testing and is authorized to perform on-site third-party evaluations that can lead to the awarding of an official Green Globe rating.

- **Green Globe professional (GGP):** An architect, engineer, builder, contractor, or green building consultant with more than five years' experience in the industry who has completed user-level Green Globe training and is qualified to fill out online evaluations and provide technical support and project management to clients going through the certification process.

You can find a Green Globe certified professional on the Green Globes Certification Personnel Search (**www.thegbi.org/green-globes/ personnel-certifications/certified-personnel-listing**).

Certification and Legal Issues

The decision to seek LEED or Green Globe certification involves not only an additional financial commitment from the building owner, but also a commitment from the design team and the construction team to fulfill the LEED or Green Globe requirements. Many things could go wrong during the construction process that could ultimately cost the building its certification. A design might prove to be less energy-efficient than expected, a contractor could decide to cut costs by using a toxic product instead of an approved one, or the construction crew could fail to observe proper procedures for disposal of waste. Such mistakes translate into financial losses for the building owner who has invested money to seek certification, as well as failure to meet the stated objectives of the building project. Who is responsible when a building fails to receive certification, and who must pay for corrections, repairs, and resubmissions? Some important legal issues to consider when seeking LEED or Green Globe certification are:

Does the language in your contracts specify each project stakeholder's role in earning the desired level of LEED or Green Globes certification?

Contracts should specify who is responsible for tracking, collecting, assembling, and submitting the supporting documentation for a certification program. Architects, engineers, and other professionals must make it clear that signing off on a document for submission to LEED or Green Globes does not constitute any other kind of warranty or guarantee.

Are your design professionals and consultants familiar with sustainable design, green building rating systems, and the corresponding certification process, and have they participated in other green certification projects?

Experienced professionals are familiar with the challenges and requirements of seeking certification for a building. They are already aware of legal pitfalls and will be careful to avoid them.

Does your contract specify green materials, systems, and products whose green performance has already been verified?

New materials, products, and innovative technologies are constantly coming on the market, but their efficiency may be untested and undocumented. If you are seeking certification, it is safer to stick to acknowledged green products and materials.

Have you carefully reviewed all federal, state, and local green building requirements and the requirements for any green building financial incentives?

Zoning laws, building codes, and requirements for financial incentives vary widely from one location to another. Failure to comply could cost you a valuable tax credit or discount.

Have you made allowances for the uncertainties and complexities of green building?

Most green building projects are covering new ground of one kind or another. Budget extra time and money wherever possible, and be especially conscious when negotiating costs and deadlines. Contracts should include provisions for resolving disparities and renegotiating budgets and schedules when necessary.

A USGBC decision not to award LEED certification or LEED points can be appealed, but the process is time-consuming. Critics of LEED have suggested that a third-party organization should review appeals instead of the USGBC, and that a standardized appeals process with time deadlines should be implemented.

Permits and Zoning Requirements

As in conventional building, permit requirements for green building vary significantly from one county, city, or town to another. Some municipalities have developed a building permit process specifically for green building projects and those seeking LEED certification. Contact your local municipal building department for information on permits and zoning requirements for your county.

Contact the Right Office

A municipal building department can be called a variety of names, including the Building and Zoning Division, the Office of Public Works, or the Office of Community Development. Call your local government headquarters and ask to be directed to the department that handles commercial building permits. In New York City, for instance, it is the Department of Buildings, which operates under the government of the City of New York.

Although the process of obtaining a permit for a green building does not differ much from the process for obtaining one for a conventional building, there may be additional requirements. The following example is a summary of the general requirements for a commercial green building project in Sonoma County, California:

Plan Requirements

- Four sets of plans signed by a licensed engineer or architect, plus two additional sets if the building will use a septic system. A set of plans must include:

  - A plot and site plan depicting property lines, lot dimensions, and drainage systems

  - A floor plan demonstrating the dimensions of the building

  - A foundation plan incorporating all crawl spaces, retaining walls, and type of foundation

  - Exterior building plans showing all windows and doors and other exterior features

  - A framing plan including all windows, doors, ceilings, roof, and stairs and the dimensions of each

  - The cross sections of the building

  - The structural details of the foundation, roof, flooring, and walls, including support beams and separation details

  - Disability access details

- A site evaluation which leads to a Building and Grading Permit, that includes a review of the drainage systems, soil, seismic zones, flood zones, and overhead power lines

- A map with the location of the property and posting of the address of the project at the site within 48 hours after the submission of the building plans

- The inclusion of the LEED checklist if the building is seeking LEED certification

- A Title 24 Energy Calculation Report, which is California's compliance document as part of its code of regulations. (All new construction must include this document.)

- An engineering report on all non-conventional construction materials, such as sand and rock materials from dredging used to make cement

- A geotechnical report from a geotechnical engineer, which details the conditions of the building site's soil and water and includes the engineer's design and construction recommendations for roadway and bridge construction

- Truss calculation and layout plans when truss engineering is incorporated

- An elevation certificate if the site is located within a flood zone, a creek setback form if the building is located next to a creek, or a grading permit if grading work will be performed on the site

Once the building has been completed, the contractor is required to coordinate an inspection and review of the building with an accredited LEED professional to ensure all requirements for points the building is seeking have been met. The LEED professional must submit a form, the Verification of Plan Reviewer by Green Point Rater, which confirms that the building has met all LEED requirements. Once the LEED professional submits the appropriate paperwork, a building inspector will issue a final occupancy permit, which will authorize the building for occupancy by people.

Just as in conventional construction, a green building project must follow local building codes and zoning laws, receive the appropriate permits and meet the requirements of the municipality in which the site is located. In New York, for instance, you are required to get approval from the state's Department of Environmental Protection to use backflow preventers on toilets to ensure they are not a threat to the potable water system. There is an additional laundry list of requirements to meet fire, electrical, plumbing codes, foundation, and safety codes. The building code and zoning requirements for your geographical area are typically available on your municipality's website. Reed Construction Data's Building Code Reference Library (**www.reedconstructiondata.com/building-codes**) contains building code requirements for each state. Permits may also be required to address water pollution control, stormwater discharge, and ground water discharge.

CHAPTER 9:

Renovating or Retrofitting an Office Building

For every newly constructed building, there are more than 100 existing buildings.

Existing buildings are likely to have older, less energy-efficient fixtures and systems than new buildings, and they can be expected to remain in use for decades. It is obvious that renovating and retrofitting existing buildings would significantly reduce greenhouse gas emissions, water usage, and pollution.

A renovation is a complete makeover of the interior and/or exterior of an existing building and may involve making structural changes, replacing old systems with new ones, removing toxic materials, and installing new fittings. A green retrofit is simpler and involves making changes to one or more building components; for example, replacing or updating the HVAC unit, adding a solar system to supply some of the building's electricity, or replacing windows or water fixtures.

The process of renovating an existing office space will differ from new building construction, but the general concepts of green building will remain the same. A remodeling project should address the three main objectives of green building: energy efficiency, indoor air quality, and water usage. Green building processes discussed in other sections of this book also can be applied to a remodeling project. LEED and Green Globes certification is available for existing buildings.

This chapter provides an overview of some of the most cost-efficient and effective strategies for making an existing building greener, as well as recommendations for minimizing disruption of the workplace, effectively managing dangerous toxins, and maintaining the quality of the air inside the building during a renovation.

Increasing energy efficiency and becoming greener does not have to be complicated. Some of the most cost-effective strategies are the simplest: installing light sensors or low-flow water fixtures and introducing a recycling program. If you are unable to undertake a large-scale renovation project, such as replacing your HVAC system or installing a stormwater management system to prevent polluted rainwater from entering the water supply, many smaller projects will make your office greener.

Planning and Designing a Retrofit or Renovation

Good planning is essential for a green retrofit or renovation. The first step is to evaluate the property and its potential for a green retrofit. If the building to be renovated is occupied by tenants, a feasibility study is particularly important. A green renovation may reduce energy costs and improve indoor air quality, but will the tenants be willing to pay higher rents for green office space, and will the building be worth more on the real estate market? Will the renovated building bring in enough income to cover the cost? If your own company occupies the building, you may be undertaking the renovation for other reasons, such as the need to establish an environmentally friendly and socially responsible image for your company or to set an example for your industry. You may expect to reap other benefits from your green building that will justify the expense of the renovation, such as reduced operating costs, increased productivity, and improved employee morale.

Because parts of the building may have to be vacated during the renovation, and construction activities may disrupt employees' normal routines, careful scheduling of the renovation work is essential. Work areas may have to be moved or rearranged, and your human resources officer will need to make arrangements so that workers can continue to do their jobs. Building occupants will have to be protected from exposure to dust and toxins during certain stages of the renovation process. Parking might have to be reorganized to provide storage and work space for the construction crews. You might lose rental income from units that are vacated during the renovation. Careful advance planning will avoid chaos and ensure that your business is not unnecessarily disturbed during the renovation.

Determining the economic feasibility of a renovation

Whether you are renovating a rental property or your own offices, you should not undertake a green renovation without understanding the economic implications. A recent statistical analysis published by Dutch economist Nils Kok showed that U.S. buildings labeled under the LEED or ENERGY STAR programs charge 3 percent higher rent, have greater occupancy rates, and sell for 13 percent more than comparable nearby properties. However, green office space is valued more highly in some areas of the United States than in others, and its value is affected by the local market for office space. Understanding how your green project will affect the value of your property will guide you in making design choices and selecting materials.

☀ Market feasibility study

Investigate the market for green real estate in your area. Compare your current rents to rents for other properties, check occupancy rates, find out if new office space is under construction in your area, if there is a demand for green office space, and whether rent for green offices is higher.

☀ Interview tenants and local real estate brokers

Survey your tenants to see if they are interested in the project and would be willing to pay higher rent if you renovate. Consult local real estate brokers to get a feel for local market conditions.

☀ Review local regulations

Identify any regulatory policies that might affect the future use of your building and its competitiveness on the market.

☀ Review your tenant leases

Look over lease documents. Identify your legal obligations and those of your tenants. See if there are any clauses that would allow you to pass the cost of improvements on to tenants.

Evaluating your property

When you have determined that a retrofit is economically feasible, it is time to evaluate the property itself to identify exactly what needs to be done during the green renovation. At this point, you might want to hire a green building professional to advise you or conduct the assessments for you.

☀ Property Condition Assessment (PCA)

A traditional PCA assesses the physical condition of the building, including the site, structure, exterior and interior, mechanical systems, elevators and escalators, and building code compliance. It estimates the cost of repairs and improvements. The PCA standards do not encompass sustainability, so additional assessments are necessary to plan for a green renovation.

☀ Sustainability profile

A sustainability profile lists the positive and negative aspects of your building in the various categories covered by green certification systems.

☀ Certification gap assessment

A certification gap assessment shows exactly where you fall short of the standards of a certification system such as LEED or Green Globes, and what you would have to do to become certified. It can be performed by a third party or by a LEED or Green Globes professional. Even if you do not plan to seek certification, such an assessment can help you set objectives for your renovation project.

☀ Energy audit

Use the ENERGY STAR portfolio manager (information later in this chapter) or another tool to compare your energy use to similar buildings. If you determine that you need to improve the energy efficiency of your building, have a professional energy audit performed to identify all the areas where energy is being lost or wasted, and where most of your energy is being used.

Water audit

A preliminary review is performed using a year's worth of water bills and a list of all the water fixtures in the building. A more detailed assessment can be done on site to identify upgrades that can be made without redesigning the plumbing system, and their estimated cost.

Indoor Air Quality Assessment

The EPA's Indoor Air Quality Building Education and Assessment Model (I-BEAM) (**www.epa.gov/iaq/largebldgs/i-beam/index.html**) takes you through the process of conducting an indoor air quality analysis.

Based on the results of this research, identify your objectives, the green features you want to include in your renovated building, and the scale of your project. You are now ready to hire a designer and a construction manager to help you plan your project and set up a construction schedule.

The Building Envelope

By renovating an existing building, you are already fulfilling one green building objective — to reduce waste by reusing a building. In a renovation, you are working with an existing building envelope. The key structural elements of a building, such as the foundation, roof, walls, and windows, protect its structural integrity, and determine the temperature, moisture, and air pressure within the building. The building envelope determines how well a building retains heat and cool air, how the building is ventilated, and how much energy is needed to operate a forced-air system. The better the building envelope functions, the more energy you will conserve, the more effective your systems will be, and the more money you will save in the long run. If your building envelope is not properly designed, systems within the building, as well as the indoor air quality and general function of the building, will not function to their optimal level.

The benefits of installing a green HVAC system that uses significantly less energy to pump cool air into your building will be canceled out if you do not use proper insulation, windows, and doors to retain the cooled air efficiently. A poorly designed building envelope, which does not properly prevent moisture from entering the building, can lead to the growth of toxic mold and mildew. The first step in achieving energy efficiency is repairing and modifying the building envelope.

Improving Energy Efficiency

Improving energy efficiency is the primary goal of many office-remodeling projects. Improved energy efficiency has a direct and very tangible effect not just on operations and maintenance costs, but also on the environment. The American Society of Heating, Ventilation, Refrigerating, and Air Conditioning Engineers (ASHRAE) is an excellent source for information on how to measure energy use and apply energy-efficiency measures (EEMs) to reduce a building's energy consumption. According to the *Energy Efficiency Guide for Existing Commercial Buildings: The Business Case for Building Owners and Managers,* published by ASHRAE, strategies to improve energy efficiency include:

- Purchasing ENERGY STAR equipment and appliances

- Installing power management systems on employee computers, which put computers into a dormant mode when they are not being used for extended periods of time

- Implementing energy saving policies, such as turning off computers, lights, and other equipment overnight.

- Promoting energy use awareness among employees

- Using lamps and lighting fixtures that can be turned on and off when a task needs to be complete (task lighting), instead of lighting the entire space throughout the entire workday (ambient lighting)

- Installing lighting sensors that automatically turn on when occupants enter a room and off when occupants leave

- Evaluating the current HVAC system and installing appropriate upgrades to enable it to operate more efficiently and/or changing the operations of the system

Energy use in a building is documented using an energy utilization index (EUI), which measures energy consumption over time. The British thermal units (Btu) consumed for each source of energy in the building are measured over a consecutive time period. Data must be monitored and collected over 12 to 24 months to gain accurate results and to create a base index for annual comparisons.

By looking at the EUI, a building owner or operator can identify areas where energy efficiency can be improved, such as the HVAC system, and develop specific cost-effective strategies. Unless yours is a green building with the highest LEED certification, incorporating almost every green system available to minimize waste across multiple platforms, there is always room for improvement in a commercial space.

ENERGY STAR *portfolio manager*

The ENERGY STAR portfolio manager is an easy and innovative way to manage this process and compare your building to other commercial buildings across the country. The ENERGY STAR portfolio manager measures more than energy consumption. It also:

- Tracks the energy and water meters for each facility

- Offers comparisons and benchmarks for different years of measurement

- Enables the monitoring of costs associated with energy and water consumption

- Enables you to view and share this data

- Allows you to include specific characteristics associated with the operations of your facility that may affect energy and water usage

- Breaks down this tailored information to each space within your building

When using this system, and other systems of energy consumption measurement, it is important to understand the difference between site and source energy. Site energy is the amount of heat and electricity consumed by a building as reflected in utility bills. Site energy may be delivered to a facility in as primary energy, the raw fuel such as natural gas or fuel oil that is burned to generate heat and electricity on site; or as secondary energy, the heat or electricity created from a raw fuel such as electricity purchased from the grid or heat received from a district steam system. A unit of primary and a unit of secondary energy consumed at the same site cannot be directly compared because one represents a raw fuel while the other represents a converted fuel. To assess the relative efficiencies of buildings with varying proportions of primary and secondary energy consumption, these two types of energy must be converted into equivalent units of raw fuel consumed to generate one unit of energy consumed on site. To achieve this equivalency, EPA uses the convention of "source energy." Source energy accounts for losses incurred by the storage, transport, and delivery of fuel to the building when primary energy is consumed on site. When secondary energy is consumed on site, the conversion to source energy accounts for losses incurred during the production, transmission, and delivery of energy to the site. The factors used to restate primary and secondary energy in terms of the total units of equivalent source energy units are called the "source-site ratios."

The ENERGY STAR portfolio manager compiles data from your building and uses statistically representative models to compare it to similar buildings from a national survey conducted by the Department of Energy's Energy Information Administration (EIA). This national survey, known as the Commercial Building Energy Consumption Survey (CBECS), conducted every four years, gathers data on building characteristics and energy use from thousands of buildings across the United States. Your building is compared to a peer group of buildings in the CBECS survey that have similar building and operating characteristics. A rating of 50 indicates that the building, from an energy-consumption standpoint, performs better than 50 percent of all similar buildings nationwide, while a rating of 75 indicates that the building performs better than 75 percent of all similar buildings nationwide.

If your building achieves a rating of 75 percent or higher, you can apply for the ENERGY STAR label, which recognizes a building as being energy efficient. The ENERGY STAR label indicates that your facility meets the energy consumption guidelines outlined by the EPA, emitting fewer greenhouse gases, costing less to operate, and using significantly less energy in comparison to most similar buildings.

Commissioning an existing building

Chapter 3 discussed commissioning, the hiring of a third-party agent (CA) to test and inspect every component and system in a new building to ensure that it is working as it was designed to. Recommissioning (RCx), sometimes referred to as "retrocommissioning," is the practice of commissioning existing buildings. RCx uses building and equipment documentation along with functional testing to adjust the building systems to meet the original design specifications or optimize the systems for current operational needs. According to the EERE, recommissioning costs between $0.05 and $0.40 per square foot. A cheaper option is value recommissioning (VCx), which concentrates on the energy-savings opportunities that promise the fastest results.

You can realize substantial energy savings by recommissioning your existing HVAC, water, and electrical systems. Many new buildings were never commissioned; they were just handed over to the occupants with malfunctions and operational problems, and operations staff was never trained to correctly maintain and adjust mechanical systems. Over time, sensors and thermostats may break, building occupants may adjust settings for their personal comfort, valves may stick, and electrical connections corrode, rendering energy savings mechanisms useless.

Typical Findings from Existing Building Commissioning

Excerpt from the EERE's *O&M Best Practices Guide, Chapter 7: Commissioning Existing Buildings* (**www1.eere. energy.gov/femp/pdfs/OM_7.pdf**)

- Many case studies of existing building commissioning efforts have been published over the years. A review of case studies for multiple buildings published by Portland Energy Conservation, Inc. (PECI), Texas A&M University, proceedings from National Building Commissioning Conferences, and FEMP Assessments of Load and Energy Reduction Techniques (ALERT) is useful in identifying measures most typically available in commercial building spaces. The most frequently cited measures and opportunities are:

- Adjust reset and setback temperatures and temperature setting. Settings are often adjusted over time based on personal preferences, to compensate for inadequate system operation, or to achieve energy savings. In addition, sensors require periodic recalibration.

- Staging/sequencing of boilers, chillers, and air handling units. Equipment should be operated in the most efficient combination of chillers, boilers, and fans at varying load conditions.

- Adjust and repair dampers and economizers. Malfunctioning or poorly tuned dampers (including seals, actuators, and linkages) and economizers result in (1) increased supply air fan energy in the closed position or require additional air heating and cooling when open too much, (2) undesired building operating conditions due to lack of outside air, and (3) premature equipment degradation and replacement.

- Modify control strategies for standard hours of operation. Motors, pumps, fans, and air handlers often operate on a 24/7 schedule even though not required by either the building tenants or the building operating plan.

- Eliminate simultaneous heating and cooling. Heating and cooling systems for the same space can compete against each other due to improper set points.

- Air and water distribution balancing and adjustments. Systems require rebalancing due to drift and changing building/workspace mission and/or tenant requirements.

Verify controls and control sequencing, including enabling and re-enabling automatic controls for set points, weekends, and holidays. Verify that overrides are released.

Improving the lighting system

Lighting can be responsible for nearly one-third of the energy consumption of your building. Making changes to your lighting system can significantly lower your energy consumption and your electric bill. There are a variety of ways to improve a lighting system, ranging from switching out your conventional light bulbs with energy-efficient compact fluorescent bulbs (CFLs) or light emitting diode (LED) bulbs to the replacement of your overhead ceiling lighting system with two-lamp T5 fixtures.

CFL bulb and LED bulbs

LED and CFL bulbs generate less heat than traditional light bulbs and give off the same amount of light while using less electricity. LED bulbs are very energy efficient and last up to 50,000 hours, while a traditional bulb lasts less than 1,000 hours. LED bulbs contain no mercury or filament (the coiled wires inside a traditional light bulb), so they are not harmful when broken, are more resistant to damage, and do not get nearly as hot as traditional light bulbs. The initial cost of LEDs can be a deterrent, but the savings on your electric bill offset the expense. LEDs are also sensitive to extreme heat, which can significantly reduce their performance and their life span.

CFLs are generally more energy-efficient than LED bulbs; they are four times as efficient as traditional bulbs. CFLs last nearly ten times longer than traditional bulbs and are very versatile. Replacing just one traditional bulb with a CFL bulb would eliminate a ½ ton of carbon emissions. CFLs contain small amounts of mercury, but low- and no-mercury bulbs are available. Some CFL bulbs cannot be dimmed, and some people complain that the light from CFL bulbs can be very bright. CFLs might not fit into some existing light fixtures.

Jay Black of Reckson Associates Realty Corporation, the east-coast commercial landlord and real estate developer featured in a Case Study in this chapter, describes how his company uses two-lamp T5 fixtures in many of his company's green building and remodeling projects. Black explains that the industry standard is a two-lamp T8 fixture, with a row of three lights that use 32 watts each, or 93 watts of power per fixture. By using a two-lamp T5 fixture with only two lights that use 28 watts per bulb instead, the wattage usage is nearly cut in half. Because these bulbs put out more light per bulb than the traditional bulbs used in the three-lamp fixture, lighting quality is actually improved. They put out more light, so the fixtures can be placed further apart on the ceiling, reducing the number of fixtures needed to light the building.

Finding Alternative Lighting Options

Arizona lighting company AEI Lighting (**www.aeilighting.com**) offers a variety of alternative and hybrid lighting options such as the two-lamp T5 systems. Its website is a good resource for researching dozens of lighting options. Lighting Services Inc. (**www.lightingservicesinc.com**) is also a good source for sustainable lighting options.

The Challenges and Elements of Remodeling

Q&A with Dan Perruzzi, principal at Margulies Perruzzi Architects, a green design and architectural firm that specializes in commercial remodeling and renovating.

What are some of the most important architectural and design elements of a green office remodel project?

There are certainly some competing concepts in a sustainable remodel. To minimize waste, you would be tempted to retain as much of the existing build-out as possible, but if you are dealing with antiquated systems, that might not be the best strategy. When space is remodeled, an important question is the condition and suitability of the existing HVAC system. Most older HVAC systems cannot deliver the quantity of outside air essential for comfort and productivity. Old lighting systems may not have the capacity to be upgraded and may have to be totally removed to make way for newer systems that will use less energy. The presence of indoor contaminants also has to be considered. Flooring containing asbestos or wood doors fabricated with urea formaldehyde might be serviceable, but their presence would be detrimental to the health and well-being of the users. The key to a successful sustainable remodel is to retain those elements that can be made to work while lacking a threat to overall sustainability and to remove those elements that, either by content or operation, do not support a sustainable design approach.

What are some of the challenges of designing a green office building or space?

The challenge of designing a green office building or space is the same as for any design project: establishing goals that are consistent with the mission and budget. Sustainability comes in many flavors, as do other design strategies. The key is identifying those that fit with the overall mission of the design and the project budget. Planning for sustainability is critical, and that planning effort needs to happen as early as possible. We tell our clients that the discussion about sustainability should be part of the programming discussion. Every space, every building has its own unique set of characteristics and challenges that shape how they are designed. The key is to understand and blend those into the discussion over sustainability. Sustainability requires some opportunism: When we realized there would be a sizable quantity of blast rock from the Hingham Building excavation, we looked for ways to use it on site. The rock retaining walls were a perfect fit. In our own space, we recognized that the great daylight coming into the space was an opportunity that could not be wasted on private offices alone, so we kept the number of private offices low and moved them all off of the exterior wall.

What are some of the challenges when it comes to working within various zoning regulations?

I think about green or sustainable strategies in three broad categories: those that are mostly transparent to local communities enforcing zoning (material selections, amount of recycled content), those that actually have a positive benefit to the local community (reduced stormwater runoff, reduced water and energy usage, emphasis on public transportation, fewer vehicle trips), and those that may require some flexibility on the part of local zoning to accept. Wind turbines and other building-mounted alternative energy sources certainly can have an impact on how a building appears or on the overall height of the structure. A project wanting to maximize the use of public transportation may ask that it be allowed to construct fewer parking spaces than required by zoning. Though these might be problematic for some communities, the overall positive benefits of a green building or development have to be weighed against the relatively small number of areas where some flexibility is needed. At the same time, proponents of green design cannot expect free reign to flout zoning ordinances.

What are some of the strategies you incorporate when designing a green space within a restricted budget?

We are seeing a trend where many clients have asked us to design a sustainable space without actually seeking LEED certification, as a way of saving money on the documentation process. Though we believe that the LEED process is beneficial in that it adds discipline, we also know that the incremental cost of sustainable design is small and getting smaller, depending on the program of sustainable strategies. We are convinced that a project with even the most restricted budget can employ some sustainable design strategies. In Massachusetts, construction debris has to be recycled by law, so that additional cost is no longer optional. The real additional cost of selecting sustainable materials is also shrinking. Designing a simple energy-saving lighting system may actually cost less than not doing so, but adding lighting controls into the mix can add significant cost. For clients who are trying to be sustainable while controlling costs, we advise them to avoid costly lighting controls until these elements become more cost effective. Another compelling argument for sustainability is to consider first cost versus life cycle cost. For example, while the added costs for including lighting controls may seem initially large you have to look at the savings over time. In many cases, that higher first cost is offset by savings over the term of use.

> **What are some innovative and unique ways to incorporate reclaimed and reused material in a remodel project?**
>
> These are virtually limitless, depending on the nature of the reclaimed material and the creativity of the architect. There are great examples of old wood windows reused as interior glazed walls, and doors used as paneling. Boston's Big Dig yielded a huge quantity of structural steel. I know of one house that is designed around reclaiming that steel as structure. Old lighting fixtures can be stripped of their wiring and sockets and fitted with new to support new lamping.

Improving the HVAC system

Programmable thermostats allow you to control the temperature when the building is not being used.

The easiest way to improve the HVAC system in your building is to change the way you use it. Many buildings continue to heat and cool the building even when occupants are not there at night and on weekends and holidays. If you calculate the energy use and the cost for this energy over time, you would probably be shocked at how much is being wasted. ASHRAE suggests that changing the operations and management of the HVAC system can realize savings of up to 20 percent.

Strategies to improve the energy efficiency of your HVAC system are defined by your heating and cooling needs, which depend largely on your geographical location. In Florida, for example, where humidity levels are high, moisture must be removed from the air to create a comfortable indoor environment. In California, on the other hand, the air is very dry and additional moisture is needed to create a comfortable indoor environment. In both locations, heating needs are very low so the HVAC systems in buildings in these states should be designed accordingly.

In warm-climate areas like Florida and California, the HVAC system can be made more efficient by painting the roof a lighter color. Most roofs are black, a color that attracts and absorbs heat. Painting the roof white significantly reduces the absorption of heat by the building, thus reducing the need for air conditioning. Replacing appliances and office equipment with ENERGY STAR or other energy-efficient appliances also can reduce cooling requirements. Lighting and equipment, especially industrial copy machines and computers, gives off a significant amount of heat. Use of energy-efficient versions reduces heat emissions and the need to subsequently cool the space.

A number of minimal changes and upgrades can be made to significantly improve the efficiency of the HVAC system. The motors, fans, and pumps used in the HVAC system also can be replaced or upgraded to more energy efficient. This will make your HVAC system operate more efficiently without having to be entirely replaced.

Another consideration during a renovation is the distribution of cool or warm air throughout the building. Some areas of the building, such as conference rooms, do not need to be cooled and heated at the same rate as other areas of the building that are occupied all day long. Many buildings pump excessive heat throughout a building during the winter and cold air during the summer, making

Using light gray roof shingles instead of black shingles can help decrease the amount of heat that is absorbed.

building occupants uncomfortable and wasting money and energy. Adjusting the temperature control on the HVAC system by even a few degrees can significantly raise the comfort level inside the building and conserve energy and money. If your HVAC system does not already have an economizer cycle, consider adding one. The economizer works by cooling a space with air from the outside when a space reaches a certain predetermined temperature (usually between 50 and 55 degrees Fahrenheit). The economizer can be used during periods of low occupancy, such as on weekends, to maintain a temperature in the building without having to use artificial air conditioning.

Another option to consider if you are replacing an HVAC system is a heat and energy recovery ventilation system (ERV), which uses energy produced by outside exhaust systems and other air streams to condition outside air as it enters the ventilation system. In a heat recovery system, heat exchangers use this recycled energy to heat or cool outside air for use in the building. Energy recovery systems employ a number of methods, including run-around coil systems, which recover energy during the process of cooling water and use it to heat water and air; regenerative heat wheels, which treat outside heat and moisture; and heat pipes, which absorb energy from exhaust streams and transfer it.

An ERV is more expensive to install than other ventilation systems, but it has a payback period of several months to three years. According to the U.S. Department of Energy, most energy recovery ventilation systems can recover about 70 to 80 percent of the energy in the exiting air and deliver that energy to the incoming air. However, they are most cost effective in climates with extreme winters or summers and where fuel costs are high. In mild climates, the cost of the additional electricity needed to run the recovery system fans may exceed the savings from not having to condition the supply air.

Adding insulation

Insulation directly affects the temperature of your building and the function of the building envelope. A poorly insulated building envelope will not efficiently retain heat in the building during the cold winter months or cool air during hot summer months.

In addition to modifying your HVAC system, you will need to examine how efficiently the heat and air conditioning produced by the HVAC system is maintained in the building. Without completely renovating a building and stripping it down to its bare structure, it is difficult to significantly change the efficiency of the building envelope. The tighter the building envelope — meaning the fewer cracks and gaps in the building — the more efficiently it will keep heat and cool air in the building.

Sealing cracks and gaps, replacing windows, and adding insulation during a renovation project can tighten the building envelope. Heat rises, so adding insulation to the roof is the most effective way to keep the heat from escaping, reducing the need for heat from the HVAC system.

Replacing windows

Replacing old windows is one way to tighten the building envelope and keep heat and air from leaking out of the building. Depending on the quality of your windows and your budget, you might decide to seal the cracks and gaps in between the windows and between the walls and ceilings instead. This will reduce waste and control leakage.

Manufacturers are now making double- and triple-paned windows, which significantly improve energy efficiency compared to single-pane windows by keeping in more heat and air. Windows with low emissivity, or low-E, glass are also an option. These windows include a very thin coating of metal to reflect heat and lower the condensation levels on the glass. Look at the window frames as well; aluminum and steel frames are not always the best choice for maintaining building temperature. Wood or fiberglass frames are less likely to conduct heat or cold to the outside of the building.

Seal Cracks and Gaps with an Environmentally Friendly Sealant

Using an environmentally friendly sealant to seal cracks and gaps around older windows and throughout the rest of your building is an excellent low-cost way to increase energy efficiency. Companies like OSI make adhesives and sealants for these purposes and have the **Greenguard®** approval, a certification from the Greenguard Environmental Institute that certifies products for low chemical emissions.

Improving Indoor Air Quality

Indoor air quality affects building occupants directly every day. Many of the processes of improving energy efficiency, such as replacing windows, sealing cracks, and adding insulation, can have a negative effect on the indoor air quality, which is why it is very important to use low-emitting and low-VOC products during a renovation. Low-VOC products, including paints, office furniture, carpets, finishes, adhesives, and flooring, help to maintain the indoor air quality of your building. This is especially important if you are renovating while occupants are in the building. With little ventilation in office buildings, toxins and chemicals emitted from paint, carpeting, and even furniture can get trapped inside the building and create a toxic environment.

The floors, carpeting, paints, and ceilings in many older buildings contain toxic chemicals. These items should be replaced instead of reused. Contractors should safely remove them from the building to protect building occupants from exposure to toxic dust or fumes that might be released into the air.

CASE STUDY: STARTING SMALL IS KEY

Jay Black, director of architectural sustainability
Reckson Associates Realty; New York, NY
www.slgreen.com

For more than six years, Jay Black has served as the director of architectural sustainability for Reckson Associates Realty, which is part of the SL Green Company, a well-respected real estate developer and real estate management company based in New York. The company has a vast portfolio of high-end commercial buildings in areas including New York City and Connecticut and has been involved with green building for many years.

Black's job as the sustainability director for Reckson is to identify and integrate green building methods and materials into the company's projects. "At Reckson, we address the entire portfolio instead of focusing on one thing," Black said. "We realize there is a lot of opportunity on the macro level."

This opportunity equates to cost savings and conservation on a variety of levels. "It is a constant peeling back of layers to find initiatives that work for our company and that make sense business-wise," he added.

These initiatives have included things like implementing construction debris recycling programs, using more sustainable building materials, and integrating efficient mechanical systems to conserve water and energy. "It is not always money driven," Black said. "It is often about making the building process easier and preventing unnecessary waste." In fact, Reckson's experience with building green was born out of one simple process it integrated into its construction work: recycling. "We were recycling scrap metal," Black said, "and we realized there were more opportunities to take advantage of."

The company quickly began recycling other materials, like ceiling tiles. "We had to find a method and a strategy that worked for us," Black said. Reckson achieved this by finding local manufacturers to recycle large amounts of materials from construction projects. Because most of Reckson's projects are located in New York City, where space is limited, the company had to find a way to recycle materials without having to hold or process the materials on site. Some manufacturers, for instance, require materials be specifically packaged and prepared to be picked up. "When you are dealing with space limitations, you do not have space to shrink wrap," Black said.

Reckon's solution was to find local manufacturers who were willing to meet the company's specific recycling needs. One of these is a carpet manufacturer based in New Jersey. In the beginning, the company was achieving these recycling goals "at a very nominal additional cost," Black said. "Now it is cost-neutral and, in some instances, we are even saving money" by avoiding the fees to deposit debris in a landfill. Since 2007, the company has successfully recycled nearly 1 million feet of carpet and tile — about 400,000 square feet of each.

Beyond recycling, Reckson has incorporated dozens of processes to meet green goals, whether these goals include obtaining LEED certification or not. "We try to fold in as many LEED points as possible," Black said. However, obtaining LEED certification is not the primary motive in many of the company's building projects. Instead, the goals are to preserve resources and use more sustainable products and materials. The company believes these goals are achieved by not only using recycled materials and reducing its own waste, but also by working with socially responsible manufacturers. The company purchases carpeting for its buildings from Cambridge Carpets, a company that manufactures its carpeting products using wind energy.

One of Reckson's recent remodel projects, an older commercial office building in White Plains, New York, was completely transformed into a high efficiency, sustainable building through the incorporation of a variety of strategies. "We brought the building back down to its structure and gave it infrastructure upgrades, redesigned it, redid all the windows to get rid of all the cracks, and created a tighter building envelope," Black said.

Reckson also replaced some of the low-efficiency motors in the HVAC system with newer, high-efficiency ones, made modifications to the elevators in the building to enable them to operate more efficiently, and repainted the roof a lighter color. "We added 4 inches of insulation. This, in combination with the lighter color roof, reduced the heat gains," Black said.

Another important system Reckson addressed in the White Plains building was the lighting system. Reckson replaced the old lighting system with higher efficiency fixtures and bulbs. Instead of using the industry-standard three-lamp T8 fixtures for ceiling lighting (which uses 98 watts of power), Reckson installed two-lamp T5 fixtures (which uses only 56 watts of power). This small change had a significant impact on electricity costs over the long term. "Light quality is not reduced because the new fixtures put out more light per bulb," Black said. "Because of this, the fixtures can be placed father apart from each other." This reduces the amount of fixtures and bulbs needed throughout the building. Although the fixtures cost more than conventional ones, "any premium is reduced by the efficiency of the fixtures." The payback for the fixtures — the amount of time it takes to earn back the initial investment — is about four years.

Reckson also looked at the big picture and considered how much these lighting upgrades could save on a larger scale. The company analyzed 20 buildings in its portfolio and replaced, upgraded, or retrofitted fixtures in the buildings. "We capitalized on incentives," Black said. The incentives included a 50 percent rebate from the local light and power company for the upgrades and retrofits. At the end of the day, Reckson would save more than $500,000 a year from these small changes. Because the project cost $1.4 million, the payback is just less than one and a half years.

Reckson is expanding on these efforts, and recently launched a mechanical retrofit pilot project that will analyze the mechanical systems of its buildings and determine what upgrades and retrofits can be made to improve the efficiency of these systems. "We are finding these amazing savings with quick paybacks," Black said. As for the future of green building, "there is a tremendous amount of opportunity that people do not realize is there. It is a matter of everyone being diligent. They key is to start small."

That is exactly how Reckson began, and in three short years, it has grown into a major player in the field of sustainable development.

Handling Asbestos and Lead during Renovation

Managing asbestos is a particular concern when remodeling an existing building to make it environmentally friendly. Hire an asbestos professional to determine whether asbestos is present and to supervise its removal. This is particularly crucial if you are doing renovations while occupants and employees are in the building. The following are EPA guidelines for handling and removing asbestos during the course of a remodel on a building:

If you hire a professional asbestos inspector

According to the EPA, you should ensure that an inspector completes a visual inspection of the area and collects samples to be analyzed in a lab. If the results indicate a presence of asbestos, the inspector should provide a written report that includes the location of the asbestos and how much of it is present. The report should also suggest procedures for removal and management of removal, as well as prevention of future exposure to asbestos. The inspector should monitor the removal process by making periodic visits to the construction site to ensure that the contractor follows the proper procedures for handling asbestos. The inspector should also inspect the area after the asbestos has been removed to ensure that no asbestos remains.

If you hire a corrective-action contractor

The EPA suggests checking with the Better Business Bureau and your local air pollution control board to ensure that the contractor has no safety violations or legal actions filed against it. Find out what notifications and procedures are required for asbestos removal by your municipal and state governments. Also, check with your EPA regional office (**www.epa.gov/epahome/regions.htm**) as well as your local Occupational Safety and Health Administration (OSHA) office (**www.osha.gov**) about specific requirements.

Your contract should stipulate that the contractor must use the appropriate asbestos removal equipment and that workers must use masks and gloves. This clause will protect you from any lawsuit arising from workers or contractors being exposed to the asbestos. The contract should state that the removal procedure as well as the clean-up process must adhere to all federal, state, and local requirements and regulations for asbestos removal. Inform the contractor that he or she will be required to provide written proof that all procedures were followed correctly.

Monitor the contractor's work to ensure that he or she does not expose other areas of your office building to asbestos dust. The area where asbestos is being removed should be sealed off to prevent the contamination of other parts of the building. Your heating and air conditioning systems should be turned off when the asbestos removal is in progress. Ensure the area of contamination is clearly marked and that all building occupants stay clear of the site until the process is complete and the area is deemed safe. The EPA suggests that your contract require the contractor to "apply a wetting agent to the asbestos material with a hand sprayer that creates a fine mist before removal. Wet fibers do not float in the air as easily as dry fibers and will be easier to clean up."

Monitor the removal process to ensure that, once it is removed, the contaminated material is not broken into smaller pieces, which would create further contamination by releasing asbestos fibers. Contaminated pieces should be removed from the site in whole parts. Monitor the clean-up process and ensure the contaminated area is cleaned up and deemed safe for occupancy. Contractors should use wet rags, mops, sponges, and high efficiency particulate air (HEPA) vacuum cleaners to clean up any dust or debris. A wetting agent should be used to minimize the release of asbestos fibers in the air. All equipment to be disposed of, including workers' clothing, gloves, and masks, should be placed in sealed plastic bags with labels stating that they are contaminated with asbestos.

A third party not associated with the original contractor who removed the asbestos should monitor the air quality after asbestos removal.

EPA Certification for Lead Removal

It is important to note that, beginning in April 2010, the law began requiring contractors be officially certified by the EPA and follow specific guidelines to handle lead removal. If you are a contractor and need to get certified for lead removal, visit **www.epa.gov/lead/pubs/renovation.htm** to download the proper forms to become certified.

These are the EPA guidelines for handling and removing lead during the course of a remodel on a building:

- Use signs to keep residents and pets out of the work area.

- Remove furniture and belongings, or cover them securely with heavy plastic sheeting.

- Use heavy plastic sheeting to cover floors and other fixed surfaces like large appliances in the work area.

- When appropriate, use heavy plastic sheeting to separate the work area from the rest of the residence.

- Close and seal vents in the work area and, if necessary, turn off forced-air heating and air conditioning systems.

- Mark off the work area to keep non-workers away.

- Cover the ground and plants with heavy plastic sheeting.

- Close windows and doors near the work area.

- Move or cover play areas near the work area.

- Mist areas before sanding, scraping, drilling, and cutting.

- Score paint before separating components.

- Pry and pull apart components instead of pounding and hammering.

- Always use a shroud with HEPA vacuum attachment when using power tools and equipment.

- Put trash and debris in heavy-duty plastic bags.

- Wrap waste building components, such as windows and doors, in heavy plastic sheeting and tape shut.

- Ensure everything, including tools, equipment, and even workers, is free of dust and debris before leaving the work area.

- HEPA vacuum the work area.

- Wash up and change out of work clothes before you and your workers go home.

- Remind residents to stay out of the work area.

Following the job completion, contractors are required to:

- Remove the plastic sheeting carefully, mist with water, fold dirty side in, tape shut, and dispose of it.

- HEPA vacuum all surfaces, including walls.

- Wash the work area with a general purpose cleaner.

- Check your work carefully for lead dust because hazardous amounts may be minute and not easily visible. If you see any dust or debris, then reclean the area.

- Perform a final clean-up check. Use disposable cleaning cloths to wipe the floor of the work area and compare them to a cleaning verification card to determine if the work area was adequately cleaned.

The guidelines stipulate that contractors do not use the following when removing lead:

- Open flame burning or torching

- Sanding, grinding, planing, needle gunning, or blasting with power tools unless equipped with a shroud and HEPA vacuum attachment

- A heat gun at temperatures greater than 1100 degrees Fahrenheit

How to Safely Dispose of Unsafe Materials

The U.S. Army Corps of Engineer's publication *Unified Facilities Criteria* is a helpful document that explains the best ways to dispose of building construction and demolition debris and prevent this material from entering landfills. The document can be accessed at **www.wbdg.org/ccb/DOD/UFC/ufc_1_900_01.pdf**. The Field Guide for Residential Remodelers, prepared by the National Association of Home Builders (NAHB) Research Center, provides guidance for the removal of debris as well. Although intended for residential remodeling projects, the guide is a helpful resource for determining cost-effective and environmentally friendly methods of disposing of construction debris. It can be accessed at **www.epa.gov/osw/conserve/rrr/imr/cdm/pubs/remguide.pdf**.

Recycling and Reusing Materials

The EPA provides guidelines for reducing costs and waste during the remodeling of a commercial building. Before you begin your remodeling project, consult your local builders association, solid waste department, and state environmental agency about the process of debris removal and recycling. They will provide you with information on recycling materials to reduce large amounts of waste. You may be able to reuse certain materials in your remodel. What you cannot reuse, you should consider donating to a deconstruction auction in which contractors and other building professionals purchase recyclable materials for use in building projects.

Organizations that solicit salvaged building materials.

ReUse People (**www.thereusepeople.org**) is a nonprofit that seeks to reduce waste in landfills by salvaging it and donating or selling it to businesses and individuals. It also donates materials to low-income families to aid them in building or remodeling their homes. You can also donate materials to Habitat for Humanity, which builds homes for low-income families and raises money by selling donated building materials.

Before purchasing new products, consider reusing products that have been salvaged. Reclaimed products such as cabinets, doors, windows, light fixtures, and wood for flooring and framing, can be purchased for much less than new ones.

Historical Preservation and Green Renovation

Sustainable preservation combines the principles of green building with the need to preserve a community's cultural heritage. Many historical buildings were built before the existence of modern construction materials, from natural, locally available products. They were also built to use daylight and natural ventilation and cooling, though alterations to the original building envelope have obliterated some of these features. A green rehabilitation of a historical building seeks to incorporate energy-saving technologies while preserving as much as possible of the original structure's aesthetic and cultural characteristics. *The following sections discuss the differences in priorities for sustainable preservation over ordinary green building renovation.*

Repair rather than replace

Wherever possible, repair and restore the building's original components, including hardware, flooring, wood and masonry, and furniture.

Redeploy the green features of the original structure

Buildings constructed before the advent of electricity and air conditioning had architectural elements that are now considered green, such as breezeways, shutters, awnings, chimneys, and operable windows. The first high-rise buildings provided light and ventilation through interior courtyards and shafts. Green restoration seeks to reinstate these elements and to uncover natural wood floors and ceilings.

Work closely with local authorities

Remain in contact with local regulatory authorities from the planning stage through completion to ensure that your design complies with building codes, zoning regulations, and the requirements of historical preservation agencies.

Look for grants and incentives to help finance the project

A green building renovation may qualify not only for green tax credits, but also for grants that support historical preservation. Do not miss any opportunity to get financing for the additional costs of restoring a historical property.

Look for ways to expand your project

If your building is situated in a historic district, look for ways to expand the project to neighboring sites. The same materials and techniques used on your building can be applied to similar buildings, and the overall cost can be lowered.

Before you hire a professional

Because the systems, methods, and considerations for green building differ so much from conventional building, it is wise to determine a professional's experience with green building before signing a hiring contract.

Consider the information in the following sections before hiring a professional.

His or her experience with and general knowledge of green building

Many green building professionals get into the business because they truly care about the environment and are passionate about the overall process and what green buildings can attain. Talk with the professional about general green building concepts — after you have familiarized yourself with them — and get a sense of how familiar he or she is with low-VOC paints, subfloor ventilation systems, and other green design elements and processes.

Samples of commercial office building projects he or she has worked on

This is the best way to gauge his or her experience and the kinds of processes, systems, and green building elements with which he or she is familiar.

Familiarity with LEED

If you are seeking LEED certification, the contractor, designers, engineers, and other professionals you hire should at least be familiar with LEED and the various requirements for certification. Having an LEED AP serve as a LEED consultant throughout the course of your project is the best way to ensure you are building in accordance with LEED requirements for certification.

His or her involvement in the business of green building and knowledge of its future

Inquire whether the professional is a member of any local or national green building coalitions or associations and what his or her involvement is in the overall business of green building.

Experience working on a green team

Green projects involve much more teamwork than traditional building projects. Experience working on a green project with other green professionals is important. Everyone should be able to work well together to meet the building's objectives.

His or her recommendations for or comments on your project

The first time you speak with a green building professional, you should discuss your general needs and outline the goals of your project. Ask how the professional can achieve these goals for you and what recommendations he or she has.

CHAPTER 10:
Financing Your Green Project

Funding and financing opportunities are available
for green and sustainable building projects, from local, state, and federal
incentives and from private and public sources. Because the environmental,
financial, and health benefits of green building are very apparent, governments
want to encourage businesses, companies, and corporations to build green.

Although more financial institutions and lenders are recognizing the value
of sustainable building and providing funding opportunities, there are still
some hurdles to overcome before such funding becomes widely available.
Lenders often find it difficult to assess the value of a green buildings and
how viable the project will be. The risk involved in a conventional building
project is easy to calculate because the associated costs, construction times,
and leasing times are well documented. Because the concept of green design
and construction is so new and unfamiliar, lenders perceive the risk as higher.
Lenders also find it difficult to translate factors like energy and water savings
into a tangible number. Determining the financial viability of a green project
and the return on investment for these projects is more difficult. As more
studies and evidence emerge to document the high rates of return on green
buildings, it will become easier to secure funding for a green building project.

A project's viability is determined using a valuation model that weighs all the risks against the potential for annual financial gain. A lender determines the amount of a loan by looking at the loan-to-value ratio — the ratio of the loan amount to the value of the property. The lower the ratio, the lower the risk for the lender, and the better the interest rates he or she is willing to offer. For almost two decades, green building advocates have been gathering data and promoting studies on the financial returns realized from green buildings to provide financial markets with solid evidence of the increased potential of green buildings to realize savings on energy and maintenance, demand higher rents, and bring higher prices on the real estate market.

Funding for green projects can be obtained from financial institutions and banks, as well as private investment companies and the federal and local government. More large banks like Wells Fargo are offering green funding as they become more comfortable with the financial benefits and high return on investment of green building. Wells Fargo has funded about $3 billion for dozens of LEED projects around the country. Some small community banks, such as Green Bank in Houston, Texas, specialize in sustainable community development.

Private funding options

Private and nonprofit organizations such as the Bridgemer Group also offer green building funding and investing opportunities because these organizations wish to tap into the financial benefits of sustainable construction. Some companies that offer funding for green building are listed below. Many financiers have specific restrictions and guidelines for receiving funding. For instance, some will only consider projects that are seeking LEED certification, while others focus specifically on nonprofits.

The amount of funding available for a certain project depends on the company, what types of funding it offers, and the specific needs of your project. Evolution Partners provides loan programs that focus on construction, short-term financing, or long-term financing. Once you have identified the specific financial needs of your project, look for companies that offer funding to meet those needs. Some companies that offer funding for green building are:

- **The Bridgemer Group (www.bridgemer.com/greenbuildings. html)** is a global real estate investment company that offers financing options for green renovation project and new green buildings. According to its website, the group created the program partly because "the usual sources of capital do not necessarily place the appropriate valuation on green features that make buildings more hospitable to their environment and the people inside and outside."

The Process of Obtaining Funding

According to Daniel Shindleman of the Bridgemer Group, "The process of obtaining green funding begins with identifying debt and equity providers interested in green buildings. Bridgemer has for many years been a green funding source because we genuinely believe in the benefits of green buildings to those people working, living, visiting, and investing in green buildings, as well as the outside community at large. Our process begins with a business plan including financial analysis, an assessment of the major project participants, schedule, and other project-specific and community matters. We strive to assist sponsors to create viable projects. A project is viable when it contributes positively to all stakeholders, namely building occupants, owners, the neighborhood, and the community. The best hint in seeking funding is to be prepared with a stress-tested business plan and commitment to see the project through to completion."

- **Bridgeway Capital Lending (www.bridgewaycapital.org)** provides loans to green companies seeking LEED certification in western Pennsylvania.

- **Evolution Partners (www.evolutionpartners.com)** specializes in high-end green real estate projects by leading developers around the country. It provides construction financing, bridge loans, and short- and long-term loans.

- **The Heinz Endowments (www.heinz.org)** provides endowment opportunities for green companies and sustainable development projects seeking LEED certification in the Pittsburgh, Pennsylvania, area.

Where to Look

Funding Green Buildings (**www.fundinggreenbuildings.com**), a website dedicated specifically to providing information and resources to companies looking for grants and other funding to construct green buildings, offers books, seminars, and other tools to help builders optimize their funding potential.

Government funding options

Federal and local governments offer a number of incentives to offset the costs of many green building initiatives. Although this is primarily achieved through tax rebates and credits, which will be discussed in the next section, there are some grants and loan programs. The following resources provide information on these opportunities:

- **The Department of Energy (www1.eere.energy.gov/financing):** Through the Department of Energy, the federal government offers several specific programs for green building funding, including:

  » **Energy Efficiency and Renewable Energy program:** The program offers funding opportunities for green energy projects for businesses, as well as a loan guarantee program.

  » **The American Recovery and Reinvestment Act of 2009:** This was established to stimulate the economy and encourage recovery after the 2008 market crash, which ultimately affected the development of infrastructure in the United States. Funds are available for businesses, for-profit, and nonprofit organizations that are investing in green energy practices and building green.

  » **The Local Government Commission (www.lgc.org/freepub/ energy/funding.html):** This website lists federal and state financing programs along with a brief description and link for each program.

The EPA also provides a comprehensive list of additional funding opportunities by state and geographical region (**www.epa.gov/greenbuilding/tools/ funding.htm**). Another good resource for finding available government grants and loans for business projects is Business.gov (**www.business.gov**).

Tax and financial incentives

Tax credits and rebates for green building are available at the local, state, and federal levels. These include property tax incentives, construction and design incentives, and rebates for increased energy efficiency of HVAC systems.

Research the local, state, and federal programs that correspond to the objectives of your project to see whether it qualifies. The Database of State

Incentives for Renewable Energy (**www.dsireusa.org**) allows you to search by geographic region and type of incentive.

One Step Farther

IRS Notice 2006-52: Deduction for Energy Efficient Commercial Buildings (**www.irs.gov/pub/ irs-drop/n-06-52.pdf?cm_sp=ExternalLink-_-Federal- _-Treasury**) and Internal Revenue Bulletin: 2008-14 (**www.irs.gov/irb/2008-14_IRB/ar12.html**) provide detailed instructions for obtaining tax credits for energy efficiency in a commercial building.

Here is a sample of some of the available federal financial incentives:

- **The Solar and Geothermal Business Energy Tax Credit.** Commercial buildings that incorporate solar and geothermal power for heat and electricity can qualify for a credit of more than $25,000 a year. This tax credit was expanded significantly as part of the Energy Policy Act of 2005 and was expanded further under the *American Recovery and Reinvestment Act of 2009.*

- **Department of Energy Tax Deductions:** Through the U.S. Department of Energy, building owners, tenants, and designers (only applicable to designers of government buildings) can receive a deduction of up to $1.80 per square foot of building space for green lighting systems, HVAC systems, and the exterior of the building. These are available for buildings constructed through 2013. This tax deduction was created as part of the *Energy Policy Act of 2005.*

- **Renewable Electricity Production Tax Credit:** This credit, initiated under the *Energy Policy Act of 2002,* applies to companies investing in alternative energy, such as wind, hydroelectric, geothermal, and hydrokinetic power.

CASE STUDY: A DETAILED LOOK AT FEDERAL INCENTIVES

MELISSA COLLAR, PARTNER
WARNER NORCROSS & JUDD LL P
GRAND RAPIDS, MI
WWW.WNJ.COM

Melissa Collar, a partner at law firm Warner Norcross & Judd LLP, provides an overview of some of the federal incentives available for green commercial buildings. *She is profiled in a Case Study in Chapter 3, which focuses on some of the legal issues of green building.* About tax and financial incentives, she explains:

The federal government is offering federal tax credits to promote commercial energy efficiency in new or rehabilitated commercial buildings. The program, which offers a sliding scale of tax deductions based on meeting certain standards, requires that new or improved construction meet or exceed the American Society of Heating, Refrigerating, and Air-Conditioning Engineers, or ASHRAE 90.1 standards for efficiency.

Owners or tenants of new or existing private commercial buildings are eligible to apply for the one-time tax credits under the Energy Policy Act of 2005, while architects and designers of new or existing public buildings may also apply. Buildings may meet one, two, or all three energy-efficiency standards, securing up to $1.80 per square foot in tax credits. Specifically the following standards apply:

- HVAC and hot water systems must be 50 percent better than ASHRAE 90.1 and can earn a credit of $0.60 per square foot.

- Building envelopes are 50 percent better than ASHRAE 90.1 and can earn a credit of $0.60 per square foot.

- Interior lighting systems that are 25 to 50 percent better than ASHRAE 90.1 can earn a credit of $0.30 to 0.60 per square foot on a sliding scale.

"Another federal program to promote energy efficiency is the Community Development Block Grants. Though these are federal dollars, they are distributed by the state at the local level by municipalities and communities. The majority of funds are being used to assist with rehabilitating public, and, in some cases, private buildings to improve their energy efficiency. To date, municipalities have done many different things, including taking lump sums and upgrading windows or HVAC systems in public buildings and establishing low-interest revolving loan programs for investments in private buildings.

"Though not a federal program, many states around the country have adopted net metering programs that allow consumers to add small wind or solar installations to their home, connect with the local energy grid, generate a portion of their own electricity, and receive a credit on their monthly utility bills. In Michigan, this program applies only to very small installations of no more than 20 kilowatts. Utilities are required to connect interested consumers and may charge a small interconnection fee."

Many states offer additional tax cuts for specific green building practices and allocate funds for grants to support water conservation and the use of renewable energy. Check with your local building department for information on the incentives offered by your state and municipality. Your local government website probably lists incentive programs on its website.

Examples of green state tax credits:

- **Renewable Energy Systems Exemption (Oregon):** This program offers property tax exemption for residential and commercial buildings for up to 100 percent for the use of renewable energy. This exemption was enacted in 1976 and currently extends through 2012.

- **The Wood Energy Production Credit (Missouri):** This program offers up to $5 per ton for companies that use biomass technology, which involves "processing forestry industry residues into fuel," according to the State of Missouri Department of Natural Resources Energy Center. This credit was created in 1997 and currently extends through 2013.

- **The New Jersey SmartStart Buildings New Construction and Retrofits Rebate Program:** This incentive is intended for commercial, education, government, industrial, and construction sectors. It provides a rebate for energy efficient water heaters, lighting systems, furnaces, boilers, heat pumps, air conditioners, and energy management systems. The amount varies by system.

As green building becomes more prominent and the industry grows, more incentives will be established by the federal, state, and local governments to encourage the implementation of green building practices. Always check with your municipality and with your state and the federal government before beginning a green project to ensure you are up to date on all of the incentives available and their accompanying requirements and restrictions.

A look at costs

The costs involved in your green project will depend greatly on your building's location, the materials available in your geographic area, what green systems and materials you are incorporating, and what strategies you will use to green your building. Some aspects of green design, such as site orientation and window and overhang placement, cost little or nothing. Other sustainable green design features, such as an insulated shell, may cost more to build, but these costs will be offset by savings on energy used to heat and cool the building. Right sizing of infrastructure and mechanical systems involves planning for future needs during the design process and incorporating the components and mechanical systems that will accommodate those needs in the original design. This saves money in the long term, by minimizing the additional expense of future expansions or modifications. Dimensional planning — creating a design that minimizes the amount of framing, plumbing, carpeting, or glazing needed to achieve the building's objectives — saves on the cost of materials.

Remember to consider the long-term cost savings involved with building green and not just the initial investment, which can typically be up to 3 percent higher than a conventional project. This percentage is becoming lower every year as green building becomes more widely accepted, and manufacturers produce lower-cost materials.

☀ Best return on investment strategies of green design

According to **www.greenandsave.com**, a website detailing the cost savings for various home and office green projects, the following green design, remodel, and retrofit strategies may yield the following returns on investment:

- **Installing compact fluorescent lighting and occupancy sensors:** This can yield a return on investment of more than 100 percent, with the up-front costs earned back in less than one year. Replacing office exit signs with CFL light bulbs can yield a 90-percent return on investment alone. Installing sensors can yield a 43-percent return on investment, and costs can be paid back in 2.3 years.

- **Retrofitting the HVAC system:** Sealing airflow ducts around your office and installing weather stripping — a tight-fitting material that reduces heat and air loss — around windows and doors can yield a 55-percent return on investment and be paid back in less than two years. Replacing a furnace can yield a 15-percent return on investment and be made back in less than seven years.

- **Reducing paper consumption:** Switching from paper towels to electronic hand dryers in bathrooms can yield almost a

120-percent return on investment, while reducing paper use for office faxes and printing can yield an astonishing 312-percent return on investment.

- **Installing on-demand water heaters:** This can yield 37.8-percent return on investment and be made back in less than 3 years.

Strategies that reduce energy consumption usually offer the best tangible returns on investment for green building. These strategies do not have to be costly or complicated: replacing light bulbs with CFLs or LEDs and installing sensors can pay for itself in just a few months and yield significant ROIs. You should also consider your company's intangible needs when assessing a green project. Increased worker satisfaction and productivity, or customer and investor loyalty due to your company's reputation for environmental responsibility are part of the returns you can expect from a green building project.

CHAPTER 11:
Making Your Green Building Work

After your building is complete, it is time to create and implement strategies and processes to support all the systems and features that make your building green. Without these strategies and processes, as well as full cooperation from your employees, the building will not achieve its optimal level of function and sustainability. You do not want to undermine your investment of both time and money by not following through with maintenance. This chapter discusses some of the ways to ensure the long-term sustainability of your green building.

Greening Your Office from Top to Bottom

Changing the way employees think about their work environment can be challenging, especially if you are instituting new processes that have never existed before. If employees are used to driving to work, for instance, it may be difficult to encourage them to take public transportation. Incentives in the form of cash and recognition help to educate and motivate employees. Even though employees may be reluctant to take public transportation because it is less convenient; for instance, they may be more willing if you offer them a cost incentive by paying for half of their commute. More incentives like these will be discussed later in the chapter.

Before you can motivate employees, however, you must establish what you are motivating them to do. Determine what you want from your employees and, ultimately, from your green facility. Here are some basic ways to create a green environment in your workplace.

Institute programs to reduce, reuse, and recycle

The three main principles of a recycling program are reducing consumption, reusing what you can, and recycling what you cannot. In California, the state has instituted specific guidelines on its website (**www.calrecycle. ca.gov/ReduceWaste/office**), which outlines a program that can be used as a model for creating your own program. Check with your local municipality to determine the recycling requirements are in your area. The reduce, reuse, and recycle model can also be used to assess and reduce energy consumption, water usage, and your carbon footprint.

☀ Reduce

- Set your photocopiers and printers to print on both sides by default. This will prevent wasted paper.

- Make computer files, not paper files, when possible. There are numerous free or inexpensive software programs, like Stickies or NoteWhen, which can reduce or eliminate the need for sticky notes and note pads. These programs, as well as most electronic calendars and task lists, can be set to remind you of some event or task with a special message at any time in the future. Small handheld computers and smart phones are especially good for reminding, note-taking, calendar scheduling, and other paper-consuming tasks.

- Recent advances in computer software make it easy to create documents that are encrypted, password protected, and safe from either unauthorized access or alteration. This can be done with very sophisticated free and low-cost software. Electronic signatures are widely accepted and legally binding. Over the long run, electronic files save floor and file space. In most cases, electronic documents are safer than paper. Backup copies can be easily transferred to high-capacity low-cost removable media, such as compact discs or removable hard drives, and stored off site. Backups can also be transferred over secure Internet connections for off-site storage.

- Decrease your paper trail. Institute a paperless policy. Prohibit employees from printing out e-mails, and use electronic faxes instead of traditional paper ones. Eliminating company memos, newsletters, notices, and Christmas cards can also help achieve this objective. Create an electronic network instead for internal communication. Take steps to reduce the amount of junk mail that your office receives. This may not yield a cost savings for you, but it will make a difference to your impact on the environment.

- Reduce your carbon footprint. Look for ways to reduce your carbon footprint and carbon dioxide emissions. The best way is to reduce the number of employees driving to work. Also assess company travel — both airplane and car travel — and consider implementing strategies such as video conferencing, for example, instead of in-person meetings. This will not only reduce your carbon emissions from travel but will also save money.

- Replace old appliances and equipment. Installing ENERGY STAR appliances and equipment that is more energy efficient will save you money on energy consumption and reduce your impact on the environment.

☀ Reuse

- Reuse envelopes and send them through the mail again whenever possible. Some businesses do not like to send some types of mail in used envelopes because they wish to maintain their corporate image. However, many businesses conduct a significant amount of mailing in which corporate image is not a factor. For this type of mailing, use labels to cover the old address on used envelopes. Some companies sell reused labels for envelopes, which have a discrete message at the bottom explaining that this envelope was reused to save trees.

- Have each staff members set aside paper that they use on only one side, so that it can be reused for printing drafts in your printer, or glued together to make scratch pads. As staff accumulates paper, they can transfer it to a centrally located storage box, possibly next to a printer or photocopiers.

- Use padding compound, the glue that holds paper together in tablets, to make scratch pads from your paper that was used only on one side. Padding compound is available from many office supply stores. You can clamp the edge of the paper together with blocks of wood and C-clamps, or you can invest in a small paper padding press. Several types are sold for well under $150.

- Buy recycled toner cartridges and send your spent toner cartridges to an office supply store to be recycled. Commercially, this is referred to as recycling, but it is actually a form of reuse.

- Encourage staff to use reusable coffee mugs when they pick up coffee in the morning on their way into the office. Hang a mug reuse poster in your break room.

- Invest in rechargeable batteries and battery chargers for digital cameras, flashlights, and other small devices.

Printing Greener

Greenprint is a computer program that helps identify pieces of a document that can be deleted or truncated before printing. It detects potential nonrelevant text and illustrations, and then highlights and deletes them to reduce the size of the document printed. The software also enables you to make PDFs out of your documents, which may eliminate the need to print altogether. To learn more about the software, visit **www.printgreener.com**.

Recycle

- Determine which material you can recycle. Different municipalities have different recycling guidelines for what they will pick up and how this material needs to be handled. Check on the guidelines for your area, and then assess how practical it is to recycle these materials.

- Find someone to pick up the material. Look for local recycling, refuse, or waste disposal businesses in your Yellow Pages or online. Call around to see who can offer you the best pickup service. Each vendor will have his or her own requirements and conditions. Schedules and prices can be negotiated.

- Put recycling bins around your office, and get staff to participate. Most vendors will supply large bins to keep in the yard. Some will provide smaller bins to place around the office. You can buy your own bins from an office supply catalogue. Encourage your managers to get staff members to participate.

Encourage employees to go green

Encouraging employees to participate and support the green systems and processes implemented in the office is essential to maintaining a green work environment. Here are some sample incentives that can be offered to employees to encourage them to go green.

- **Public transportation, carpooling, and bike riding incentive:** Depending on where your building is located, there are a number of tax incentives for employees who use public transportation to get to and from work. Know about these, and educate employees on how much money they can save by taking public transportation instead of driving. You can also create a carpooling sign-up program that is accessible to all employees and groups employees according to where they live. At Google, employees who do not drive to work can earn money throughout the year from the company to be donated to a charity of the employee's choice.

- **Conservation incentives:** Canadian company LoyaltyOne has tapped into this concept of motivating employees to conserve at work and at home. Employees are pitted against each other to see which floor can make the most positive changes at work and at home. The floor with the highest number of changes receives free lunches, giveaways, and other incentives throughout the year. The incentive motivates workers to meet your bottom line in a fun, interactive way.

- **Green renovation incentives:** Some green companies have extended employee incentives beyond work to home life. Companies like NRG Systems offer employees money toward home renovations to make their homes greener. For example, the company will contribute $1,000 per year toward the installation of a solar hot water system.

- **Stay-fit incentives:** Some companies like Green Mountain Energy offer employees incentives to exercise. This company organizes local group hikes and workouts as well as deeply discounted gym memberships.

Whatever incentives you use to motivate employees, integrate a program for feedback and comments so that they can voice their opinions on how well each incentive is working and make suggestions.

CASE STUDY: PASSIONATE EMPLOYEES MAKE ALL THE DIFFERENCE

Debbie Baxter,
chief sustainability officer
LoyaltyOne
www.loyaltyone.com

It is little wonder that LoyaltyOne, a marketing and customer loyalty company based in Canada, was recently voted one of the top 50 employers to work for. As part of its significant efforts to become a green company, LoyaltyOne has integrated a variety of techniques, systems, and processes that have not only saved money and reduced its impact on the environment but also have stimulated employees to get involved as well. "Our employees are very passionate about our green initiatives," said Debbie Baxter, chief sustainability officer at the company.

Getting employees involved in the company's movement has paid off for LoyaltyOne. The company has two LEED certified buildings, one in Mississauga and one in Calgary. Employee involvement in initiatives has resulted in increased productivity, especially at the company's Mississauga location, which has LEED gold certification. The building has Canada's largest solar photovoltaic power generation system on its roof, consisting of 800 solar panels that generate 165 kilowatts of energy during every hour of sunlight. Employees can see the 23 invertors located throughout the building measuring the energy generated by the solar panels, and even compete to see which ones will generate the most in one day.

In addition to the solar panels, the Mississauga building has a thermal system to generate hot water, as well as light sensors, motion detectors, and solar tubes to decrease electricity consumption from lighting. The solar tubes are reflective fixtures resembling typical light fixtures that run through the center of the building on the ceiling. Sunlight and natural daylight are reflected off the tubes to illuminate a space. "Even on a cloudy day, they shine," Baxter said. The building also instituted a recycling program with a popular coffee house in the area to collect employee coffee cups and lids from the store and bring them back to the coffee shop, where they are recycled and made into carrying trays for coffee. "Our Mississauga building is a zero percent waste facility."

At the company's Toronto location, employees can participate in a transit pass program that offers a significant discount for taking public transportation instead of driving to work. The company found that employees still needed access to cars for off-site business meetings, however, so they bought a fleet of smart cars, small three-cylinder cars that are currently the most efficient cars on the road. "The employees see this as a perk," Baxter explains, because they get access to the cars for free and still receive a significant discount for using public transportation to commute to work. LoyaltyOne even branded the cars with its company logo, an additional way to promote itself.

LoyaltyOne has also teamed up with other organizations in an effort to get employees engaged. They recently teamed up with the World Wildlife Federation (WWF) to participate in its pilot Living Planet at Work program, which encourages employees to make "planet-friendly changes at home and at work," to decrease energy consumption and ultimately conserve resources and improve the planet. "Employees choose actions in their work and home life," Baxter said. At LoyaltyOne, different floors of employees compete with each other to see which floor can make the most changes at work and at home. The floor with the highest number of changes receives free lunches, giveaways, and other incentives.

At the Calgary location, similar programs have been integrated into the daily work life. Unlike the Mississauga building, the Calgary building was already silver LEED certified for its core and shell when LoyaltyOne moved in. "The envelope was certified, but the tenants had to get the interiors LEED certified," Baxter said, which is exactly what the company did. The result was better than the company initially expected. "One of the unexpected benefits was the quality of air. There was no smell in the air when we moved in." This contributed to employees' level of comfort and ultimately, their productivity.

With all these initiatives in their various locations, LoyaltyOne has four main objectives as a company: to reduce their carbon footprint, to create environmentally friendly facilities, to help employees live sustainable lives both at home and at work, and to adopt a leadership role and collaborate with other businesses, schools, and companies to promote sustainable development. By including employees in many of its incentives, it creates a sense of pride and purpose. "There is a tremendous sense of pride," Baxter said. "We get lots of employee feedback. We found that they are so proud of the work we have done, it really helps them feel engaged, and they are really proud to work here."

As for the future, LoyaltyOne has big plans. "In 2010, we are turning our focus internally," Baxter said. In addition to small changes like going paperless, the company has set a goal of having 85 percent of their staff in LEED certified buildings by the end of 2010.

"We are looking at the whole spectrum."

Pest Control

Commercially sprayed pesticides and pesticide bombs contaminate everything in an office space. They linger on flooring and walls and become imbedded in carpeting and other furnishings. The chemicals remain for several weeks afterward, and many pose serious health risks and significantly deteriorate the quality of your indoor air. Traditional forms of pest control can seriously threaten the health of your building occupants and your employees. Poor health from exposure to chemicals and toxins means more sick days and future liability, which means a loss of revenue for the company. As with all the other aspects of your green building, it is important to take a green approach to pest control.

Integrated pest management (IPM)

The EPA emphasizes the need for environmentally friendly products to handle insects and other pests. The current approach is called integrated pest management (IPM), defined by the EPA as "an effective and environmentally sensitive approach to pest management that relies on a combination of common-sense practices." IPM programs use pest-specific information, such as the pests' life cycles and their means of interacting with the environment. The information is combined with the least hazardous means of dealing with the pests in question. IPM applies to both agricultural and non-agricultural settings. The EPA recommends using these principles and practices in the home, garden, and the workplace. The practices are based on a four-tier approach. The steps include:

1. **Setting action thresholds:** Before taking any action in regards to pest control, IPM suggests determining the need for action and setting guidelines called an action threshold. This is the point at which pest conditions require action. A single pest sighting does not necessarily mean control is needed. The number of pests and the threat they pose should be taken into consideration.

2. **Monitoring and identifying pests:** According to the EPA, not all pests require control, so you will need to decide on an appropriate course of action, if you are going to take any. Many organisms are harmless, and some are even beneficial.

3. **Prevention:** The IPM approach suggests working to manage indoor and outdoor areas in a way that prevents pests from becoming a threat in the first place. This involves minimizing exposure of garbage, food, and other things that attract pests both on the interior and exterior.

4. **Control:** When pest control is necessary, the most cost-effective, least risky manner of handling or controlling the threat should be used.

CASE STUDY: WE STRIVE TO BE SOCIALLY RESPONSIBLE

Steven Brewster, sustainability
manager, Kimball® Office
www.kimballoffice.com

Kimball Office is a furniture designer and manufacturer that specializes in green and sustainable office furniture, from chairs and desks to tables and storage cabinets, with showrooms around the country. The company's sustainability manager, Steven Brewster, describes how the company strives to reduce the environmental impact of each product it manufactures, subsequently improve the indoor air quality of office spaces, and contribute to a healthier environment. "For 40 years, Kimball Office has manufactured sustainable office furniture, including desks, seating, and panel systems. Our products are manufactured with high recycled content using wood, steel, and aluminum. Kimball Office has always been committed to sustainable business practices, which is why we are actively involved in the U.S. Green Building Council (USGBC) and the Business and Institutional Furniture Manufacturers Association (BIFMA) Furniture Emissions Standards. More than 95 percent of Kimball Office products are BIFM-level certified," he said.

BIFMA certification measures the VOC emissions of furniture products and other factors to verify the impact the product has on the environment and the indoor air quality of a space. For products to be BIFMA certified, companies must submit to a third-party independent certification process that incorporates organizational, facility, and product-related aspects.

Although the company has been in business for 40 years, it is only recently that the company has seen a significant increased interest in green office building. "Recently, Kimball Office has seen more interest in office furniture contributing to the improved indoor air quality of office spaces and a renewed interest in the potential to recycle everything from packaging to the product itself at the end of its life cycle. Kimball Office is also seeing a growing interest in ways office furniture contributes to lowering a building's energy usage," he explained.

The company has also witnessed the changing trends over the past years as the movement to go green has gained momentum. "Over the years, Kimball Office has seen the size and layout of office furniture change to accommodate different styles of work. We have seen lower panel cubicle heights and more collaborative layouts and workstations. All these trends work together to reduce the amount of materials used and allow greater opportunities for employees to interact and share knowledge," Brewster said.

The lower cubicle walls are a result of increased use of natural sunlight as well as a more collaborative work environment. "Workplace collaboration has led to reducing cubical panel heights. Companies are realizing that to compete in the global economy, they must leverage the collective intelligence of their entire workforce. One way to accomplish this is to lower panel heights, which encourages employees to collaborate," Brewster said. "Obviously, there are some industries and functional areas within different businesses where privacy trumps collaboration. However, there are trade-offs that companies must consider when evaluating whether to lower panel heights, with the main one being visual and acoustical privacy. There is no one-size-fits-all solution."

Kimball has practiced what it preaches and has built its own office buildings and showrooms to meet LEED certification. The company has ten office buildings and showrooms across the country that are LEED certified and the company works hard to continuously improve its design and manufacturing process. "When designing our own office spaces with a goal of LEED certification, Kimball Office takes advantage of the recycled content of its products and packaging. The selection of furniture heights and surface materials offered by Kimball Office also play a part in creating open workspaces, which allows natural light to penetrate more deeply into the building and provide outdoor views to the occupants. The fact that Kimball Office systems products are Indoor Advantage™ Certified also contributed to the indoor air quality, and the high efficiency and LED task lighting contributes to energy efficiencies," Brewster said.

The manufacturing process at Kimball begins with design and the selection of materials and processes that minimize waste and reduce any environmental impact. "It is called design for the environment," Brewster said. "Once in production, all manufacturing processes are subject to Kimball Office's continuous improvement efforts, and all process changes are again evaluated to gauge any significant environmental aspects. This is a part of Kimball Office's ISO 14001 Environmental Management System, or EMS, where we routinely establish environmental improvement goals."

"Kimball Office takes pride in the fact that it manufactures durable products with a long life expectancy. One of the easiest ways to recycle product is to plan for its reuse in another project. We provide online disassembly instructions for our products, and engineer them so they can be disassembled at the end of their useful life with simple hand tools. Because Kimball Office products start their life with a high-recycled content and they are easily disassembled into their component types, they can easily be recycled in most markets," Brewster said.

To Kimball, one of the most important elements about manufacturing green products is commitment and involvement of the entire company. "We have a strong heritage of environmental stewardship and that heritage encompasses every functional area of the company, from the design of products and processes to our procurement practices, recycling, waste reduction, and our continuous improvement efforts. Operating as a socially responsible and sustainable company has always been part of our culture," Brewster said.

The materials used in Kimball products are also carefully selected. "Kimball Office offers a number of textiles made from renewable materials, and the option of Forest Stewardship Council (FSC)-certified wood on select product series. FCS-certification provides a chain of custody assurance that products come from sources practicing responsible long-term and sustainably managed forestry," Brewster said. "All products are fabricated from recycled and recyclable materials including metal, wood, glass, and aluminum, all of which are highly recyclable in most major markets. Surface materials options include 100 percent recyclable fabrics, and packaging is 100 percent recyclable. Nearly all products are created using recycled, renewable, and reclaimed materials. This includes guest, lounge, office, and executive seating, as well as panel systems, desks, independent and open workstations, and tables."

The company has been very successful in large part due to its long-term commitment to sustainability in every phase of production. "For decades, Kimball Office has implemented waste-to-energy practices by capturing wood dust and wood waste in the fabrication process and incinerating it to generate steam for use in other manufacturing processes and to heat facilities," Brewster explained. "Wood fuel is a renewable energy source, and it has been determined to have a lower greenhouse gas emission than fossil fuel. Since the 1970s, Kimball Office has successfully removed more than 99 percent of particulate matter from the air of manufacturing facilities, which improves the air quality for employees. In the winter, purified heated air is returned into manufacturing areas, thus reducing the demand for energy and decreasing greenhouse gas emissions."

Part of Kimball's commitment to sustainability includes a corporate recycling center, which recycles 65 different items in more than 15 categories. "The amount of recycling at the plants has increased steadily since its inception in 2002. Recycled products include steel, aluminum, glass, oil, fabric, printer cartridges, various types of plastics, wood, cardboard, and electronic equipment. Since 1997, Kimball International, including Kimball Office, has recycled or reused approximately 85.8 percent of all solid waste generated from its facilities, and prevented more than 465,000 tons of waste from placement in landfills," Brewster said.

When it comes to renovating an existing building to become more environmentally friendly, Brewster advises each company to begin the process by researching and understanding how work is performed and what is needed to support the work of the employees. "This may include a need for various layouts within an office to provide collaborative areas as well as more private spaces for individual focus work," Brewster said. This may also mean providing more natural light and outside views to employees. "Studies have shown companies that provide well-designed spaces with natural lighting and views to the outside have higher retention rates and less absenteeism."

As green building becomes the way of the future, Kimball remains at the forefront of the sustainable manufacturing movement and remains committed to reducing pollution and carbon emissions as well as to creating a more sustainable world. "By incorporating sustainable thinking into the entire process, we can focus on eliminating pollution issues at the source whenever possible," Brewster said. That means a better work environment for employees and a better world for all of us.

At the very beginning of the design process, you must determine how your green building will impact company policies and daily operating procedures. Every aspect of your green design should be thought through to its ultimate consequences. If you plan to incorporate a large recycling program into your day-to-day operations but fail to designate an area of the building in which to accomplish this during the planning and construction process, the success of the program will be limited. The environmental benefits of spending millions of dollars on designing and building a green office space could be offset by a failure to implement simple procedures, such as recycling and turning off lights when they are not in use.

Hiring a green cleaning service

In addition to using green cleaning materials, you will also want to hire a green cleaning service for your building to maintain the integrity of the indoor environment. Companies such as Green Clean USA, a green cleaning company that provides commercial green cleaning services to the Washington, D.C., area, specialize in green cleaning. Some green cleaning companies are listed on **www.ecobusinesslinks.com/green-cleaning.htm**.

If you are hiring a cleaning service for the first time, interview a representative from the service either in person or over the phone. Here is a list of questions to ask:

- How long have you been in business?
- What do you charge? To determine what is reasonable, compare other services in your area.

- Are you bonded? If someone is bonded, it means the employee has insurance through a bonding company that will cover any damages incurred, either intentional or accidental.

- Do you carry insurance for any problems that may occur? If you are employing a single person, rather than a well-known company who may be connected with a bonding company, you should ask if he or she carries this type of insurance. You should make sure he or she is covered for damage and loss.

- How often do you come to the office and what days are you available to come?

- How many customers do you currently have?

- Is there any flexibility in scheduling if I have something come up and need to change my allotted time or have a function coming up?

- Have you ever had any customer complaints? If yes, what have they been?

- May I have a list of references? Make the effort to contact other customers and find out if they have been satisfied with the service. Remember to ask about the products that have been used and their effectiveness in other customer's homes.

- Do you provide any kind of guarantee for services provided?

You should also ask about the cleaning products and equipment that they use. Here is a list of questions to ask:

- Do the business owners consider themselves an eco-friendly cleaning service?

- Do you bring your own products or will you use products I have?

- If you bring your own cleaning products, what are they? You may need to supply your own products, especially if you want to use specific ones.

- Are the products and equipment you use considered environmentally safe? If you are unfamiliar with the products they will use, research the product names online.

- If the products are green, what is their effectiveness in cleaning pathogens such as staphylococcus and E. coli?

- Is your company green certified? If they use green products, they need to go through a certification process to receive a green seal of approval. Determine if each of the cleaning products has been certified.

CASE STUDY: WORKING IN A GREEN BUILDING MAKES ME EAGER TO WORK

Jodi Scott, ASHRAE communications manager

Jodi Scott is a communications manager at the headquarters of the American Society of Heating, Refrigerating, and Air-Conditioning Engineers (ASHRAE) in Atlanta, Georgia. The building underwent a renovation in 2008 to meet the standards and guidelines it provides to building professionals to help create a more sustainable environment. Scott describes some of the features of the buildings, saying, "Every work space has plenty of daylighting and views of the outside; it is a very bright place to work.

"I am proud that ASHRAE, which funds research and sets standards for energy efficient buildings and HVAC&R systems, has three advanced systems of its own. The first is variable refrigerant flow equipment, which, unlike traditional air-conditioning systems, can adjust the compressor speed and the amount of refrigerant in the system automatically to meet changes in the indoor load and conserve energy. The second is a geothermal system, where pumps harness energy stored near the surface of the earth, providing high-efficiency heating and cooling. The last is a dedicated outdoor air system, which has increased our ventilation rate by nearly 30 percent above current minimum requirements specified in ASHRAE's Standard 62.1 on ventilation and indoor air quality."

Beyond the HVAC&R systems, the building incorporates a variety of green features that make the building green. "ASHRAE also has lots of other green features. We do not call it the sustainability showcase for nothing. We have a bioswale system where runoff water is naturally filtered of pollutants. This system also gradually releases water back into the sewer system to prevent overload. We have a solar panel array on our roof that produces electricity during daylight hours, which we sell back to the utility grid," Scott said.

The building has also incorporated low-flow water fixtures to reduce water consumption. "We have reduced our water consumption by 53 percent for bathrooms — 46 percent in comparison to typical office buildings of this size — by using low-flow toilets and waterless urinals and by eliminating our landscaping irrigation system through proper plant selections. Our site is 45 percent above minimum code requirements for vegetated open space; we have a green roof and reduced the parking lot heat island effects (a real plus in our hot, humid climate!)." The building also incorporated a green cleaning program, an integrated pest management system, and a recycling program. Employees are also encouraged to use filtered water instead of bottled water dispensers. "Some 23 percent of the material cost for the project came from recycled content." This recycled content includes the marble wall panels in bathrooms.

So how have these green features benefited Scott and her employees? "We have access to much more daylight than prior to our renovation in 2008. Every workstation has a view to the outdoors, so whenever the sun is shining, so is our office. Before we renovated, few of us had views to outside. It is like going from a cave to working outside."

The improvements have made the employees' work life easier in many ways. "ASHRE has new recycling stations so recycling cans, plastic bottles, paper, and cardboard is as easy as taking a few steps. Other sustainable measures that also make our lives easier include dedicated parking spaces for carpools, fuel-efficient vehicles, changing rooms, and showers for those who exercise during their lunch hour or bike to work on warm days."

The improvements have also made employees' lives healthier and promoted a quality indoor work environment. "Providing a healthy and productive workplace and meeting space for employees and members was one of the major goals of renovating. Through measures such as views to the outside, better filtration, and increased ventilation, we have improved our indoor environmental quality, which has been tied through research into increased productivity. ASHRAE employs low-emitting materials, such as furnishings and carpet, throughout the building to reduce indoor air contaminants. This is equivalent to filtration in patient rooms in hospitals. We also have touch-free bathroom fixtures and reverse osmosis/UV sanitizing water coolers/warmers. In addition, a new patio area was added next to the green roof where we can go to decompress and enjoy the fresh air as needed."

According to Scott, the biggest benefit is pride. "I am proud that my organization renovated with a goal of sustainability. Because of ASHRAE's commitment, I feel more committed to coming to work each day to assist our members in developing technology that will contribute to sustainable build design, operation, and maintenance around the world. I feel much more productive; the design of the workstations provides a much more efficient use of workspace than our previous cubes. The daylighting makes me feel more alert and eager to work."

Scott said working for an environmentally friendly company would be a very important factor for her in the future. "I cannot imagine working for a company that does not ensure a sustainable workplace or that does not show concern for their environmental footprint. Stewardship of natural resources for the future should be a top concern for all — both companies and individuals."

Conclusion

Though the green building industry is relatively new, it has expanded rapidly during the last decade and some of its principles and methods are being adopted by the conventional building industry. No one can deny that waste of any kind results in financial and material losses that ultimately affect everyone. The idea of being as efficient as possible, even in the planning and design stages, is very attractive. It is clear, as competition for finite resources and materials increases that we cannot afford to throw away anything that could be reused or recycled. The rapid growth of technologies over the past century has resulted in an unprecedented level of human consumption, and it is now evident that this level cannot be maintained indefinitely. Some green building practices that still are regarded as novelties or luxuries by many in the business community soon will become mandatory.

This book has demonstrated that the concept of green is not simple, and the motives and principles of green building sometimes come into conflict with one another. There are many reasons for building green, including financial incentives, the need to project a positive corporate image, a desire to be socially responsible, and a deep concern for the future of our planet. However, each green project has its own priorities. It can be difficult to determine which products, methods, and materials are the most environmentally sound and to predict their future impact on the environment. Products that are successful in reducing the consumption of electricity, such as solar panels and ERVs, may create new problems when they come into widespread manufacture and use and eventually are discarded. Every new product has to be scrutinized from its raw materials to its dismantling. Many green choices involve trade-offs. In addition to fulfilling its environmental objectives, a green project has to be tailored to fit the available financial resources.

New materials and technologies are being developed continually. National governments and international bodies, anxious to reduce carbon emissions and conserve energy and water, have invested heavily in research and in producing standards, regulations, and incentives to encourage green building. It is now difficult to conceive of the breakthroughs in fields such as solar energy, low-emitting materials, and heat transfer that will occur during the next few years. Another interesting field is the development of living, organic building materials and of materials that can be completely recycled.

Preliminary studies have shown that a well-planned green building project is economically viable and pays for itself in a relatively short time. New information is regularly emerging on the effects of work environments on the health of building occupants. In the near future, practices that improve indoor air quality may become standard for all buildings, and employers may be legally obligated to implement them. By building green now, a building owner can avoid expensive retrofits in the future.

This book is only an introduction to green building concepts and practices. A vast amount of information is available on green building on the Internet, from various government agencies and green building associations, and from the green building professionals who will advise you during your green building project. You are on the threshold of an exciting experience through which your knowledge and understanding will be greatly expanded. Your green project will demand creativity, ingenuity, wisdom, and the assistance of people who know more than you. You will be truly proud of the result.

APPENDIX A:
Useful Websites

Building Codes and Legal Issues

Green Building Law Update (**www.greenbuildinglawupdate.com/**)

Reed Construction Data's Building Code Reference Library
(**www.reedconstructiondata.com/building-codes**)

Building Commissioning

Associated Air Balance Council (AABC) (**www.aabc.com**)

Building Commissioning Association (BCA) (**www.bcxa.org**)

The Building Commissioning Guide Version 2.2 (**www.cecer.army.mil/
kdsites/hvac/commissionpedia/Publications/Reports/Building%20
Commissioning%20Guide.pdf**)

The Continuous Commissioning Guidebook for Federal Managers
(**www1.eere.energy.gov/femp/pdfs/ccg07_ch5.pdf**)

Certification

BREEAM (**www.breeam.org/index.jsp**)

Green Building Certification Institute (GBCI) (**www.gbci.org/**)

Green Globes Overview (**www.thegbi.org/assets/pdfs/GreenGlobes_ CIEB_Technical_Overview.pdf**)

Green Globes Trial (**www.thegbi.org/green-globes-tools/free-trial.asp/**)

Green Globes Certification Personnel Search (**www.thegbi.org/ green-globes/personnel-certifications/certified-personnel-listing**)

LEED Professionals Directory (**http://gbci.cyzap.net/gbcicertonline/ onlinedirectory/**)

LEED Regional Priorities (**www.usgbc.org/DisplayPage.aspx? CMSPageID=1984**)

Daylighting

Daylighting Collaborative (**www.daylighting.org/what.php**)

Health benefits of daylighting EERE (**www1.eere.energy.gov/femp/pdfs/ buscase_appendixf.pdf**)

Solatube International daylighting tubes (**www.solatube.com**)

Environmentalism

Buildings and their Impact on the Environment: A Statistical Summary. Revised April 22, 2009 (**www.epa.gov/greenbuilding/pubs/gbstats.pdf**)

Carbon Dioxide Emissions per Country (**http://rainforests.mongabay. com/09-carbon_emissions.htm**)

EERE, Energy Savers (**www.energysavers.gov/**)

Environmental History Timeline (**www.radford.edu/~wkovarik/envhist/**)

History of Energy (Timeline) (**www.shell.us/home/content/usa/
environment_society/education/student/energy_timeline/**)

U.S. Energy Information Administration (EIA) State and Historical Energy
Information and Statistics (**www.eia.doe.gov/overview_hd.html**)

Oil Depletion Analysis Centre (ODAC) (**www.odac-info.org/**)

Financing

Federal Tax Credits for Consumer Energy Efficiency, ENERGY STAR
(**www.energystar.gov/index.cfm?c=tax_credits.tx_index**)

Database of State Incentives for Renewable Energy (**www.dsireusa.org**)

IRS Notice 2006-52: Deduction for Energy Efficient Commercial Buildings
(**www.irs.gov/pub/irs-drop/n-06-52.pdf?cm_sp=ExternalLink-_-
Federal-_-Treasury**) and *Internal Revenue Bulletin: 2008-14* (**www.irs.
gov/irb/2008-14_IRB/ar12.html**) *P.L. 110-343 | THE EMERGENCY
ECONOMIC STABILIZATION ACT OF 2008: ENERGY TAX
INCENTIVES* (**www.energy.gov/media/HR_1424.pdf**)

Finding Green Building Professionals

Acentech consultants in acoustics, audiovisual, and vibration
(**www.acentech.com**)

Architect Finder, American Institute of Architects
(**http://architectfinder.aia.org/**)

Green Professionals Directory for California
(**www.builditgreen.org/en/directories/search.asp**)

LEED Professionals Directory
(**http://gbci.cyzap.net/gbcicertonline/onlinedirectory/**)

The Blue Book Building and Construction Network
(**www.thebluebook.com**)

Design

Athena Institute Eco-Calculator
(**www.athenasmi.org/tools/ecoCalculator/**)

Architectural Record (**http://archrecord.construction.com/**)

EERE, Integrated Building Design
(**www1.eere.energy.gov/femp/pdfs/29267-4.1.pdf**)

IISBE – International Initiative for a Sustainable Built Environment SB
Tool for rating sustainable buildings (**www.iisbe.org/sbtool**)

National Charrette Institute (**www.charretteinstitute.org**)

National Institute of Building Sciences (NIBS) Whole Building Design
Guide (**www.wbdg.org/references/mou_lem.php**)

Rocky Mountain Institute — white papers on green building
(**www.rmi.org/rmi/pid174**)

Rutgers Center for Green Building
(**http://rcgb.rutgers.edu/faq.asp?Level2ItemID=23**)

Whole Building Design Guide, a program of the National Institute of
Building Design (**www.wbdg.org**)

Writing the Green RFP, The American Institute of Architects (**www.aia.org/
practicing/groups/kc/AIAS074658?dvid=&recspec=AIAS074658**)

Government Agencies

Building Energy Codes Program, DOE (**www.energycodes.gov/**)

ENERGY STAR, U.S. Environmental Protection Agency and the U.S. Department of Energy (**www.energystar.gov/**)

National Center for Photovoltaics (**www.nrel.gov/ncpv**)

U.S. Department of Energy (DOE) (**www.energy.gov/**)

U.S. Department of Energy Energy Efficiency and Renewable Energy (EERE) (**www.eere.energy.gov/**)

U.S. Environmental Protection Agency (EPA) — green building (**www.epa.gov/greenbuilding/index.htm**)

U.S. Energy Information Administration (EIA) (**www.eia.doe.gov/**)

Global Warming and Climate Change

Buildings and Climate Change — Industry Call to Action, UNEP-SCI (**www.usgbc.org/ShowFile.aspx?DocumentID=6506**)

Eco-rate.com building statistics (**www.ecorate.com/40/green_building_statistics**)

Intergovernmental Panel on Climate Change (**www.ipcc.ch/**)

National Aeronautics and Space Administration's (NASA) *Surface Temperature Analysis* (**http://data.giss.nasa.gov/gistemp/**)

National Oceanic and Atmospheric Administration's (NOAA) *State of the Climate Report* (**www.ncdc.noaa.gov/sotc/index.php?report=global&year =2006&month=ann**)

Carbon Catalog (**www.carboncatalog.org**) and

CarbonFund.org (**www.carbonfund.org**)

EPA: How to Calculate your Carbon Footprint
(**www.epa.gov/climateleaders/smallbiz/footprint.html**)

Pending legislative initiatives on climate change
(**www.usgbc.org/DisplayPage.aspx?CMSPageID=2124**)

The Climate Trust Carbon Footprint Calculator (**www.climatetrust.org/
content/calculators/Business_&_Org_Calculator.pdf**)

Locating Green Materials and Suppliers

AEI Lighting (**www.aeilighting.com**)

AquaPro Solutions LLC (**http://aquaprosolutions.com/**)

Blue Book Building & Construction Network (**www.thebluebook.com**)

Building Block LLC. ICFs (**www.buildblock.com/greenbuilding.asp**)

Carpet and Rug Institute (CRI) (**www.carpet-rug.org/index.cfm**)

EcoRock (**www.seriousmaterials.com/html/ecorock.html**)

ERVs and HRVs "Recovery Time," *EcoHome Magazine*, Fall 2009
(**www.ecohomemagazine.com/green-products/recovery-time.aspx**)

Green Builder (**www.greenbuilder.com/general/greendbs.html**)

Green Building Supply (**www.greenbuildingsupply.com**)

Green cleaning companies
(**www.ecobusinesslinks.com/green-cleaning.htm**)

Green Fiber cellulose insulation (**www.greenfiber.com**)

Green Manufacturer (**www.greenmanufacturer.net/directory**)

Green Product Directory
(**www.builditgreen.org/green-product-directory**)

Kimball Office (furniture) (**www.kimballoffice.com**)

Lighting Services Inc. (**www.lightingservicesinc.com**)

Low-Emitting Materials. Whole Building Design Guide
(**www.wbdg.org/references/mou_lem.php**)

OSI Professional Grade Adhesives and Sealants (**www.osipro.com/**)

Tate Access Floors (**www.tateaccessfloors.com**)

Why Not Green? (**www.whynotgreen.com**)

Certification of Materials and Products

Forest Stewardship Council (**www.fscus.org**)

Green Seal (**www.greenseal.org**)

Greenguard Environmental Institute
(**www.greenguard.org/en/index.aspx**)

Institute for Market Transformation to Sustainability
(**www.mts.sustainableproducts.com**)

Scientific Certification Systems (SCS) certifies for low emission
(**www.scscertified.com**)

SMaRT rating system developed by the Institute for Market
Transformation to Sustainability (**www.sustainableproducts.com/mts/
smartstandards.html**)

Sustainable Forestry Initiative (SFI) (**www.sfiprogram.org/**)

Professional Associations and Organizations

Acoustical Society of America (**http://asa.aip.org/**)

American Institute of Architects (**www.aia.org**)

American National Standards Institute (ANSI) (**www.ansi.org**)

American Society of Heating, Refrigerating and Air-Conditioning Engineers (ASHRAE) (**www.ashrae.org**)

American Wind Energy Association (**www.awea.org/**)

Business and Institutional Furniture Manufacturer's Association (BIFMA) (**www.bifma.org**)

Carpet and Rug Institute (CRI) (**www.carpet-rug.org/index.cfm**)

Center for Community Action and Environmental Justice CCAEJ (**www.ccaej.org**)

Committee on the Environment (COTE) AIA (**http://network.aia.org/ AIA/CommitteeontheEnvironment/Home/Default.aspx**)

Environmental & Water Resources Institute (**http://content.ewrinstitute.org/**)

Environmental Working Group (**www.ewg.org**)

Florida Green Building Coalition (**http://floridagreenbuilding.org/**)

Forest Stewardship Council (**www.fscus.org**)

Greenguard Environmental Institute (**www.greenguard.org**)

Indoor Air Quality Association (**www.iaqa.org/**)

International Initiative for a Sustainable Built Environment (iiSBE) (**www.iisbe.org/**)

International Organization for Standardization (ISO) (**www.iso.org**)

Institute for Market Transformation to Sustainability (**www.mts.sustainableproducts.com**)

International Agency for Research on Cancer (IARC) (**www.iarc.fr**)

National Institute for Occupational Safety and Health (NIOSH) (**www.cdc.gov/niosh**)

Rocky Mountain Institute (**www.rmi.org**)

Sustainable Forestry Initiative (SFI) (**www.sfiprogram.org/**)

The Natural Step (**www.naturalstep.org/the-system-conditions**)

U.S. Green Building Council (USGBC) (**www.usgbc.org**)

World Wildlife Federation (WWF) (**www.worldwildlife.org**)

Recycling

Habitat for Humanity (**www.habitat.org**)

ReUse People (**www.thereusepeople.org**)

Renewable Energy

American Solar Energy Society (ASES) (**www.ases.org**)

Institute of Electrical and Electronics Engineers (IEEE) (**www.ieee.org**)

Interstate Renewable Energy Council (IREC) (**www.eren.doe.gov/irec**)

National Fire Protection Association (NFPA) (**www.nfpa.org**)

North American Board of Certified Energy Practitioners (NABCEP) (**www.nabcep.org/**)

North Carolina Solar Center, North Carolina State University (**www.ncsc.ncsu.edu**)

Solar America Board for Codes and Standards (**www.solarabcs.org/**)

Solar Energy Industries Association (SEIA) (**www.seia.org**)

Solar Energy Technologies Program (**www.eere.energy.gov/solar**)

Trade Shows

Green Manufacturing Expo (**www.canontradeshows.com/expo/gmx10**)

Greenbuild (**www.greenbuildexpo.org**)

Lean to Green (**www.sme.org/cgi-bin/get-event.pl?--001981-000007-home--SME-**)

Water Conservation

AquaPro Solutions LLC (**http://aquaprosolutions.com/**)

CalRecycle (**www.calrecycle.ca.gov**)

Environmental & Water Resources Institute (**http://content.ewrinstitute.org/**)

Water Conservation. Whole Building Design Guide (**www.wbdg.org/resources/water_conservation.php**)

Water Management Guide, General Services Administration (**www.gsa.gov/graphics/pbs/waterguide_new_R2E-c-t-r_0Z5RDZ-i34K-pR.pdf**)

Renovation, Retrofitting, and Sustainable Preservation

Commissioning Existing Buildings, EERE (**www1.eere.energy.gov/femp/pdfs/OM_7.pdf**)

IAQ Assessment. EPA. (**www.epa.gov/iaq/largebldgs/i-beam/index.html**)

LEED Renovation Standards Checklist (**www.anjec.org/pdfs/ WorkshopMaterials33009LEEDSChecklist.pdf**)

"Non-green Office Buildings Sacrifice 8% in Rent Revenues," *Environmental News* (**www.buildinggreen.com/auth/article.cfm/2010/ 11/9/Non-Green-Office-Buildings-Sacrifice-8-in-Rent-Revenues/**)

Sustainable Preservation Initiative (**www.sustainablepreservation.org/**)

Toxins, Pollutants, and Waste Disposal

A Field Guide for Residential Remodelers, prepared by the National Association of Home Builders (NAHB) Research Center (**www.epa.gov/osw/conserve/rrr/imr/cdm/pubs/remguide.pdf**)

EPA lead certification (**www.epa.gov/lead/pubs/renovation.htm**)

Lead, Environmental Protection Agency (**www.epa.gov/opptintr/lead/index.html**)

National Pollutant Discharge Elimination System (**http://cfpub.epa.gov/npdes/stormwater/cgp.cfm**)

U.S. Army Corps of Engineer's Unified Facilities Criteria, *Selection of Methods for the Reduction, Reuse, and Recycling of Demolition Waste* (**www.wbdg.org/ccb/DOD/UFC/ufc_1_900_01.pdf**)

Case Studies in this Book

Acentech Inc. (**www.acentech.com**)

American Society of Heating, Refrigerating and Air-Conditioning Engineers (ASHRAE) (**www.ashrae.org**)

Bohdan Boyko, building science manager at GreenFiber (**www.greenfiber.com**)

Breaking Ground Contracting; Jacksonville, Florida (**www.breakinggroundcontracting.com**)

Kimball Office (**www.kimballoffice.com**)

LoyaltyOne (**www.loyaltyone.com**)

Maia Gilman — owner and founder, Maia Gilman Architect (**www.maiagilman.com**)

Margulies Perruzzi Architects (**www.mp-architects.com**)

Melissa Collar, partner, Warner Norcross & Judd LLP (**www.wnj.com**)

Mike McNatt, attorney, Roetzel & Andress LPA (**www.ralaw.com**)

Reckson Associates Realty, part of the SL Green company (**www.slgreen.com**)

Streamline Material Resourcing (**www.streamlinemr.com**)

APPENDIX B:
Acronyms Found in This Book

AIA — American Institute of Architects

ANSI — American National Standards Institute

BEE — built environment efficiency

BIFMA — Business and Institutional Furniture Manufacturer's Association

BOMA — Building Owners and Manufacturers Association of Canada

BREEAM — Building Research Establishment's Environmental Assessment Method

BRE — Building research establishment

BRI — building related illness

Btu — British thermal unit

CASBEE — Comprehensive Assessment System for built environment efficiency

CBECS — Commercial Building Energy Consumption Survey

CCAEJ — Center for Community Action and Environmental Justice

CDM — clean development mechanism

CFL — compact fluorescent lamp

CLC — closed loop cycle

CLMC — closed loop material cycle

COTE — Committee on the Environment

CRI — Carpet and Rug Institute

DEP — Department of Environmental Protection

DfE — Design for the Environment

DOE — U.S. Department of Energy

EEA — European Environmental Agency

EEM — energy efficient measure

EERE — U.S. Office of Energy Efficiency and Renewable Energy

EIA — Energy Information Administration

EMS — Energy Management System

EPA — U.S. Environmental Protection Agency

ERV — energy recovery ventilator

EUI — energy utilization index

FEMP — Federal Energy Management Program

FSC — Forest Stewardship Council

GBCI — Green Building Certification Institute

GBI — green building initiative

GEM — global environmental method

HBA — Home Builder Association

HEPA — high efficiency particulate air

HVAC — heating, ventilation, and air conditioning

GGA — Green Globe assessor

GGP — Green Globe professional

GWP — global warming potential

I-BEAM — indoor air quality building education and assessment model

IARC — International Agency for Research on Cancer

ICF — insulated concrete form

IEQ — indoor environmental quality

IFMA — International Facility Management Association

iiSBE — International Initiative for a Sustainable Built Environment

IPM — integrated pest management

IUA — International Union of Architects (IUA)

LCA — life cycle assessment

LED — light-emitting diode

LEED — Leadership in Energy and Environmental Design

LEED-AP — LEED-accredited professional

MIPS — materials intensity per unit service

MSDS — material safety data sheet

NAHB — National Association of Home Builders

NAPCA — National Air Pollution Control Administration

NASA — National Aeronautics and Space Administration

NOAA — National Oceanic and Atmospheric Administration

NPDES — National Pollutant Discharge Elimination System

O&M — operation and maintenance

OSHA — U.S Occupational Safety and Health Administration

PCA — property condition assessment

PCM — phase change material

PV — photovoltaic system

RCx — recommissioning

REC — renewable energy credit

RFP — request for proposal

RFQ — request for qualifications

SBS — sick building syndrome

SFI — Sustainable Forestry Initiative

SPI — Sustainable Preservation Initiative

TAB — testing and balancing

TIF — tax increment financing

UFAD — under-floor air distribution

UHI — urban heat island

ULF — ultra-low flush

UNEP — United Nations Environment Programme

USGBC — United States Green Building Council

VCx — value recommissioning

VOC — volatile organic compound

WBCSD — World Business Council on Sustainable Development

APPENDIX C:
Green Building Glossary

Acoustics — The science of managing noise levels in a building.

Action threshold — The point at which a situation requires action.

Active living wall — A vegetative wall incorporated into a building's air conditioning and filtration system and used to clean and depollute the indoor air.

Active solar heating — A solar heating system that collects heat from solar radiation and uses a system of mechanical pumps and fluids to transfer it to the interior of a building.

Aerator — A low-flow fixture that mixes air with water to slow down the water without affecting the pressure.

Ambient lighting — Lighting systems that provide illumination for an entire space. A typical example of ambient lighting is a florescent overhead lighting in an office space.

American Institute of Architects — A professional association of architects in the U.S.

Asbestosis — A lung disease that involves scarring of lung tissue caused by inhaling asbestos fibers.

ASHRAE — American Society of Heating, Refrigerating, and Air Conditioning Engineer.

BIFMA — Business and Institutional Furniture Manufacturer's Association.

Biodiversity — The diversity of life forms, ecosystems and species that exist in the world.

Biophilia hypothesis — The concept that human beings have a genetically based need to interact with nature.

Blackwater — The excess waste water generated by toilets, showers, faucets, and other water systems.

BOMA — Building Owners and Managers Association.

BPA — bisphenol, the most common building block of plastics and a known toxin.

British thermal unit (Btu) — The amount of heat energy needed to raise the temperature of one pound of water by one degree Fahrenheit.

Brownfield sites — Abandoned industrial and commercial facilities and plots of land that can be cleaned up and reused for a new building.

Building commissioning — The verification by a third party that all the systems of a building are operating as designed.

Building envelope — The space between the interior and exterior of a building, which determines how well a building retains heat and cool air and how much energy is needed for forced air systems.

Building information modeling (BIM) — Three-dimensional building software that enables designers to manage the building design process.

Building related illnesses (BRIs) — Advanced forms of SBS that are diagnosed when the air quality of a building and its contaminants can be directly linked to specific illnesses.

Bioswale — A landscape feature designed to remove soil and silt from storm water runoff.

By-products — Secondary products created as a result of manufacturing.

CFL — compact fluorescent lamp, a lamp that uses a spiral fluorescent tube.

Carbon offsetting — The practice of investing in renewable energy in order to compensate for using energy generated from fossil fuels.

Cast-in-place concrete — A system where concrete is made and poured on site into its final form.

Certificate of insurance — A legal document verifying that an insurance policy has been taken out on a property.

Clean development mechanism (CDM) — A program established by the United Nations as part of the Kyoto Protocol that certifies green projects in developing countries.

Color rendering index (CRI) — A way of measuring lighting levels in light bulbs that can be equated to different levels of natural sunlight.

Commercial Building Energy Consumption Survey (CBECS) — An assessment of the energy consumed in a commercial building.

Committee on the Environment (COTE) — A committee of the American Institute of Architects that advocate for buildings that are environmentally responsible.

Construction delivery system — The procedure for designing and constructing a building.

Corporate social responsibility (CSR) — The commitment by a corporation to positive and ethical business practices.

Cradle-to-cradle — A method for evaluating the impact of a product on both human life and the environment by assessing every synthetic and natural material and process associated with the product from inception through the manufacturing process, use, demolition, recycling, and ultimately to its non-use.

Daylighting — The process of using natural sunlight to illuminate space.

Deconstructability — Construction of a building using components that can be removed and re-used when the product becomes broken or obsolete.

Detention pond — Ponds designed to temporarily hold stormwater runoff.

Dimensional planning — Creating a design that minimizes the amount of materials needed to achieve the objectives of a building.

Dioxins — Carcinogenic or teratogenic heterocyclic hydrocarbons that occur as impurities in petroleum-derived herbicides.

Direct exchange system — A system in which energy is transferred directly from one medium to another, such as when a thermal wall heats a room.

DOE — U.S. Department of Energy

Dredging — The deepening of a pond or waterway by scraping earth from the bottom.

Dual plumbing system — A plumbing system that provides clean water for drinking and washing, and recycles water from sinks and showers (gray water) for purposes like flushing a toilet or irrigating landscape.

Ecological rucksack — The total quantity of natural material (in pounds of kilos) that must be physically displaced to produce a particular product.

EPA — U.S. Environmental Protection Agency.

Eco-friendly — Causes little or no harm to the environment, minimally interfering with natural ecosystems

Eco-roof — Vegetative roof.

Embodied energy (embedded energy) — An assessment of the amount of energy consumed during the manufacture, transportation and installation of all of a building's components and materials.

Energy Information Administration (EIA) — A federal agency responsible for independent statistics and analysis.

Energy utilization index (EUI) — A measure of the energy consumption over time for each source of energy in a building.

Environmentally friendly — Causes little or no harm to the environment, minimally interfering with natural ecosystems.

Evapotranspiration — The plant process of transferring water from a surface to the atmosphere.

FEMP — Federal Energy Management Program.

Footprint — The area of land required to sustain a human activity or an individual human's lifestyle.

Forced air system — A heating, cooling, or ventilation system that uses pumps to move air through a building.

Formaldehyde — A toxic chemical used in many wood products and adhesives.

Free cooling — The process of cooling water and air by using the natural cooler external air temperatures.

Federal Water Quality Administration (FWQA) — A division of the U.S. Department of Labor, replaced in 1970.

Gallons per minute (gpm) — The rate at which water flows from a water faucet or through a plumbing system.

Geothermal heat pump system — A system that extracts and transfers heat and cool air from the earth to a building.

Geothermal energy — Heat stored in the earth from the decaying or organic matter, absorption of solar energy, and heat from the interior of the earth.

Green Building Certification Institute (GBCI) — An independent third-party organization that administers LEED certification.

Green roof — Vegetative roof.

Greenfield sites — Building sites that have not been previously occupied by an industrial building and are used for new construction are called.

Greenhouse gases — Gases that retain solar energy in the earth's atmosphere.

Greenwashing — The false advertisement of products, services or companies as environmentally friendly when they are not.

Ground-source heat pump system — A system that extracts and transfers heat and cool air from the earth to a building.

Hard costs — Costs that can be clearly quantified and calculated.

High efficiency particulate air (HEPA) filter — A high-performance filtration device.

High global warming potential gases (high GWP gases) — Synthetic gases such as hydrofluorocarbons, perfluorocarbons, and sulfur hexafluoride that are powerful greenhouse gases.

Hybrid heating systems — Passive solar heating systems assisted by mechanical fans and blowers.

Hydroelectric power — The generation of electricity through water movement. It is one of the most used forms of alternative energy production.

IFMA — International Facility Management Association

Inactive living walls — Vegetative walls that do not contribute to air filtration and are typically not hooked up to the building's air filtration system.

Indirect gain passive solar heating system — A passive solar heating system that uses a south-facing wall to absorb heat from radiation and gradually transfer it to the interior of a building.

Indirect heat exchange — A system that uses a transfer medium to carry heat.

Insulated concrete forms (ICFs) — Blocks of expanded polystyrene, a form of recyclable plastic, which incorporate bars of reinforced steel.

Integrated pest management (IPM) — A pest control technique using knowledge of the biological cycles of insects and a minimum of pesticides.

Isolated gain solar heating system — A system that collects solar heat energy in a designated space, then circulates it out into the rest of the building.

Lateral framing — Horizontal framing that provides resistance to wind and can comprised a number of different systems or materials, depending on the building type.

LEED — Leadership in Energy and Environmental Design, a set of official guidelines for designing and building a green building.

LEED AP (LEED accredited professional) — A professional who has passed the LEED AP examination, demonstrating his or her knowledge of green building and LEED requirements.

Light emitting diode (LED) — A lamp that emits light when electricity passes through a semi-conductor.

Living roof — A vegetated roof.

Living wall — A vertical system of living plants that helps clean stormwater or filter air in the interior of a building.

Low emissivity (low-E) glass — Window glass with a very thin coating of metal that reflects heat and lowers the condensation levels on the glass

Low-flow orifice — A control at the bottom of a detention pond that regulates the egress of water.

Material safety data sheet (MSDS) — An information sheet required by the government that provides information on chemicals contained in a product.

Material efficiency — A measure of how efficiently a material fulfills its function.

Mesothelioma — A form of cancer directly linked to asbestos exposure, found most often in the lining of the lungs, abdomen, and heart.

MIPS (materials intensity per unit service) — A measure of the amount of service delivered by a product.

Modular block vegetated roofs — A garden of plants placed in smaller sections around the roof of a building.

Net metering — An arrangement that subtracts the amount of electricity supplied to a power grid by a building's solar system from the amount of electricity supplied to the building when the solar system is not operating.

Noise travel — A situation in which noise is audible at a distance from its source.

Occupancy sensors — Motion detectors that turn lights on automatically when someone enters the room and turn them off when the room is empty.

Off-gassing — The release of chemicals into the air from building materials, paints, flooring, and carpet.

Orientation — The position of the building on a plot of land and its position in relation to roadways, sidewalks, and landscaping.

OSHA — U.S. Occupational Safety and Health Administration.

Passive solar heating — Heat radiated from surfaces that absorb solar radiation.

Pervious paving — A specialty pavement that enables water absorption and prevents runoff.

Phase change material — A material that is capable of storing and releasing large amounts of energy as it freezes and melts.

Photovoltaic system (PV) — The system that obtains, processes, and transfers power from the sun to usable energy within a building or home.

Point-of-use hot water system — Water heaters installed at faucets that heat water as it flows out.

Postconsumer waste — Waste that is discarded after the consumer is done with it.

Pre-consumer waste — Waste that is created during the product's manufacturing period before it reaches the consumer.

Primary energy — Raw fuel such as natural gas or fuel oil that is burned to generate heat and electricity on a building site.

Reclaimed materials — Materials that can be reused in their original form for a new purpose.

Recyclable materials — Materials that can be recycled and used to manufacture new products.

Retention pond — A pond built to hold excess stormwater runoff.

Right sizing — Designing infrastructure and mechanical systems to accommodate future plans so that future modifications can be done with little additional cost.

Secondary energy — Heat or electricity created from a raw fuel and purchased by a building site.

Sick building syndrome — An illness that can be directed correlated to working in a specific building, but generally cannot be attributed to specific sources.

Site energy — The amount of heat and electricity consumed by a building as reflected in utility bills.

Soft costs — Costs associated with benefits that are not easily measured, such as the cost of improving productivity or reducing absenteeism.

Source-site ratios — The factors used to restate primary and secondary energy in terms of the total equivalent source energy units.

Stakeholder — Anyone who is involved in the planning, design, and construction of a building, or who is affected by it in any way.

Stormwater management — The science of controlling excess water runoff from storms.

Stormwater runoff — Water from rain and melted snow that carries pollution from parking lots, fertilizers, and pesticides into the water table.

Subfloor air distribution system — A heating and cooling system that is installed beneath the flooring.

Sun tempering — Solar heating by means of enlarged south-facing windows and other simple measures.

Testing and balancing (TAB) — The traditional procedure for verifying that a building's HVAC system is operating as it was designed to.

Task lighting — Lighting that can be used for specific tasks. An example of task lighting includes lamps and small light fixtures at an employee's desk that can be turned on and off only when needed.

Tax increment financing (TIF) — A public funding method that uses future income from taxes to fund development projects.

The Natural Step — A framework developed by Swedish oncologist Karl Henrik Robert for evaluating the health effects of materials selected for a building.

Thermal bridging — The process of heat loss or gain through a material.

Thermal storage wall — Trombe wall.

Trombe wall — An exterior wall that collects solar heat energy and transfers it to the interior of a building.

Under-floor air distribution (UFAD) — A heating and cooling system that is installed beneath the flooring.

Urban heat islands (UHIs) — An area that has a higher temperature than areas around it. Heat islands are the result of solar radiation that becomes absorbed by all the buildings, sidewalks, and rooftops in a particular area, contributing to elevated temperatures in that area.

USGBC — United States Green Building Council.

Vegetated roof — A roof covered with plants growing in specially designed plastic trays that absorb rainwater and help insulate the building.

Volatile organic compounds (VOCs) — Harmful carbon-based toxins found in paints and plastics that cause long-term damage to the health of humans and animals.

Xeriscaping — Landscaping with plants that thrive naturally without irrigation or fertilization.

Zero landfill policy — A commitment to recycling all waste products from a building so that nothing is disposed of in a landfill.

Bibliography

"A Short History of Energy (in the US)." theWatt.com (**www.thewatt.com/node/153**)

"Buildings and Climate Change: industry call to action." United Nations Environment Programme Sustainable Buildings and Climate Initiative. 2010. (**https://www.usgbc.org/ShowFile.aspx?DocumentID=6506**)

"Buildings and their Impact on the Environment: A Statistical Summary." EPA. Revised April 22, 2009 (**www.epa.gov/greenbuilding/pubs/gbstats.pdf**)

Del Percio, Stephen. "The Top 5 Legal Issues to Consider on Green Construction Projects." *gbNYC Magazine.* November 1, 2007. (**www.greenbuildingsnyc.com/2007/11/01/the-top-5-legal-issues-to-consider-on-green-construction-projects**)

Fosdick, Judy. "Passive Solar Heating." WBDG. National Institute of Building Sciences. June 2010. (**www.wbdg.org/resources/psheating.php**)

"Green Building: Basic Information." U.S. Environmental Protection Agency. (**www.epa.gov/greenbuilding/pubs/about.htm**)

"Greenhouse Gases, Climate Change, and Energy." Energy Information Administration (EIA). (**www.eia.doe.gov/bookshelf/brochures/ greenhouse/Chapter1.htm**)

"Greening the Building and the Bottom Line." RMI and the DOE. 2004. (**www.rmi.org/rmi/pid174**)

Hirst, Eric, and O'Hara, Frederick M. *Energy efficiency in buildings: progress and promise.* Series on energy conservation and energy policy. Washington, D.C.: American Council for an Energy-Efficient Economy, 1986.

"History of Energy." Shell.com. (**www.shell.us/home/content/usa/ environment_society/education/student/energy_timeline**)

Kibert, Charles J. *Sustainable construction: green building design and delivery.* Hoboken, N.J.: John Wiley, 2005.

Lewis, Jack. "The Birth of EPA." *EPA Journal.* November 1985. (**www.epa.gov/ history/topics/epa/15c.htm**)

Makower, Joel. *The E-factor: the bottom-line approach to environmentally responsible business.* New York: Times Books, 1993.

Mills, Evan. "Building Commissioning: The Stealth Energy Efficiency Strategy." *Climate Progress.* August 12, 2009. (**http://climateprogress.org/2009/ 08/12/building-commissioning-energy-efficiency-lbnl-evan-mills**)

"Non-Green Office Buildings Sacrifice 8% in Rent Revenues." *Environmental Building News.* (**www.buildinggreen.com/auth/article.cfm/2010/11/9/ Non-Green-Office-Buildings-Sacrifice-8-in-Rent-Revenues**)

"Oil Depletion Analysis Centre (ODAC *Peak Oil Primer.* (**www.odac-info.org/ peak-oil-primer**)

Russo, Michele A., Gaudreau, Chris, and O'Shaughnessy, Catlin. *Green outlook 2009: trends driving change.* Bedford, Mass.: McGraw-Hill Construction, 2008.

Tobias, Leanne, and Vavaroutsos, George. *Retrofitting office buildings to be green and energy-efficient: optimizing building performance, tenant satisfaction, and financial return.* Washington, D.C.: Urban Land Institute, 2009.

Author Bio

Jackie Bondanza is a developmental book editor and a freelance writer. She has written about real estate, education, entertainment, travel, health, and lifestyle for iVillage, MSN, *Online Degrees Magazine*, *Hemispheres Magazine*, *Southern California Senior Life*, *Northridge Magazine*, and *College Bound Teen Magazine*. She has a master's degree in journalism and has written copy for both television and radio. She has also appeared as an education and lifestyle consultant for a variety of national television programs.

As a developmental editor, Jackie works with authors to develop books ranging in genre from historical non-fiction and reference to pop culture and literature. In addition to her editorial work, Jackie writes a blog on international aid issues for Globalhood, an international consultancy firm, and she also leads workshops for homeless writers around the country. She currently lives in New York City with her husband and her dog. Visit her at **www.jackiebondanza.com**.

Index

7285